The Future of Union Organising

The Future of Union Organising

Building for Tomorrow

Edited by

Gregor Gall
University of Hertfordshire

First published 2009 by
PALGRAVE MACMILLAN

Palgrave Macmillan in the UK is an imprint of Macmillan Publishers Limited,
registered in England, company number 785998, of Houndmills, Basingstoke,
Hampshire RG21 6XS.

Palgrave Macmillan in the US is a division of St Martin's Press LLC,
175 Fifth Avenue, New York, NY 10010.

Palgrave Macmillan is the global academic imprint of the above companies
and has companies and representatives throughout the world.

Palgrave® and Macmillan® are registered trademarks in the United States,
the United Kingdom, Europe and other countries.

ISBN-13: 978–0–230–22242–7 hardback
ISBN-10: 0–230–22242–0 hardback

This book is printed on paper suitable for recycling and made from fully
managed and sustained forest sources. Logging, pulping and manufacturing
processes are expected to conform to the environmental regulations of the
country of origin.

A catalogue record for this book is available from the British Library.

Library of Congress Cataloging-in-Publication Data

International Labour Process Conference (2007 : Dublin, Ireland)
The future of union organising : building for tomorrow / edited by Gregor Gall.
    p. cm.
Papers presented at a special stream at the 2007 International
Labour Process Conference in Dublin.
Includes bibliographical references and index.
ISBN 978–0–230–22242–7 (alk. paper)
    1. Labor unions – Congresses. 2. Labor unions – Organizing – Congresses.
3. Labor unions – Case studies – Congresses. 4. Labor unions – Organizing –
Case studies – Congresses. I. Gall, Gregor. II. Title.

HD6483.I634 2009
331.87—dc22   2009013667
10 9 8 7 6 5 4 3 2 1
18 17 16 15 14 13 12 11 10 09

Printed and bound in Great Britain by
CPI Antony Rowe, Chippenham and Eastbourne

To Bob Crow, general secretary of the National Union of Rail, Maritime and Transport Workers – probably one of the finest union leaders of his generation in Britain today

Contents

Illustrations

Tables

Figures

Contributors

Kieran Allen is a Senior Lecturer at the School of Sociology in University College Dublin. He is the author of *Fianna Fail and Irish Labour: 1926 to the Present* (Pluto Press, 1997), *The Celtic Tiger: the Myth of Social Partnership* (Manchester University Press, 2000) and *The Corporate Takeover of Ireland* (Irish Academic Press, 2007). His current research is on economic globalisation.

Francisco Arqueros-Fernández is a doctoral candidate at the Department of Anthropology, National University of Ireland, Maynooth. Previous published work includes 'Low Wages, Migrant Labour and Politics in the Irish Mushroom Industry' in the *Irish Journal of Anthropology* (2006).

Dale Belman is a Professor of Labor Relations and Human Resources, School of Labor and Industrial Relations, Michigan State University. He has carried out extensive research on wage issues and the construction and transport sectors. He is co-editor of a number of books, such as *How New Is the 'New Employment Contract'?: Evidence from North American Pay Practices* (Upjohn Institute, 2002) and *Trucking in the Age of Information* (Ashgate, 2005), and co-author of a number of books, such as *Sailors of the Concrete Sea: A Portrait of Truck Drivers' Work and Lives* (MSU Press, 2004).

Donna Buttigieg is an Associate Professor in the Department of Management and the School of Business and Economics at Monash University. She is the Director for the School of Business and Economics (Gippsland) and is the Acting Director of the Family and Small Business Research Unit. Her research interests include union participation and exit behaviour, community unionism, vulnerable workers (including women and older workers), bullying and strategic HRM. She has recent publications in the *Journal of Applied Psychology*, *British Journal of Industrial Relations* and *Work, Employment and Society*. Earlier publications include the *Journal of Management Studies*, *Human Relations*, *Relations Industrielles* and *Journal of Industrial Relations*. She has also recently co-edited a book on community unionism.

Dr Iona Byford is a Senior Lecturer in the Human Resources and Marketing Department at Portsmouth University Business School. She has recently completed her PhD thesis entitled: 'A comparative study of trade union renewal strategies: partnership, organising and social unionism'. This is her first publication. Her next publication (forth-coming) is a chapter on the Canadian Auto Workers' union and Social Unionism in Canada in an edited volume on *Community Unionism* (Palgrave Macmillan, 2009). Her current research interests include union renewal and union democracy.

Dr Sandra Cockfield is a lecturer in the Department of Management at Monash University and a member of the Australian Centre for Research on Employment and Work (ACREW). She has published in the *Journal of Industrial Relations, Labour History* and the *Labor Studies Journal*. She also has a recent co-edited book on community unionism. Her current research focuses on the possibilities and limitations of information and communication technologies in relation to union renewal strategies, including in the hospitality and higher education sectors, and on com-munity and social movement unionism.

Dr Sheila Cohen is a Visiting Lecturer in Industrial Relations and a Senior Research Fellow at the Centre for Research in Employment Studies, University of Hertfordshire. She is the author of *Ramparts of Resistance: Why Workers Lost Their Power and How to Get It Back* (Pluto Press, 2006) as well as numerous articles and pamphlets on trade union-ism, working-class activism and the nature of work.

Michael Crosby is the Director of the Change to Win Organizing Center in Amsterdam. He was formerly the Director of the ACTU Organising Centre in Australia and has been for many years a leading advocate in that country of the need for unions to change to an organising focus. He was the coordinator of CleanStart between 2005 and 2007, and is the author of *Power at Work: Rebuilding the Australian Union Movement* (Federation Press, 2005). He recently chaired the Irish union SIPTU's Commission of Review and works with a range of unions in Europe advising on union change and strategic campaigning.

Dr Tony Dundon is College Lecturer in the J.E. Cairnes School of Business and Economics at the National University of Ireland, Galway. He is co-author of *Employment Relations in Non-union Firms* (Routledge, 2004) and *Understanding Employment Relations* (McGraw Hill, 2007) and editor of the *Human Resource Management Journal*.

Peter Fairbrother is Professor of International Employment Relations at RMIT University, Victoria, Australia. For most of his academic life, he has worked at the University of Warwick and more recently at Cardiff University. He has published widely on unions, the state and labour, and workplace recomposition, training and workplace learning in the steel sector. His work focuses on Australia, Britain and Europe more generally, addressing the interrelationship between the local and the global. He has co-edited a number of books on globalisation, the state and labour (Routledge, 2006) and union renewal (Continuum, 2002, 2003) and is author of numerous books on unions, such as *Trade Unions at the Crossroads* (Continuum, 2000).

Gregor Gall is Research Professor of Industrial Relations and Director of the Centre for Research in Employment Studies at the University of Hertfordshire. His previous work includes three edited volumes on union organising (Routledge, 2003, 2006; Palgrave, 2009) and books on postal workers (Ashgate, 2003), the labour movement in Scotland (University of Wales Press, 2005), sex workers (Palgrave, 2006) and finance workers (Ashgate, 2008). He writes regular columns for the *Morning Star, Respect Paper, Solidarity* and the Guardian's *CommentisFree.*

Dr Maria-Alejandra Gonzalez-Perez is Professor of International Business in the Department of International Business, Eafit University, Colombia. She is the director of the International Studies research group at the same university. She has published in the areas of international labour migration, corporate social responsibility and civic engagement of higher education.

Marjorie Jerrard is a Senior Lecturer in the Department of Management, Monash University, and is Deputy Director of the Australian Centre for Research on Employment and Work (ACREW) and President of the Pacific Employment Relations Association (PERA). She has published on union strategies, community unionism, unions and employment rights, and industrial relations in the Australian and New Zealand meat processing industries. She has recently co-edited a book on community unionism and has forthcoming work on community unionism published in *Labor Studies Journal.* She is currently engaged in research projects with a number of Victorian unions and is also working on a project examining careers in the Australian meat processing industry.

Dr Terrence McDonough is Professor of Economics in the J.E. Cairnes School of Business and Economics at the National University of Ireland, Galway. He has published in American economic history, colonialism in Ireland, public policy, and labour education. A new volume extending the arguments in his co-edited *Social Structures of Accumulation: The Political Economy of Growth and Crisis* (Cambridge University Press, 1994) will shortly be published by Cambridge University Press.

Kim Moody is a Senior Lecturer in industrial relations and a Senior Research Fellow at the Centre for Research in Employment Studies at the University of Hertfordshire. He is the author of three books on American labour relations (Verso, 1988, 1997, 2007), as well as a book on New York City politics (The New Press, 2007) and recent articles on trade union mergers, immigrant labour, and US labour history.

Adam Mrozowicki is doctoral researcher at the Centre for Sociological Research, the Catholic University of Leuven. His research explores the problems of the agency and subjectivity of blue-collar workers in Poland after the end of state socialism. The selected results of this study have been recently published in *European Journal of Industrial Relations* (2008).

Valeria Pulignano is Professor of Sociology of Labour and Industrial Relations at the Katholieke Universiteit in Leuven, Belgium, and Associate Fellow at the universities of Warwick and West of England. She is also Co-researcher of the 'Interuniversity Research Center on Globalisation and Work' (CRIMT) at the University of Montréal. Her research focuses on comparative European industrial relations such as systems of employee representations, social dialogue and collective bargaining, changes of employment relationships within new European socio-economic and productive models, and MNCs and employment relations. Among her recent publications are an edited volume on *Labour Flexibility* (Palgrave, 2008) and an edited special issue in *Transfer* (2007) on industrial restructuring and unions. She has extensively published in international journals and is Belgian expert in the Societae Europea network at the ETUI-REHS.

Dr Allen Smith is currently a consultant for various building trades unions and labour compliance organisations. He is also founder and president of Innovative Construction Research, Washington DC. Previously, he worked for the Food and Allied Service Trades Department, the Building Trades Organizing Project, the Sheet Metal Workers' International Association, and the Building and Construction Trades Department. He received his PhD in American History in 1995.

Wim Sprenger is a researcher in industrial relations and work organisation (Amsterdam, Opus 8). He worked with STZ Advies & Onderzoek in Eindhoven (2005–8) and before that as a researcher and policy officer with the FNV union confederation in the Netherlands. He was a member of the Administrative Board of Eurofoundation, Dublin, and participated in a series of European and international projects. His main research interests are self-employment, participative work redesign, age-proof work organisations, training/employability, and the informal economy.

Dean Stroud is a lecturer at Cardiff School of Social Sciences, Cardiff University. He is also Centre Manager of the Regeneration Institute and member of the Centre for Global Labour Research, both at Cardiff University. He has recently published on training and trade union strategy in the *Journal of Education and Work* (2006), *Policy Studies* (2008), *Studies in Continuing Education* (2008) and the *Journal of Workplace Learning* (2008). He is currently involved in a project looking at the organisation of women in ports.

Geert van Hootegem is Professor of Sociology of Work and Organisation at the Centre for Sociological Research, the Catholic University of Leuven. His main areas of research include labour market analysis, team-based work, job and organisations redesign, flexibility and well-being at work. He has published in *International Journal of Management Reviews*, *European Journal of Industrial Relations*, *Work, Employment, and Society*, and *Journal of Management Studies*. Currently, he leads a research project on the interrelations of globalisation and labour market changes and has co-established a consortium (with the participation of the Flemish government) which aims at supporting organisational innovation and workers' well-being at work.

Maarten van Klaveren works at the Amsterdam Institute for Advanced Labour Studies, University of Amsterdam, Netherlands and at the STZ consultancy and research, Eindhoven. He is author of numerous research outputs on unions, work and employment in the Netherlands. He is co-editor of *Low-Wage Work in the Netherlands* (Russell Sage Foundation, 2008).

1

'Union Organising' – Past, Present and Future

Gregor Gall

Introduction

By the beginning of 2009, the working populaces of the developed capitalist nation states were beginning to experience (again) a severe economic downturn, affecting their jobs, incomes, pensions and housing.
Only in retrospect will it be possible to assess the true depth and extent
of this downturn. But, regardless of this, the downturn presents a further, and huge, challenge to the projects of 'union organising' taking
place in many of these countries. This challenge arises not just because
of the weakening of any extant labour market power that workers may
wield and the diversion of union attention and resources towards dealing with redundancies and closures and away from 'union organising'
per se. It also arises because the destruction of capital – through firm
closure and downsizing – and the then consequent emergence of new
units of capital (as slump provides the conditions for the next boom)
will represent the destruction of unionised enterprises and the emergence of non-unionised enterprises. Enterprises do not as a rule emerge
as unionised; this has to be struggled for to be achieved. In other words,
the ways in which capitalism and units of capital respond and act will
force 'union organising'[1] back several, if not many, steps. And, of course,
there is an obvious sense in which workers need the protection of labour
unionism[2] even more at such a time of downturn and yet, paradoxically,
this is often the time this protection can least be proffered because of
the weakening of the power of organised labour. So, and notwithstanding that some sectors are more resistant to recession than others, union
organising, at the time of its greatest need, may also be at its most impo-
tent. There is, then, the sense that labour unionism, trying to become a
master of its own destiny, will be blown asunder. Historically speaking,

1

it is arguable that this will be the case unless labour unionism replicates militant struggles such as those of the 1930s (in the US) and the 1970s (in Britain) by deploying tactics like occupations and sit-down strikes to prevent the flight and destruction of capital by increasing the costs of closure and by making a political crisis out of an economic crisis.

Aside from this contemporaneous dimension, and despite many positive developments and advances (see Gall 2009a), most nationally based union organising projects have merely staved off further or greater decline rather than reversing it. 'Running very fast merely to stand still' seems an appropriate assessment. But, as is clear from its title, this collection seeks to assess what lessons can be learnt from the successes, failures, context, nature and dynamics of extant projects (of a national and subnational nature) in order to inform future practice. In other words, the focus of this collection is upon trying to identify models of 'best' and 'better' practice for the future rather than just examining, in the rather dry academic way, what has happened and why. Of course, in order to inform the judgements of what are, and should be, the 'best' and 'better', consideration of what has been 'union organising' and what should be 'union organising' are both implicit and explicit in the chapters. So too is whether union organising has been too radical for unions as relatively conservative organisations or whether it has been managerialised to become a form of managed activism of lay and employed union officers (EUOs).

While the prior edited collection, *Union Revitalisation in Advanced Economies – Assessing the Contribution of 'Union Organising'* (Gall 2009a), contained chapters on Canada, New Zealand and the US, their purpose was primarily to help contextualise the studied body of developments which focused upon Britain. This collection, *The Future of Union Organising: Building for Tomorrow*, by contrast, has three distinctive features. First, the collection covers a wider array of countries, providing both country-based assessments of union organising in the form of national case studies and consideration of subnational units and processes. Thus, the collection breaks new ground by having a collection of chapters on Eire, the Netherlands, Poland and two pan-national studies (cleaning, steel). The second feature concerns surveying, analysing and critiquing current practice with a view to informing the prospects of future 'best' or 'better' practice. Third, the collection considers hitherto unexamined areas and issues like organising migrants, atypical workers, insecure workers and young workers. All but two of the chapters in this collection are from a selection of papers presented at a special stream at the 2007 International Labour Process conference in Dublin called 'Assessing "union organising"'.

Beyond this, the collection offers chapters which converse with each other in a number of ways, sometimes directly, sometimes indirectly. For example, chapters by Belman/Allen and Stroud/Fairbrother examine what could be called a new, non-traditional and possibly heterodox agenda for union organising of skills, training and professional development, indicating that labour unions as a labour market actor can obtain mileage from operating as a body which has some role normally associated with professional bodies or craft unionism, namely, regulating entry and standards of behaviour. Meantime, issues such as neutrality agreements with employers (Crosby; Moody, both this volume) and organising migrant workers (Arqueros, Gonzalez-Perez *et al.*, both this volume) span chapters. Also, the activities of the SEIU have a prominent place in this collection by virtue of not only the strategic leveraged sectoral campaigning approach which it has pioneered but also its dissemination, with SEIU help and funding, to other labour unionisms in other countries around the world. SEIU activity here would seem to provide a clear case of organising for partnership, where leverage is enacted upon recalcitrant employers in order to recalibrate their calculations about the costs and benefits of 'going union'. Indeed, it is not just the SEIU but sometimes one of the contributors to the collection – namely, Michael Crosby – who features in chapters such as those on Britain, Eire and the Netherlands.

Limited gains and external organising

An analysis of the TUC *Organising Academy* in Britain, commissioned by the TUC, estimated that, since its launch in 1998, the 270 organisers enrolled in the Academy had recruited around 50,000 new members and 4,500 new union activists during their training (*TUC press release* 14 October 2008). Recognising the limitations of what could be achieved through an academy which trained paid organisers, the TUC launched a new organising and campaigning initiative for lay reps and stewards called the *Activist Academy*. It aims to train 1,000 lay workplace organisers between 2008 and 2011. While welcome, this again is but a drop in the proverbial ocean when one considers that there are already around 200,000 lay workplace representatives in Britain and – setting aside issues of their qualitative nature – these existing numbers are insufficient to the task of significant union revitalisation.

This brief snapshot indicates that the task of trying to create a cog (the employed organisers) to identify and train a bigger cog (the lay activists) to turn an even bigger cog (the members) is not an easy one, and may take more than one way to crack the nut as well as indicating variance on whether future union organising is based on expansion (new 'greenfield', non-union workplaces) or consolidation (existing 'brownfield' unionised workplaces).[3] And, whilst there are salient issues of sufficient resourcing and the appropriateness of top-down command structures (for a discussion, see Gall 2009b), it is becoming more evident that the way in which union organising has been practised in Britain as well as Australia, New Zealand, Canada and the US has involved EUOs bringing the 'union' as an outside body into workplaces. This has several dimensions. The tangible presence of the union in the workplace emanates from outside even where there is an initial approach from workers in the workplace to the union. Consequently, and despite the professed mantra of self-activity where the 'members are the union', the union is often either brought to workers and into the workplace by EUOs or created in the workplace by EUOs. This means that the EUOs are the centre of the cog from which the members – the spokes – emanate out, with the result that the links between the members are few and far between and the trajectory of relationship between members and EUOs is rather unidirectional, inasmuch as the EUOs are the leaders and the members are the followers. *In toto*, members are organised into a union but they are not organised within a union *as* a union of members in the traditional sought-after means.[4]

There is an absence of an authentic organic process of workplace union creation and building in this method. The riposte to any implied criticism here is that this – union organising as practised – is what is needed and appropriate in the situation of depleted labour unionism, atrophied grassroots members' collective confidence and consciousness and so on. Whilst this can be accepted, it still cannot avoid the significance that the outcome of this kind of labour unionism – no matter the good intentions – is unlikely to be the very type of self-sustaining, self-confident, self-assertive and self-reliant grassroots unionism that union organising is supposed to aspire to create. Indeed, it would not be pushing things too far to venture that this *modus operandi* of union organising has the potential to replicate the much criticised 'servicing' orientation, albeit where members are more mobilised behind the union, because initiation and direction are provided by a body external to the workplace union (as opposed to from within it). Evidence of this can also be found within a number of the chapters in this collection and the previous ones (see Gall 2003, 2009a).

The import of this discussion leads to a necessary consideration of the organisational culture and dimensions of union organising. It constitutes an act of national leadership – often after *de facto* factional struggles at this level to establish its providence. In this sense, union organising is both imposed upon and followed by those sections of union organisation and membership underneath the national leadership. And, while 'buy in' has obviously been sought from these lower orders, it is clear that this has not been a bottom-up initiative from any section underneath the national leadership. Consequently, union organising has the hallmarks of being a centralised, command operation. This jars with the professed decentralised and autonomous characteristics of union organising, and starkly contrasts with the attempts at sponsored democracy in a number of British and US unions in the 1970s, where a greater number of spaces for the empowerment of members were opened up by national leaderships. Thus, the resources of national unions are being expended – to the degree that they are – on a different goal but in the same way as on other goals and within the same organisational framework.

Union organising is not union organising

Adapting the *Star Trek* observation on life but not as we know it, union organising is no longer union organising as we know it. Initially, union organising was a fairly tightly defined set of principles and practices drawn up in contradistinction to 'servicing'. Whatever its failings at a conceptual level, it seemed to be clear what it should look like in practice, except that transition to practice has involved so much variation and adaptation, as well as insufficient success, that union organising has transmuted into a broad hook on which to hang many ideas and practices. One example is the advocacy of social movement unionism because union organising stood accused of being too narrowly focused on the workplace whilst there were levers for acting upon the workplace which existed well beyond the confines of the workplace. Yet here, as elsewhere, some of the extra-workplace levers have become rather divorced from the agency in the workplace, so that corporate campaigns can operate pretty much on their own but still be called union organising. This is not an argument for a narrow-minded return to the workplace as the singular focus, but rather an appreciation that, when union organising is said to be practised on a now much wider canvas, discordance and dilution can exist. More pertinently, it calls for some theorisation of how, where and when union organising can be positively part of a wider strategy or aligned to other strategies.

New environments, same directions?

There are no signs that union organising is going away or will shortly be challenged by an alternative emerging strategy. Indeed, in piecemeal ways, it is spreading internationally. For example, the SEIU strategic model has been transposed into Australasia, Britain and Ireland (see Allen, Cohen, and Crosby, all this volume). But diffusion to new environments does not seem to have proffered the outcomes of positive adaptation and innovation for generic union organising. Rather, there seems to be a continuation of what has, in practice, become union organising, and a tendency to fit union organising into existing discourses and methods. While not to be unexpected, and reflective of the relationship between agency and environment, this is still somewhat disappointing.

In Ireland, a 'union outreach service' was launched by the peak federation, the ICTU, on behalf of SIPTU, IMPACT, CWU, TEEU and Mandate unions in 2007 as a recruitment vehicle (EIRO 2007b). Since 2003, SIPTU has employed dedicated organisers, now numbering 12, with an Organising Department to focus on gaining membership and recognition in construction, security, hotels/catering, cleaning, and nursing home sectors (EIRO 2005b, 2008b). It gained some success by achieving a partnership agreement with DHL Express (Ireland), which provides for recognition covering about 1,000 workers. Meantime, the finance union, IBOA, began a new recruitment campaign in 2004, as did Mandate. More recently, SIPTU, Mandate and CWU unions have agreed to put greater resources into organising (EIRO 2008b). Finally, Unite, which operates throughout the British Isles, has rolled out its organising strategy to its Irish region. This brief summary as a taster for the subsequent three chapters dealing with themes within Ireland (Allen, Arqueros, Gonzalez-Perez *et al.*) raises the issue of to what extent union organising is union organising or merely recruitment. To the extent that the latter exists, it could be taken as evidence of unions being more concerned with membership numbers and financial viability than developing collective strength and bargaining prowess.

In Germany and the Netherlands, union organising is, as with Ireland, a more recent phenomenon. In these two countries, one could expect a concentration on workplace union organising as *de facto* union recruitment given the relatively centralised and supportive institutions of industrial relations in these countries. The rationale here is that emphasis on the collective organisation and mobilisation of members is less required, certainly at the workplace level, for political exchange within the institutions is the preferred and effective *modus operandi*. In Germany, membership decline has been stabilised in recent years (EIRO 2003, 2005a,

2006, 2007a, 2008a) and affiliates of the peak federation, the DGB, have taken initiatives to recruit young workers, strengthen ties between members and unions, and organise new economic sectors and employment groups (Behrens *et al.* 2003; EIRO 2006). Whilst many of these initiatives appear to be based on recruitment primarily (Behrens *et al.* 2003; EIRO 2005a), there is at least some evidence of workplace union organising in regard of, for example, the supermarket, Lidl, security guarding and construction. This may indicate that union organising has become seen as necessary because of the general erosion of corporatism and codetermination and/or because of their fragmentation at the edges where new players and new sectors develop outwith the extant systems of industrial relations regulation. In the Netherlands (van Klaveren/Springer, this volume, and http://unionrenewal.blogspot.com/[5]), there is again evidence of the tension between recruitment and organising in this way, with recruitment to the fore.

But, whether priority is given to recruitment (with or without attention to retention) or workplace or extra-workplace union organising, it is clear that both practices are very resource-intensive because of the heavy emphasis on the deployment of EUOs to conduct this work. This in turn limits the spread of organising and brings with it certain features (see Gall 2009a). Although of a more sporadic nature, little research (save, for example, McCarthy (2009) on the PCS union in Britain) has examined whether mobilisation, through strikes in particular, presents an alternative or additional means of recruitment and support to organising. For example, in the 2006 one-day strike by Unison members over public sector pensions in Britain, 30,000 workers joined Unison (which has about 1.3 million members). Other such strike examples are known of in the CWU and UCU unions in recent years. The general salience of this type of recruitment is that workers tend to approach the union in these mobilisation instances (rather than *vice versa*) and approach the lay workplace and activists to join as well. With regard to organising, some new members have shown a preponderance to become active in the run-up to, during and after the strike mobilisations. This brief consideration would seem to indicate that mobilisation as a perpetual cycle of means and ends should receive more attention by the union-organising strategists within unions.

A politics of union organising?[6]

Whilst there are politics of union organising – the professed, the actual, the implicit and the explicit, and often reflecting the politics of unions as organisations as well as the individuality of specific unions – what union organising arguably still lacks is a macro-world view by which to provide its clarion calls with an extra-work and extra-workplace foundation in social justice and social democracy. In other words, an underlying ideological perspective is required (see Cohen, this volume, *cf.* Baccaro *et al.* 2003). Too often union organising replicates the narrow, economistic agendas of unions and remains aloof from the wider political processes because it is part of, and emanates from, labourism, where economic and political representation of workers are separated through a division of labour of agencies. This *modus operandi* of labour unionism no longer has the property of appropriateness or effectiveness of the past. Even where there is a political engagement, the terms of this engagement are centred upon slight progression from, and adaptation of, the politics of governing parties rather than those emanating from a radical and independent basis. This has the effect of facilitating union engagement *within* the parameters of neoliberalism rather than using the sharper, cutting edge of socialised democracy as a means by which to create leverage *vis-à-vis* ideology and mobilisation. So, for much of what passes for union organising, the lack of overt political and politically conscious labour unionism appears to act as a constraint on the ability to raise worker consciousness and capacity to struggle and organise. This us returns to the point of departure for this introduction, whereby the presence and dissemination of such an ideology might provide union organising with greater purchase in these times of economic turmoil.

Notes

My thanks are to Jack Fiorito for comments on an earlier draft of this introduction. Further information and interpretation on union organising in countries like the Netherlands and Germany can be found in at http://unionrenewal.blogspot.com/2009/03/membership-growth-despite-crisis.html and in Gajewska and Niesyto (2009).

1. The term 'union organising' is presented as such in order to denote the complexity of the social phenomenon which it is, being a conflation of theory, practice and praxis, from which many variants arise. With that said, the term will henceforth be used without such denotation.
2. The term 'labour' unionism is used because in the contemporary period the term 'trade' unionism has become inappropriate, for most major unions are increasingly general or conglomerate, rather than 'trade' (see Gall (2008:1) for a brief consideration of the issues).
3. Because training lay workplace reps is an easier task to accomplish where the employer dispenses facility time and this, in turn, presumes the employer has agreed to union recognition.

4. This trajectory of union organising has become very evident in both the Amicus and TGWU sides of Unite, the GMB, RMT and CWU unions from observation and discussion with key participants. The case of the PCS union is interesting, for it appears to diverge somewhat from these aforementioned unions' experiences. PCS appears to have achieved a higher level of grassroots activist involvement in its union-organising activities (see, *inter alia*, PCS 2008) and this may be attributable to much of its focus being on workplaces which have long-standing union recognition and workplace structures which, in turn, exist in the public sector. In other words, its efforts have been targeted towards not only a slightly more favourable environment compared with many private sector enterprises but also one where the baseline it is operating upon is higher (or in existence). Nonetheless, even here and with amongst the most militant and former and current lay-based national leadership, it is clear that the union organising is very much senior leadership-conceptualised, formatted and driven. It will be interesting to see what kind of organising the biggest public sector union in Britain, Unison, implements and what its experience of that will be, because the union began to expend considerable resources within its branches on organising in 2008, and concomitant branches were to be subject to centrally organised branch assessments.

5. The unionrenewal.blogspot is run by Dirk Kloosterboer and Tonny Groen of the FNV union federation (see van Klaveren/Springer in this volume for more information on the FNV).

6. If it is correct to talk of a politics of union organising, it must also be correct to talk of an economics and sociology of union organising too. In regard to the former, and while the resource intensiveness has already been noted, the means for calculating 'expenditure', 'revenue' and 'profit' are not well developed amongst unions. Consequently, the economic sustainability of union organising can be questionable (even where the political will exists to fund it).

2
Union Organising in the US: New Tactics, Old Barriers

Kim Moody

Introduction

A 2005 survey by Peter D. Hart Research Associates (2005: 6) showed that 53% of non-managerial employees in the US would, or probably would, vote for union representation at their workplace. This figure was up from 39% in 1996 and 30% in 1984 (Harcourt and Lam 2007: 334). This suggests support for unions has risen in the US over the past two decades. As Robinson (2008: 238) argued, the pressures of a quarter-century of 'neoliberal restructuring' have moved more workers to view unions positively. Yet, union membership and density declined over these years, leaving more and more workers without union protection. This decline is most dramatic in the private sector, where losses account for almost twice the net decline since 1970. What is to explain this 'representation gap'? Despite much rhetoric about accelerated organising, new approaches such as 'neutrality' and card-check agreements, and large amounts of financial resources shifted from 'servicing' to organising, the results have been too meagre to reverse the downward trend. Using academic, union, and government sources, this chapter will examine the course of this decline, the shift in organising efforts from state-sponsored elections under the National Labor Relations Board (NLRB) to voluntary 'neutrality' and card-check agreements, the extent and effectiveness of these new approaches, and the internal barriers to more rapid growth embedded in the American business union model. The focus will be on the private sector, both because this is the location of the decline and because it is the heart of the US economy and, hence, the key potential source of labour's renewed power. The chapter will conclude with a look at some of the alternatives, some of which are already practised by some unions.

Contours of union decline

Between 1970 and 2007, US unions lost just over 5 million members, while the proportion of union members in the workforce dropped from 27.3% to just 12.1%. In the private sector, however, the plunge was far greater: from 16.9 million members in 1970 to 8.1 million in 2007, a loss of over 50%. Density slumped from 29% in the private sector to 7.5% over those years (Goldfield 1987: 10–11; Troy 1986: 81; US BLS 2000, 2002, 2004, 2006, 2008b; USDOC 1972, 1991, 2001, 2004–05). Total membership continued to grow until 1980, reaching a high point of over 20 million in that year. As Table 2.1 shows, however, membership in the private sector began its descent after 1970. Between 1970 and 2006, when private sector membership hit its lowest point so far, 8.997 million members 'disappeared'. Not often noted is the fact that the biggest single slump in members came in the three years between 1980 and 1983, when 3.3 million members were 'lost'. Another 1.4 million members were lost from 1983 to 1989, bringing the total loss for that decade to 4.7 million. That is, over half of the private sector loss to 2007 occurred in the first decade after 1980, with losses slowing down

Table 2.1   Private sector union membership

Year	Membership	Change	Density (%)
1970	16,978,000		29.1
1980	15,264,000	−1,714,000	20.6
1983	11,933,600	−3,330,400	16.8
1989	10,520,000	−1,413,600	12.4
1991	9,909,000	−611,000	11.9
1995	9,432,000	−477,000	10.4
1996	9,415,000	−17,000	10.4
1997	9,363,000	−52,000	9.7
1998	9,306,000	−57,000	9.5
1999	9,419,000	+113,000	9.4
2000	9,148,000	−271,000	9.1
2001	9,141,000	−7,000	9.0
2002	8,652,000	−489,000	8.6
2003	8,452,000	−200,000	8.2
2004	8,205,000	−247,000	7.8
2005	8,255,000	+50,000	7.9
2006	7,981,000	−274,000	7.4
2007	8,114,000	+133,000	7.5

Sources: Troy (1986: 81), Lewin (1986: 244), USDOC (US Department of Commerce) (1991, 1992, 2001, 2004–5) and USBLS (2000–2008b).

thereafter – a trend that should have made growth possible if effort had been increased.

The fall in manufacturing that accounts for much of the drop in the number of private sector members came after 1980, but does not fully explain the loss of members. From 1980 to 1992, 1.9 million production jobs in manufacturing disappeared, 80% of them concentrated in three industries: primary metals, textiles, and garment (Moody 2007: 102; USDOC 1993, 2001). But the number of union members lost in manufacturing in those years was over 3 million (US BLS 2008a, b; US Department of Commerce (USDOC) 1972). Shrinking membership in industries with growing employment can be partly explained by a geographical restructuring of several industries, notably automobiles, meatpacking, trucking and construction. In these cases, it was the unions' inability to follow the work to new sites, often in the non-union South, that led to declining membership (Moody 2007: 99–106). The rising opposition of employers to new unionisation also explains some of the difficulty of organising. Using back-pay awards due to Unfair Labor Practice claims with the NLRB as a proxy measure of employer resistance, Meyer and Cooke (1993: 533) noted a dramatic rise in their incidence in the 1970s. Similarly, they showed a fourfold increase in decertification elections. While these external explanations for decline are relevant, Bronfenbrenner (2003: 39) argued:

> *Yet, unions in the USA cannot simply blame external factors for their failure to organize. They themselves must take a significant share of the blame. In the 1950s and 1960s, when unions had the resources and power to launch massive organizing campaigns, taking on entire industries, they failed to do so.*

It is certainly true that organised labour in the US did not undertake any 'massive organising campaigns' following the Second World War, but beginning in the late 1950s and into the 1970s the number of NLRB certification elections rose significantly. It reached its peak in 1973 at 8,526, but remained well above 7,000 elections a year until 1980 (Goldfield 1987: 90–1). Then, in a period of three years from 1980, the number of NLRB elections fell by more than half to 3,241, never to recover to earlier levels (Meyer and Cooke 1993: 533; Moody 2007: 139). As NLRB elections were virtually the only way in which unions conducted new organising in those years, union efforts to recruit new members fell by half. Suddenly, in the early 1980s, most unions all but abandoned new organising. By the 1990s, labour's decline and crisis could no longer be ignored. This gave rise to the 1995 campaign of John Sweeney for AFL-CIO president on the promise to make organising a priority, urging affiliated unions to 'organize at a pace and scale that is unprecedented' (Hurd 2004: 8). As Fiorito and Jarley (2008), Hurd (2007) and others have argued, organising decisions lie with the affiliated unions and not the federation, and the overall record of both organising efforts and growth remained poor for all but a handful of unions. Hurd (2004: 13, 17) showed that, despite much talk and some effort by a few unions, private sector union density continued downward from 1995 through to 2002, falling by 16.5%. So too did density in all of the industries considered a major private sector organising target except for hospitals. Similarly, in closely related occupational groups, only nurses and nurses' aides showed increases. Other well-known targets of active organising such as janitors, carpenters, and construction labourers continued to show declining density from 1998 to 2003.

The rise of card-check and neutrality agreements

The number of NLRB representation elections held from 1999 to 2006 fell by 43% as unions downplayed this traditional approach to new organising (NLRB 1999–2006). Not surprisingly, the number of workers organised through this method dropped steadily from just over 100,000 in 1999 and 2000 to 67,468 in 2006. Beginning in the mid-1990s, in an effort to bypass the NLRB, several unions turned increasingly to non-NLRB methods of gaining recognition (Brudney 2007: 11–12). Most common are neutrality agreements and card-check recognition procedures. These are essentially voluntary forms of recognition long upheld by the NLRB (Becker *et al.* 2006: 118) and by the Supreme Court since 1981 (Jordan and Bruno 2006: 182–3). Hurd (2008) breaks them down into two broad categories – those resulting from collective bargaining with a company with which the union already has an established bargaining relationship, and those that stand alone. The approach of extending recognition to non-union units of the already unionised companies is sometimes called 'bargaining to organise'. Benz (2002: 96) described it as 'the leveraging of existing contractual relations with a company in order to make it easier to organise other workers in the company, its joint ventures, or its suppliers'. Examples of this kind include the CWA's neutrality agreement with Southwestern Bell's Cingular Wireless, now part of AT&T, which brought it 40,000 new members between 1997 and 2007, UNITE-HERE's agreements with the Hilton and Starwood hotel chains which netted 6,000 members from 2004 to 2006 (Hurd 2008: 37–9), and the UAW's eleven agreements with major auto-parts suppliers which brought it 20,000 new members between 2002 and 2006 (UAW 2006: 103). In a similar vein are voluntary agreements reached with employers in markets where the union has significant density or a pattern agreement (Jordan and Bruno 2006: 187). The second or stand-alone type involves convincing or forcing an employer with whom there is no previous bargaining relationship to sign such an agreement. Most of these procedures include both a neutrality agreement, in which the employer agrees not to openly attack the union or use the extreme tactics associated with NLRB elections, and a procedure to grant recognition upon verification of cards signed by a majority of the workforce.

It is, however, not only the employer who agrees to mute criticism of the union in most neutrality agreements. Three-quarters of the voluntary agreements studied by Eaton and Kriesky (2001: 48) set limits on the union's behaviour: 'Most commonly the union agreed not to attack management.' Yet, it is precisely the 'us-versus-them' and the 'industrial conflict' that build the sense of solidarity required to build a strong union and display the power needed to win a first contract (Jordan and Bruno 2006: 188). Furthermore, there is always a temptation to seek voluntary recognition by giving the employers much of what they want, such as lower real wages, and bargain away benefits. For example, a sort of *quid pro quo* that borders on a 'sweetheart deal' has been criticised in the SEIU's deals with a California nursing home chain (Hurd 2008: 41–2). Hurd (2008: 41–2), who uses that example, goes further, stating: 'There is no denying that most neutrality agreements are achieved through top-down methods; the bargaining, corporate campaigns, and political initiatives associated with neutrality are typically controlled by national union leaders and staff.' This does not mean that the various mobilisation and 'leverage' tactics that have become more widely used in recent years are not deployed. It does mean they are typically at the initiative and under the control of full-time organisers and high-level officials.

Bold claims are frequently made about the increased use of voluntary agreements. A widely cited figure from the AFL-CIO is that, between 1998 and 2003, 80% of the nearly 3 million workers organised by AFL-CIO affiliates were recruited outside NLRB procedures (Brudney 2007: 12). This figure, however, includes public sector workers who are outside the NLRB framework and for whom we have no figures. Similarly, it would include the 400,000 or so newly unionised home health and childcare workers who are outside the NLRB's jurisdiction because they are either public employees or considered domestic workers. Another claim from the AFL-CIO is that in 2005 their affiliates recruited 150,000 private sector workers outside the NLRB procedures (*New York Times* 11 March 2006). In that year, AFL-CIO unions recruited some 70,000 workers through the NLRB (2005: table 13) for a total of 220,000 new private sector members. Clearly, the non-NLRB approach was more effective. In terms of the number of elections, Martin (2008: 1081) found, in his sample of 70 local unions between 1990 and 2001, that NLRB elections composed almost 90% of organising drives, but that 42% of the new members came from the non-NLRB campaigns. To get an overview of the frequency of voluntary recognition agreements and campaigns, the Federal Mediation and Conciliation Service's figures for private sector voluntary recognition, and comparing them with the NLRB and National Mediation Board (NMB) elections – the latter covering rail and airline employees under the *Railway Labor Act 1926* (RLA) – can be used. The FMCS requires unions that achieve recognition by whatever means to file an F-7 form in preparation for first contract negotiations. The recognition agreements reported to the FMCS are only those from successful recognition campaigns, so an adjustment of these numbers was made to match up to the nearly 70% success rate of campaigning for such voluntary agreements found by Eaton and Kriesky (2001: 51). The results for the late 1990s are similar to those found by Martin (2008: 1081). Unfortunately, this breakdown of voluntary private sector F-7 referrals was discontinued after 2004.

Table 2.2 shows that the frequency of voluntary recognition efforts doubled from 1998 to 2001, but slackened off thereafter. As a proportion of all organising efforts in those years, voluntary recognition

Table 2.2 Organising efforts by type

Type	1988	1999	2000	2001	2002	2003	2004
NLRB	3,339	3,162	2,983	2,694	2,604	2,797	2,565
FMCS/Voluntary*	227	260	381	420	273	240	258
FMCS adjusted	324	371	544	600	390	343	369
NMB/RLA	91	72	74	73	70	55	63
Total efforts	3,754	3,605	3,601	3,367	3,064	3,195	2,997
Voluntary % total	9	10	15	18	13	11	12

Note: * includes voluntary recognition under neutrality, card-check, voluntary election, or some combination.

Sources: NLRB (1998–2004), FMCS (2000, 2004) and NMB (2001, 2006).

efforts never surpassed 18% and for the years 2000 to 2004 averaged about 14% a year. Three things seem clear from this. First, NLRB elections remain by far the favoured approach to organising. In fact, with the exception of UNITE-HERE, even the unions that claim to bypass NLRB elections in favour of voluntary procedures still use the NLRB more frequently. The Teamsters claim to seek neutrality agreements in their national campaigns (Hurd 2008: 39), while the SEIU says it 'infrequently uses legal mechanisms provided by the federal government' (Woodruff 2008: 2). Yet, these two unions were the top two users of NLRB elections from 1999 to 2007, when these two Change To Win (CTW) unions accounted for more NLRB elections than all AFL-CIO unions (Fiorito and Jarley 2008: table 1, NLRB 2006–7). Second, the addition of voluntary recognition to the organising repertoire has not been enough to replace the decline in NLRB elections. In other words, the declining use of NLRB elections is not simply the result of a switch to voluntary procedures. Furthermore, it is only a small number of unions that use these with any frequency. A survey of the *Daily Labor Report* from 1997 to 2004 by Brudney (2005: 26, n28, n29) revealed five unions as regularly pursuing voluntary recognition. These were HERE with 46 citations, CWA with 25, the UAW with 21, the SEIU with 15, and the USWA with 11. Bronfenbrenner and Hickey (2004: 41) produced a list of the most frequent users of the NLRB procedure, which included the Teamsters, SEIU, USWA, UAW, and UFCW. Here again with these unions, the number of NLRB elections outstrips that of voluntary agreements significantly. Third, the frequency of voluntary agreements is not great enough so far to produce the sort of gains that can sustain significant growth despite the high 'win' rate, identified as 67.7% by Eaton and Kriesky (2001: 51) and 83% by Martin (2008: 1082). There are no figures for the number of workers recruited in this way, but Martin (2008: 1086) found that the average in his sample was 357 new members for voluntary procedures compared with only 83 for NLRB elections. This indicates the more general finding that voluntary efforts are almost always directed at larger targets. The question has to be asked: if voluntary procedures are so much more efficient a way to bring in new members, why do not more unions use them more often?

Why so few voluntary recognition agreements?

The problem with voluntary recognition agreements, outside those negotiated with companies that already have an extensive bargaining relationship with unions, is simply that employers are intensely anti-union. Most see no advantage in accepting a union into their operations and, given the continued union premium in wages and benefits of about 28% for both, many disadvantages (Mishel and Walters 2003: 1). For those confronted with a union-organising campaign, a broad repertoire of union avoidance tactics will be deployed. The SEIU (Woodruff 2008: 2) estimates that 80% of employers hire union-busting consultants in NLRB elections, 91% engage in captive audience meetings, and 31% illegally fire union supporters during a campaign. As shown in the successful, but long, hard-fought SEIU campaign for voluntary recognition and a first contract among 5,000 building service workers, such campaigns can drag out as long as any NLRB election. In the latter case, it took many months of mobilisation, community support, and a ten-day strike to gain recognition, and then another year and a strike to win a contract (SEIU 2005, 2006a,b). Even where a prior bargaining relationship exists, it is not always a simple matter of gaining employer agreement. As Benz (2002: 104–5) pointed out, the CWA's pioneering 1997 neutrality/card-check agreement with SBC 'was the result of a long, hard won struggle'. She injected a realistic tone into the oft-cited ease of card-check procedures: 'to evaluate the usefulness of the bargaining-to-organise strategy, we have to look at the process it takes to get *to* neutrality or card-check agreements as well as the results from such agreements'.

Employer resistance in voluntary recognition campaigns, as well as in NLRB elections, prolongs and raises the costs of such efforts. Bronfenbrenner and Hickey (2004: 45) noted: 'the utilisation of a comprehensive union building campaign incorporating most, if not all, of the elements of our model has been critical to the success of many of the most significant non-Board victories.' In other words, voluntary recognition campaigns often require the same extensive effort as NLRB elections when the entire process is looked at. Fine (2007b: 38) calculated it took SEIU 10 years to organise 900,000 workers for a net gain of 600,000 at a cost of $1 billion, concluding that at this pace: 'To reach the same goal in health care, it would take upwards of thirty years, at a cost of three bn.' Thus, even such a fast-growing union as the SEIU, using many of the latest tactics including neutrality and card-check agreements, is unlikely to reach the sort of density goals it has set itself even with above average effort using the current methods. Rendering things even more difficult, in 2007, the NLRB delivered a blow to voluntary recognition when it ruled in *Dana/Metaldyne* (NLRB 2007: 351) that the 'recognition bar', which prevented anti-union employees or employers from petitioning for decertification for a reasonable amount of time, would no longer apply to card-check recognition. This meant that 30% of the workforce could now petition for decertification soon after the employer had granted voluntary recognition. In the first test of this ruling, a CWA local in New Hampshire had to postpone negotiations for a first contract during the 45-day period granted by the NLRB for a decertification challenge and only became recognised in January 2008 (Gaus 2008a). In April 2008, another CWA local in New York State won an NLRB election after their card-check recognition was challenged (American Rights at Work 2008). Prior to the *Dana/Metaldyne* decision, the UAW had won NLRB elections in three auto-parts suppliers in the South when a challenge to their card-check procedure by the anti-union National Right to Work Committee led to NLRB-ordered elections (UAW 2006: 104). It appeared unions can overcome this new barrier, but it is also clear it can add time and expense to voluntary organising efforts, somewhat reducing the differential between these campaigns and NLRB elections.

A closer look at progress

Table 2.3 shows the density changes in most of the major targeted industries and occupations between 2002 and 2007. Like Hurd's (2004) earlier assessment of the gains in density by those unions with the most

Table 2.3   Density by industry and occupation (%), 2003–7

Union	Industry/occupation	2003	2004	2005	2006	2007
SEIU	Hospitals	14.1	14.0	13.7	13.6	15.3
SEIU	Nursing care	9.4	8.7	8.4	8.4	9.1
SEIU	Home health care	7.6	10.0	9.8	7.9	10.2
SEIU	Building service	5.6	4.9	6.3	5.5	5.1
IBT	Trucking	12.2	11.0	10.9	12.0	10.6
UFCW	Grocery stores	24.0	21.8	18.2	19.1	18.9
UFCW	Meat packing	16.1	16.6	18.8	18.8	20.1
CWA	Telecom (wired)	23.3	22.3	22.8	23.3	23.6
CWA	Telecom (other)	11.3	23.2	18.1	14.1	7.8
SEIU	Registered nurse	16.9	16.7	16.6	16.7	17.4
SEIU	Nurses' aide	13.9	12.9	12.2	13.4	13.1
SEIU	Security guard	10.2	12.1	12.7	10.4	11.9
SEIU	Home care aide	8.2	9.6	11.4	8.9	9.1
UBCJA	Carpenter	17.4	15.2	13.4	13.2	15.6
LIUNA	Construction labourer	16.0	11.7	11.0	11.1	11.9

Source: Hirsch and Macpherson (2008a).

aggressive organising programmes, these more recent figures show little progress outside three industries – and in those there are only modest gains. Gains in health care may be the result of several unions' efforts in those industries and occupations. These unions include not only the SEIU, which is the dominant union in health care, but the California Nurses Association/National Nurses Organising Committee (CNA/NNOC), the USWA, CWA, AFT, and UAW among others. The same has to be said for the three occupational groups that showed increases in density: registered nurses, home health care aides, and security guards. All three are SEIU targets, but are also sought by other unions. The largest gains were in meatpacking, where the UFCW is the major player. After having lost thousands of members during industrial restructuring in the 1970s and 1980s, its fortunes began to change in 2000 when it organised a number of plants in Omaha, Nebraska, with the help of a community organisation and an immigrant workforce that was already organising itself, a phenomenon noticed in this and several other industries (Gabriel 2006: 343–4; Fink 2003; Ness 2005). According to Hirsch and Macpherson's (2008a) figures, the UFCW has gained about 18,000 members between 2003 and 2007, while the industry's workforce remained basically stable.

Who is growing?

Despite this lack of progress in density, 19 out of some 56 unions saw net gains in membership from 2000 to 2007. Table 2.4 looks at the membership of these unions based on their LM-2 reports to the Department of Labor. What is surprising is that a number of those unions usually designated as 'organising unions' are missing. The CWA, UAW, LIUNA, UFCW, and UNITE-HERE all failed to show net growth. Some of those that did make this list must be disqualified because their growth in this period was more than accounted for by mergers with or affiliations by other unions. The USWA gained 291,000 members through two mergers in this period, while the IBT gained 125,000 with three mergers. The growth of the NEA must be modified as it gained about 400,000 members in 2006 through the affiliation of the AFT-affiliated New York State United Teachers, now a joint affiliate of NEA and AFT (NEA 2006). Its real gain would have been 237,612 or a jump of 9.4%.

Eight of the 17 unions that grew other than by mergers were in the public sector: IAFF, AFT, AFGE, ATU, TWU, AFSCME, NEA and NATCA. The eight private sector unions with net gains seemed to defy the conventional wisdom that size and resources are what count in the growth

Table 2.4   Unions with net gains, 2000–7

Union	2000	2007	Net gain
SEIU	1,374,300	1,691,973	317,673 (23.1%)
IBT	1,402,000	1,423,038	21,038 (1.5%)
USWA	612,157	722,545	110,388 (18.0%)
IFPTE	43,571	61,767	18,196 (41.8%)
CNA/NNOC	61,000	80,000	19,000 (31.1%)
ALPA	49,224	61,235	12,011 (24.4%)
IUOE	379,309	403,927	24,618 (6.5%)
OPCM	40,339	43,671	3,332 (8.3%)
PPF	307,454	332,205	24,751 (8.1%)
IATSE	100,000	108,386	8,386 (8.4%)
UWU	42,065	50,000	7,935 (18.9%)
AFSCME	1,300,000	1,433,688	133,688 (10.3%)
AFT	706,973	832,058	125,085 (17.7%)
IAFF	241,933	283,932	41,999 (17.4%)
AFGE	197,096	235,678	38,582 (19.6%)
NATCA	13,682	14,648	966 (7.1%)
TWU	109,000	115,145	6,145 (5.6%)
ATU	170,466	183,781	13,315 (7.8%)
NEA	2,530,000	3,167,612	637,612 (25.2%)

Sources: USDOL (2000, 2007), CNA/NNOC (2008).

game. The fastest-growing union in the US was not the SEIU, as it routinely claims, but the IFPTE, which grew by 42% from 2000 to 2007. Other unions with high growth rates are also occupationally based – the three construction unions, and the other professionally based unions such as the nurses, stagehands, and airline pilots. Most of these growing occupational unions are quite small, and even large percentage gains cannot turn labour's fortunes around. Clearly, something more and different is needed.

Business union barriers to growth

American business unionism has long been characterised by rigid hierarchical structures that mute debate and limit membership involvement, an ideology that denies a fundamental conflict between capital and labour, and an almost exclusive dependence on long-term, formal collective bargaining relationships. The original debate over the 'servicing model' versus the 'organising model' – internal participation at the local level – in the 1980s and early 1990s attempted to address some of the problems that flowed from this form of unionism. With its emphasis on member participation, the original organising model aimed to replace the dependence on top-down servicing with workplace self-organisation and activity. By the late 1990s, however, the debate was transformed into the later duality of servicing the membership versus external organising (Hurd 2004: 7–8). In this phase of the debate, the 'organising model' became, as Fletcher and Gapasin (2008: 200) describe it, 'focused on retooling existing unions to make them more effective organising machines'. This later version of the 'organising model', they argue, 'holds that organising workers into unions is, in and of itself, a progressive, if not revolutionary, action'. In this view, 'one chooses to ignore the character of the union or unionism and proceeds with the conviction that things will work out in the end.' This debate was well within the parameters of American business unionism. Business unionism perpetuates a bureaucratic form of organisation that both insulates leaders and breeds passivity among members (Moody 1988: 55–65). The 'servicing model', which places power in the hands of officials and professionals, fosters the notion of the union as something other than the workforce it represents, while the new 'organising model' bypasses the current members (Moody 2007: 187). As de Turberville (2004: 782) concluded, however, 'the two models are not opposites.' Bureaucratic business unionism has always practised both. The ultimate 'organising model' union, the SEIU, continues to provide services from above, recently carrying this practice one remove farther from the membership by initiating a grievance servicing call centre (Brenner 2008: 10). Now, however, the emphasis, deployment of resources, and tactical repertoire have changed significantly for some unions.

There are certain practices in the US business union model that have arisen since the 1930s which were encouraged, though not required, by the legal framework of the *National Labor Relations Act* (NLRA) as it has been interpreted by most labour leaders. As a result, they are deeply engrained in both the mentality of most leaders and the daily practice of most unions. The broadest of these has been the structural and political limitations on union democracy and member participation in union affairs beyond the workplace or local union. Various efforts have been made in recent years by some unions (CWA, USWA, UNITE-HERE, SEIU) to overcome this through mobilisation tactics while seldom addressing the structural problem. Hence, there is a tendency for mobilisations and member involvement in new organising or contract campaigns to be tightly controlled by officialdom. Lustig (2002) suggested:

> *increased activism and recruitment turn out to bear no necessary connection to decentralizing initiative, promoting internal debate or developing new organizational structures. Ironically, the multitude of new tasks mandated by the model ... can actually provide a new rationale for centralization to coordinate it all.*

Yet, it was a great deal of spontaneity and grassroots initiative that created most unions in the first place (see later). Here, the focus will be on four structural features of business unionism as barriers to organising: (i) defining membership as those under a collective bargaining agreement; (ii) separation of 'recognition' and 'representation' phases in organising; (iii) choices made by cost–benefit analysis – money; and (iv) lack of horizontal communications within the union.

Most unions count as members only those already covered by a union contract. A few count those involved in winning a contract. Fewer still include those who choose to be members within a workplace where no majority or recognition has been established. Almost none open their membership simply to workers who are looking for a union even if they are in an industry or occupation covered by that union. If 53% of non-managerial workers (50 million employees) are willing to vote for a union, it is likely that a smaller number (perhaps one in ten or 5 million) would be willing to actually join one at their workplace or in a geographical area that included their job. Self-organisation led by activists without benefit of professional organisers or a government-sponsored procedure was done prior to the ratification of the NLRA by the Supreme Court in 1937, after the great upheaval of that year. Outside rail workers covered by the RLA (Bernstein 1960: 215–20), there was no state-sponsored procedure nor any thought of 'neutrality' agreements, though 'sweetheart' deals by AFL unions in competition with more militant CIO unions were not uncommon. By requiring workers to be part of a workplace or group that is already in the union sights, organised labour is certainly limiting its potential growth.

For most unions the phase of 'organising', that is, seeking recognition, is a totally different function from 'representation', which might begin with the negotiation of a first contract or even after that. Organising is perceived as a specialised function or skill, and negotiating and representation as another. In most organising drives, this separation is embodied by different staff personnel. When recognition is achieved, the organisers exit and the full-time negotiators enter. Jordan and Bruno (2006: 194) found that: 'In most of the unions, organising and negotiations remain separate functions and seldom are they unified as a strategic plan.' Yet, summarising many studies of organising, Bronfenbrenner (2003: 41) argued that unions are most likely to achieve recognition 'when they run aggressive and creative campaigns utilizing a rank-and-file, grassroots intensive strategy, *building a union and acting like a union from the very beginning of the campaign*' (emphasis added). Acting like a grassroots intensive union from the start also increases the chance of winning a good first contract. Jordan and Bruno (2006: 182–5) pointed out that the choice between NLRB and voluntary procedures 'is not as stark as some have suggested'. In both cases, pressure is required. Bronfenbrenner's (Bronfenbrenner and Juravich 1998: 19–36, Bronfenbrenner 2003: 41) call to act like a union from the start would end this dichotomy and engage the members from the beginning. But, as she points out, few unions follow this prescription.

Another limit to organising is the exclusive emphasis on cost–benefit analysis of most unions. Of course, unions have limited financial and human resources and must make choices as organising is done under today's staff-driven model. On average, however, unions still spend only 10% of their resources on organising, far less than the 30% Sweeney once called for or the 50% the SEIU spends. So even here there is room for greater effort (Bronfenbrenner 2007a: 144). There are, however, also alternatives to high-cost campaigning, mostly involving activation of existing members. At a 2003 AFL-CIO summit on organising, Paul Booth (Early 2003: 7) of AFSCME argued: 'what we need is an army, and that can only come from our underutilized membership ranks'. Fletcher and Hurd (1998: 48–51) argued, among others, that current members and even stewards resist taking on external organising and this is no doubt a problem. But the same authors found examples of local unions drawing members into organising. Some local unions make this a matter of principle (Rosenstein 2008: 12). As long as US unions see new organising as primarily a professionalised, budget-driven activity in opposition to 'representation', Fine's (2007b: 38) observation on the high-cost, decades-long trek to density will be valid. To be sure, such ambitious and costly national campaigns as UNITE-HERE's 'Hotel Workers Rising' are having an effect (*In These Times* 19 April 2006). Ironically, this campaign also provides an example of how grassroots leaders can take over a campaign and reduce staff costs. Talking about the recent UNITE-HERE victory at a Hilton hotel in California, the leader organiser said 'the [grassroots] leaders were in the forefront, training workers to be organisers. It got to the point where we didn't have a lot of staff on it because the leaders were pushing each other' (in Gaus 2008b: 5).

Another barrier to organising, if it is to become a grassroots-based activity, is the lack of horizontal communication between locals of the same union. Many cities will have several locals of the same union that could coordinate efforts on a geographic or industrial basis. But communications in most unions run from local to international and back – if, indeed, there is even two-way communication. There are, of course, some structures such as Central Labor Councils (CLCs), the AFL-CIO Union Cities programme (AFL-CIO 2005: 55–7) and a number of Industry Coordinating Committees (Hurd 2007: 317) that bring together locals for organising and campaign purposes. But direct contact between locals of the same union is seldom encouraged. This, too, limits low-cost local organising possibilities.

Alternative approaches

If NLRB procedures are, as AFL-CIO Organising Director (Acuff 2006) puts it 'broken', neutrality agreements and card-check procedures do not seem to provide a fast track to growth either. What are needed are institutional changes within the unions to enlist a broader layer of the membership in organising new members. This would resemble the original 'organising model' of local member participation in both recognition and representation. Some of the alternative approaches that could expand and speed up the organisation of workers who say they want a union are: (i) open source/non-majority unionism; (ii) 'federal' or local CLC charters; (iii) ending the separation of recognition and representation; and (iv) activating and empowering members. Some of these are already practised by a few unions in limited cases. The idea is to generalise them.

Freeman and Rogers (2002: 8–40) argued for what they call 'open source' or non-majority unionism not based exclusively on bargaining units recognised by majority vote or a show of cards. It is a unionism that would be open to 'any worker, anywhere, everywhere in the economy'. It is a practice that could have brought many of the 366,000 workers into membership who participated in lost NLRB elections between 2003 and 2006, those disqualified under *Dana/Metaldyne*, and those from the 30% or so of card-check efforts that failed into the 'house of labour'. It could reach out to the 53% of non-unionised workers who say they want a union if it were widely used and defended.

The organising process would typically be initiated by groups of workers seeking a union, who could be issued a charter by international unions, CLCs, or one of the two federations. The charter could be specific to a workplace, an occupation, a geographical area, or a partially organised industry. This is precisely how many unions in the US were organised until after the Second World War. According to Cobble (2001: 87), between its founding in 1886 and the merger with the CIO in 1955 'the AFL chartered some twenty thousand federal or directly affiliated local unions'. The practice was abandoned after the Second World War in favour of the self-imposed model of growth exclusively through the international unions and NLRB channels. While such workers will certainly face intense employer opposition, Freeman and Rogers (2002: 25–8) argued that non-majority unionism is supported by NLRA Section 7, which is supposed to protect 'concerted activities' by any group of workers. Reinstatement and back pay for workers fired for union activity through the NLRB are fairly common. More reliable support could come from CLCs, other unions in the area, or directly from the federations. Examples of this type of union presently include the New York Taxi Workers Alliance, UE Local 150 at the University of North Carolina, and the CWA's Washtech at Microsoft, WAGE at General Electric and Alliance@IBM.

Another self-limiting practice, described above, is the separation of the recognition phase from the representation phase. Bronfenbrenner (2003: 41) found over and over that unions are most likely to win recognition by acting like a union from the start. Further, the militancy and experience accumulated in the organising phase need to be carried over into the day-to-day practice of representation. All of this implies member activation and participation in bargaining, representation and grievance-handling, not simply occasional mobilisation. This goes back to what Fletcher and Gapasin (2008) argued about a union's purpose: it cannot be just an organising machine or servicing agent. Rather, it must be a workers' organisation that defends and advances their interests and those of the broader working class in the workplace and society in general.

Conclusion

Unionism in the private sector remains in crisis despite some increased effort by several unions. As neutrality and card-check efforts move beyond companies with previous bargaining relationships or areas with significant density, they run into the same intense employer resistance experienced in NLRB elections. The time, effort, and resources required to win in stand-alone situations are likely to increase. Neutrality and card-check agreements are not a panacea, despite their more efficient outcomes. Industry-wide campaigns like 'Hotel Workers Rising' and Justice for Janitors are certainly part of the way forward, but labour needs to cast the net wider if it is to regain power across the private economy. Some of the barriers to union growth inherent in the business union model can be overcome if alternative methods of growth are more widely employed. More research into both organised labour's internal barriers and the alternatives to majority bargaining unit organising could help advance the possibilities for union growth in the US.

Appendix of acronyms

AFGE	American Federation of Government Employees
AFL-CIO	American Federation of Labor-Congress of Industrial Organizations
AFSCME	American Federation of State, County, and Municipal Employees
AFT	American Federation of Teachers
ALPA	Air Line Pilots' Association
ATU	Amalgamated Transit Union
CWA	Communication Workers of America
FMCS	Federal Mediation and Conciliation Service
HERE	Hotel Employees, Restaurant Employees
IAFF	International Association of Fire Fighters
IAM	International Association of Machinists
IATSE	International Association of Theatrical Stage Employees
IBT	International Brotherhood of Teamsters
IFPTE	International Federation of Professional and Technical Engineers
IUOE	International Union of Operating Engineers
LIUNA	Laborers' International Union of North America
NATCA	National Air Traffic Controllers' Association
NEA	National Education Association
OPCM	Operative, Plasterers and Cement Masons
PPF	Plumbing and Pipe Fitting Workers
SEIU	Service Employees' International Union
TWU	Transport Workers' Union
UAW	United Automobile Workers

UE	United Electrical Workers
UFCW	United Food and Commercial Workers
US BLS	United States Bureau of Labor Statistics
USDOC	United States Department of Commerce
USDOL	United States Department of Labor
USWA	United Steel Workers of America
UWU	United Utility Workers

3
Opening Pandora's Box: The Paradox of Institutionalised Organising

Sheila Cohen

Introduction

In the literature on the prospects for union renewal, the approach now widely known as the 'organising model' (OM) has emerged as a leading contender to facilitate such renewal. By contrast, initial responses to the declines in union density produced unproductive recruitment campaigns, accompanied or supplanted by equally ineffective forms of 'credit card unionism' (Waddington and Whitson 1997: 516). During the 1990s, these gave way to widespread official and theoretical support for 'partnership' (see Heery 2002). Yet, paradoxically, only after the OM received TUC endorsement with the founding of its *Organising Academy* in 1998 did union membership begin to stabilise, although density continued to decline, albeit more slowly. These developments in membership and density might also be attributed to external factors such as the Labour government's union recognition legislation (for a discussion see Gall 2004, 2007) and increases in the extent of employment and size of the labour force. The comparatively energetic, mobilising *zeitgeist* of the OM would seem to be particularly compatible with notions of union renewal based on membership activism (Fairbrother 2000), suggesting that the model has had at least some influence in regenerating union membership 'from the ground up'.

Yet, despite optimistic claims made for a renewed and resurgent unionism, the model appears so far to have failed to resolve the current impasse in which, while remaining relatively stable, union membership shows little signs of any widespread revival. Such relative 'failure' has led, more recently, to some critical interrogation of the model itself.

A number of contributions (such as de Turberville 2004; Holgate and Simms 2008) have noted its inherent ambiguity, while an inherent 'paradox' has been identified at the heart of the OM (de Turberville 2007) whereby the OM is premised on an undermining of 'bureaucratic' leadership control in favour of membership-led activity, but if such a shift is initiated by those 'bureaucracies' themselves 'it must paradoxically be assumed that those same bureaucracies must be emancipatory... It follows they should not be removed' (de Turberville 2007: 573).

This argument is strengthened by the evidence that most, if not all, initiatives in the direction of the OM, including the TUC's *Organising Academy*, have stemmed from union leaderships rather than from grassroots activists. As another contribution points out: 'Contrary to the conceptualisation of "union organising" being characterised by high levels of lay activism... the practice comprises... substantial FTO [full-time officer] involvement' (Gall 2005: 211; see also Gall 2009b). Additionally, while lay activists themselves might be expected to support the approach, research has demonstrated that many have professed hostility to 'organising' (Heery and Simms 2008). The conception of a paradox at the heart of the OM may thus be utilised at least in part to account for its disappointing results to date. Interrogation of such contradictions was a key purpose of the research undertaken for this chapter into one of the most well-resourced examples of the model, the organising strategy adopted by the Transport and General Workers' Union (now T&G-Unite) beginning from 2003–4. Before presenting these results, a number of salient themes present within the literature are examined. These are then utilised to structure the chapter.

'Organising model': Key themes

The widespread adoption of an 'organising' perspective within British unions in the late 1990s was encouraged not only by US initiatives such as those of the AFL-CIO's *Organizing Institute* and *Union Summer* (Foerster 2001; Heery *et al.* 2000), but also by influential US research (Bronfenbrenner *et al.* 1998) which highlighted the key role of 'union tactics' in influencing union growth. Such research directed attention away from more pessimistic perspectives based on 'environmental' factors (see, for example, Charlwood 2004) and emphasised the salience of union grassroots mobilisation and action in building membership. Here, the more successful 'union tactics' revealed a repeat of the historical pattern in which traditionally 'strong' sectors of the movement have, at grassroots level, generated the spread of membership to weaker sections. One important example is the 'worker to worker' campaigns cited by Bronfenbrenner and Juravich (1998: 24–5) in which well-organised groups visited or otherwise engaged non-members in their immediate areas.

The twin factors of grassroots efficacy and the 'strong-to-weak' dynamic are confirmed in more recent British accounts of 'greenfield' organising in which successful campaigns involved the support of networks of activists (Findlay and McKinlay 2003; Simms 2007). In general, research shows that already-existing and committed activists are crucial to recruitment and organising (Heery *et al.* 2000; Kelly 1998). The point is also emphasised in studies of union joining propensity which demonstrated that unfulfilled desire for union representation is high (see Verma *et al.* 2002: 377). However, this potential has to be contextualised in view of 56% of non-members never having been asked to join (TUC 2003: 32). Again, this points to the role of activists to locate, recruit and organise such potential members (see Gall 2007: 103). Nonetheless, significant hostility to union organising has been found amongst lay activists (see Heery and Simms 2008: 32, 39) and this is explored in the research. The notion that leadership-sponsored organising initiatives somehow conflict with the perspectives of those at the grassroots of the union is also explored in this chapter.

An emphasis on existing activists is also a key element of the reformulation and development of 'mobilisation theory' (Kelly 1998), which marks a further key theme in the salient literature. Cited by numerous writers, the re-emphasis on worker mobilisation points to a reversal of earlier invocations of 'environmental' and institutional factors in examining patterns of union growth. While often somewhat mechanistic and 'stage-ist' in its approach (*cf.* Gall 2005: 220–1), the focus of mobilisation theory on patterns of worker self-activity rooted in workplace experience encapsulates the redirection embodied in the OM towards 'bottom-up' rather than 'top-down' conceptions and patterns of union renewal. Such repositioning also places issues of membership involvement and union democracy at the centre of analysis.

Two related themes found within mobilisation theory indicate further directions for research *vis-à-vis* union organising strategies. First, a recapitulation of theories of leadership both affirms the role of left-wing union militants in building and sustaining union organisation and suggests a new emphasis on the 'charismatic' nature of successfully 'transformational' grassroots leadership (see Kelly 1998: 34–5). As shown below, this innovative approach to workplace leadership strongly influenced the organising strategy of the union under investigation. Second, the dynamics examined in patterns of worker mobilisation reaffirms the continuing pertinence of industrial action as a key source both of worker power and of union renewal. Kelly's (1998) analysis correlated patterns of strike activity and union growth. Despite legislative impediments, the continued salience of industrial action within processes of organising and mobilisation was clear within the research findings (see below).

Further pertinent literature themes include that of union effectiveness. Findings within mobilisation studies and work by Waddington and Whitson (1997), Greene *et al.* (2000) and Waddington (2006) demonstrated that even relatively high levels of density do not signal union growth and renewal where workplace unionism appears unable or unwilling to win manifest gains for members and resist managerial attacks. Again, membership involvement and union democracy are key variables within these processes. As this chapter will indicate, reduced levels of such involvement emerged as union organisation became less effective in the workplace. Another is the suggested tension between conceptions of 'organising' and 'servicing' (see Heery *et al.* 2000). This was not borne out by the research for this chapter. Perhaps most significant for the chapter's argument is the conception of contradiction between two interlinked facets of unions, namely, 'union-as-institution' and 'union-as-movement' (Cohen 2006). This counterposition depicts these trajectories as dialectically interwoven rather than diametrically opposed. Yet the trajectories point in different directions for strategies of union renewal. The relevance of these directions appears marked in terms of the largely 'top-down' direction of current union organising strategies in Britain (Carter 2006: 422; Gall 2007: 105; Heery *et al.* 2000: 43). In the case of the SEIU, a major progenitor of 'organising' (Bronfenbrenner *et al.* 1998; Foerster 2001), these tendencies and contradictions have by now worked themselves out in a marked suppression of membership democracy (de Turberville 2007; Moody 2007). Yet even in British unions, where bureaucratic tendencies tend to be less hegemonic, the same contradictions are arguably apparent, and it is these which frame the account of the research here.

The 'organising model' in T&G-Unite[1]

The T&G-Unite Organising Strategy (OS) was selected as a site for examination of these issues for three reasons, namely, the relative newness of the strategy, the significantly greater proportion of union resources devoted to organising compared with other unions, and its grassroots, workplace-based orientation. Graham (2006: 4), the T&G/T&G-Unite Director of Organising, argued the key objectives were 'rebuilding the...shop stewards movement' and building 'self-led industry-wide combine[s]'. This invocation of the type of independent, workplace-based shop steward organisation last seen in the 1968–74 'upsurge' (Cohen 2006, 2008; Lyddon and Darlington 2001) raises the possibility of a potentially more movement-oriented example of union organising.

The fieldwork for the research involved interviews with, and observation of, a number of individuals and groups identified as key actors in relation to the OS. Interviews were carried out with the Director (DoO) and Deputy Director (DDoO) of Organising and with six Regional Organisers (ROs), in addition to observation of Field Organisers (FOs) and attendance at relevant meetings in three of the regions concerned. This was followed by interviewing of convenors, shop stewards and 'workplace leaders' at two key workplace sites involved in the Organising Strategy, and with activists in non-OS sectors. The OS itself is currently directed towards four sectors – meat processing, avionics, building service (cleaning) and logistics – identified through the union's 'mapping' techniques. As a result of the merger, some areas of the car industry were added in. With a relatively short research timeframe, not all areas covered by the OS were investigated, and priority was given to those areas signalled by the Organising Department, such as meat processing and, at the suggestion of a Regional Organiser, a car plant newly involved in organising. To provide a counterpoint, the research also included observation and interviewing of six activists in non-OS sectors.

Strategic and resource-intensive organising

The OS drew significantly on the union's central financial and institutional resources, rather than on workplace-based or membership-led activity, giving rise to contradictions between institutional and membership-based aspects of unionism. Asked to identify the central features of the OS, both directors of organising placed immediate emphasis on a 'sectoral' rather than workplace-based approach. Based on macroeconomic analysis provided by the union's research department, sectors were identified as eligible for inclusion within the OS through 'mapping' the economy and selecting targets on the basis of 'filters' such as size, technical change and the economic viability and stability. Thus: 'We do all that – reduce it to seven or eight possible sectors...and then the leadership picks which we do.'

The 'leadership' referred to is that of the TGWU's lay National Executive Committee, making this process highly democratic in formal terms.

However, it stands in contrast to earlier 'spontaneous', workplace-based dynamics which had once stimulated considerable membership growth in the union. Any suggestion of extending the OS to more 'traditional' or member-led areas was rebutted in terms of the union's resources: 'What we can't do is take 14 groups or 23 sectors, we just haven't got the resources to do that.' The main dimension of the reliance on employed union personnel was stark. The DoO stated: 'The fact is we've got suf-ficient resources. And that's both organisers and money. [We employ] more organisers than any other union – 102 – and it'll probably rise to 130, 140 within another 12 months. The commitment is to spend £10–20m a year on organising.' The necessary dependence upon such union resources indicated the emphasis on a 'top-down' approach. Thus, the DoO argued: 'It's got to be led from the top, it's about prioritising organising in the union…because it takes a lot of resources to create an organising union…which means the leadership of the union…has to drive it effectively.'

Coupled to the resource intensiveness was the strategy of external leverage. Employing a range of activities such as demonstrations, inter-ventions at shareholders' meetings and general 'pestering' of corporate CEOs, this means sought to exert pressure for improvements in the con-ditions of workers in OS sectors by damaging brands and reputations. The DDoO outlined an example: 'We've particularly targeted [a lead-ing supermarket chain] and we've used a whole capital leverage strat-egy against them – protests around the world – Hong Kong, Moscow, Indonesia.' Such activities would not have been possible without the considerable financial resources of the union at extra-workplace level. A shop steward who participated in such a campaigns described how: 'A hundred of us bought shares in [the supermarket chain] and were ready to move a motion [at a shareholders' meeting] and I think that was the straw that broke the camel's back…It's the union that paid [for the shares], I can't remember how much but it would be in the tens of thousands of pounds that was spent on it.'

Workplace density and leadership

Such resource-based 'leverage' strategies exist on a financial scale well beyond the reach of shop steward milieus which were rhetorically invoked by the DoO, and this lends support to the notion of the contra-dictory trajectories of unions. But unions cannot function without mem-bers, and the workplace-based dimension of the OS existed in terms of the need to build levels of membership density that would both impress recalcitrant employers and fulfil the fundamental purpose of the OS by 'putting on' members. As one RO argued: 'If we go to [employers] saying we've got 60% membership and here's a petition signed by 80% of the workforce, and if we don't get this dealt with, we will be starting a campaign and targeting your clients [supermarkets] then they have to listen.' So workplace organisation was, in turn, necessary to secure the desired membership growth. As such it figured in a curious reverse dynamic whereby, rather than organising being required to win victories, leverage-based victories required organisation. As the DoO put it: 'The key thing is if you don't have the density before you move on the issue ... you either lose the issue ... or you win it and you're teaching workers that they don't really have to be collectivised in order to win'. It is notable that this process stands in direct contrast to historical patterns of union formation in which workers self-organise before formal unionisation takes place.

The OS deemed that initial or primary focus on the workplace would mean 'if you didn't take the sector then effectively this isolated workplace [becomes] the most expensive concept for the company, becoming vulnerable and probably going to close'. Nevertheless, the orientation on the workplace was clear, albeit mediated by an Organising Department (OD) strategic approach which emphasised centralised planning: 'You get the issues, you identify the leaders, you build your organisation, you get in some self-education and *they* win it by collective action. It's got to be them winning it ... We're trying to rebuild shop steward confidence and power here so it's got to be them.' The emphasis on leadership identification drew attention to the OS adherence to ideas of 'charismatic' leadership which led organisers to take action beyond existing patterns of lay representation in the workplace in order to encourage the development of alternative workplace-based leaders: 'Other unions talk about activists, Unite concentrates on leaders. Workplace leaders [are] different from activists ... you've got to have workplace leaders and they may or may not be our shop stewards'. Some may conclude from this that the national union in its institutional capacity was playing an important role in helping workers decide who their leaders should be.

Emphasis on organiser-identified 'workplace leaders' by implication challenged the role of existing activists who, however unsatisfactory, had been chosen by fellow workers in some manner. This neglect of a potential source of support and activism for the OS lends some support to the emergence of activist opposition. The basis for this neglect was predicated on the lethargy of shop stewards from 'brownfield' sites. In the words of one RO, they were shop stewards 'for the wrong reasons', summed up as work avoidance. But the basis of activist opposition was also highlighted by this RO in terms of resentment against young, inexperienced, upstart 'Turks' coming into the workplace and telling others how it was to be done.

The 'reverse dynamic' of purportedly member-led strategies being designed and conducted by employed union officers might seem countered by the OS championing combine committees, that is, bringing it close to the 'traditional' agenda of building shop steward strength and solidarity across different workplaces. However, again the research revealed a relative lack of efficacy in combine organisation, which might have been expected given the much more oppositional employer environment compared to that experienced in the previous period of the combine organisation. This was, of necessity, enhanced by OD's caution over industrial action, which while understandable in the context of the salient legislation, acted as an inhibitor on more traditional, and effective, forms of worker resistance (see below).

Organising strategy effectiveness

While density is, perhaps, a necessary condition for, or aspect of, the revitalisation of unions, situations of 'shallow power' (Moody 2007) where unions are recognised and have majority density but little bargaining effectiveness are currently widespread (see Waddington 2006; Kersley *et al.* 2006). This lack of effectiveness was evident in two aspects of the OS – its inability to build density and loss of effectiveness even in pre-existing areas of majority density. In many ways, the damage had already been done by 'partnership' deals, an approach the current TGWU leadership, which had initiated the OS, had specifically repudiated (Graham 2006). Nevertheless, the difficulty in building density in many OS areas highlights the absence of a 'strong-to-weak' perspective as a consideration in choosing targeted sectors, for the principal determinants for selection were economic. Thus the criteria lacked recognition of key internal dynamics of union renewal, shown historically when unions 'move out' from strong to weaker sections (Cohen 2006: 12–13; Kelly 1998: 96). Within the OS sectors and regions studied, the weakness of many targeted groups was evident. ROs presided over areas in which organised unionism was scanty or non-existent; one estimated the extent of density as '10%–20%, maybe a little bit higher [but a] lot of individual sites are completely greenfield or we [have] one or two members'. In this context, some sophisticated organising techniques were utilised. Thus, selection of 'minor issues' seen as 'widely felt', 'deeply felt' but 'winnable' by newly organising groups of workers occurred and low-risk actions (such as petitions) were encouraged in order to build density without undue danger of victimisation. Concrete results, in many cases, were impressive. For example, contract cleaners at Stanstead airport had been without an across-the-board pay rise for four years but shortly after gaining union recognition, the workers there received pay rises of between 4% to 8%.

Yet judged by the criteria such as wider advances in membership, recognition and working conditions, these techniques were, comparatively, limited. In one region, for example, only 35 out of a target of 1,116 sites in grocery retail had been organised, indicating the limits on union capacity and time delays in the capability for deploying sectoral leverage. In another two regions, consistent effort could not overcome lack of organisation in a deindustrialised area suffering widespread and long-standing unemployment. Three targeted meat-processing sites remained unrecognised, with membership density rates ranging from 12% to 17%. At the highest-density site, an outbreak of anger over fake 'redundancies' revealed widespread grievances. But, while this episode invoked processes identified within mobilisation theory as central to the dynamic of organising, the 'collective actions' encouraged by ROs along OS lines, such as petitions, lacked the efficacy of traditional 'spontaneous' expressions of mobilisation like walking off the job.

By contrast, success was more obvious in already unionised sites (see also Waddington and Whitson 1997). At a logistics company, organisers had worked with existing stewards on the company council to make it 'more agitational', encouraging in the process a rise in density – from 30%–40% to 70%–80% – and the creation of ten new stewards. In similar terms, the example of FlyBe in the same region showed how recognition could be achieved from a base of young, non-traditional workers who had assumed that they 'didn't need a union'.

Drawing attention to these successes, both the directors of organising emphasised ongoing net gains in membership: 'We started with nothing, gained 5,000 in the first year, by [the end of 2008] it should be over 50,000...' (see Table 3.1). These were unquestionably impressive gains when compared to those of the earlier (but now repudiated) 'partnership' means. However, such undoubted gains were counterbalanced by losses in other, non-OS areas of the union (see Table 3.2), underlining the pertinence of complaints by activists of neglect within these sectors. As the convenor of a non-OS site put it: 'The organising campaigns have been very successful in gaining new members [but] the problem is...a lot of the time they've...overlooked the people that are leaving. They've got to back up their leavers, track them and find out why they're leaving.' Interviewees cited a lack of support from the national union in

Table 3.1 Net organising membership gains, 2005–8

Year	Members recruited
6/05–12/05	4,284 (food only)
2006	10,211
2007	15,106
1/08–8/08	9,502
Total	39,103

Source: Unite-TGWU Organising Department.

Table 3.2 TGWU membership

Year	Numbers
2000–1	858,804
2001–2	848,809
2002–3	835,351
2003–4	816,986
2004–5	806,938
2005–6	777,325
2006–7	761,336
Net loss	97,468

Source: *Annual Reports*, Certification Officer.

these areas as a key explanation for problems with retention. And this may take the form of the much maligned 'servicing'. In the words of another non-OS activist:

> *The Organising Department is very dynamic, but the main body of the union still has to service existing unionised workplaces. Organising can't be divorced from the main body of the union ... If the union position is accepting concessions too easily, not advancing struggle, the Organising Department will recruit members but what will they be recruited to? There's nothing wrong with organising but it could be a revolving door syndrome.*

The highly concrete nature of the issues raised by these 'already-existing' activists appeared absent from the OS priorities, even in relatively strong, high-density areas, again indicating the relative distance of the OS from ongoing forms of self-activity and organisation, rooted in the material, exploitation-related preoccupations of workers.

In the workplace

Proximity to the workplace generates an ability to detect the concrete realities of working conditions and bargaining, revealing the more 'organic' bases for collective efficacy and action. At the meat-processing factory, a membership density of almost 100% membership was presided over by a dedicated and experienced convenor. This strong position was based on its previous history of company-wide collective bargaining, which was then disrupted when a new owner had dismantled this structure in favour of site-by-site negotiations. According to the convenor, this spurred activists 'to organise ourselves a bit more effectively and reach out to other sites... to try not just to bring back the collective bargaining we had... but to extend it'.

This suggested that forms of company-wide organisation had been generated before the inception of OS. Indeed, the convenor noted that, 'our attempts to organise [following the company's attempt to change the final salary pension scheme] probably led to us become part of the Organising Strategy'. The building of a cross-site combine proved its worth in a company-wide dispute sparked when the new employer contradicted its own insistence on negotiating 'site-by-site' by instigating a pay freeze across all plants. Although all 12 sites voted for the action, workers walked out at only half, a weakness attributed to the 'very early stages' of combine development. Nevertheless, the action was enough to break the pay freeze and compel the employer to negotiate on other matters.

Yet signs of diminished effectiveness emerged even within the strongest organised site. One employee identified as a 'workplace leader' appeared unaware of or at best confused as to the role of the OS: 'I don't really have an opinion. Whatever's going to benefit the workforce and the members.' But, when asked about the main issues facing workers, she became more engaged: 'They expect you to do more and more, take on more and more.' The union's effectiveness in combating such problems was attributed almost entirely to the convenor. So was the convenor himself 'the union'? 'He says – You're the union. And if you have a problem, you come to me and I'll see what I can do about it. It's up to the person to go and see him.'

Such comments bore relevance to issues of membership involvement and union democracy which are central to worker mobilisation and union effectiveness. Belying the passivity and reliance on the 'servicing' relationship was a dynamic in which conditions angered workers to the extent of saying: 'We should just walk out.' Yet such spontaneous triggers for mobilisation were vitiated by obstacles of legal and institutional dimensions: 'We speak about...strik[ing]...But [the convenor] will say you have to go through the procedures.' Thus, while the convenor was praised for his consistent record in fighting for the members, such aspirations were understood as inevitably limited: 'You just wish he could have more elbow grease but his hands are tied a lot of times.' Such constraints were at the root of the lessened union effectiveness in this high-density plant. The response to these constraints by OS leaders invoked an arguable weakness and contradiction within 'organising' identified by the convenor himself:

> As well as organising being a challenge for the employers it can be a challenge for the union...Sometimes you can march people up to the top of the hill and then the union has got to...take them back down the hill...It can be a difficulty at times, you lose control of the reins...It can run away from you. A Pandora's Box maybe?

Efficacy of industrial action

The issue of industrial action, and its role in union renewal and mobilisation (Buttigieg *et al.* 2007; Kelly 1998), recurs because of the central place given to sectoral combines by the OS. While considerably weaker than their historic counterparts (see Beynon and Wainwright 1979), they point to workplace-led action. Yet, although industrial action was acknowledged by both organising directors as a possible and powerful aspect of extant combines, its use was treated with extreme caution. Conceding that 'at times we have had to hold industrial action ballots', the DoO firmly situated potential deployment of industrial action within the existing framework: 'We will use [it] but it has to be within legal boundaries.' Striking was characterised as 'a last resort...if employers refuse to do the right thing'. By contrast, preference was expressed for alternative, more propagandistic forms of pressure like leverage acting upon corporate reputation and brands. Within this context, the prioritisation of a formal, institutionally led approach was again asserted: 'Sometimes it's not enough to just have workers doing things.'

The same reservations concerning worker-led instances of direct action were exhibited by ROs of a car plant where attempts to build up its minority union membership were still trammelled by the no-strike agreement of all three Japanese car companies operating in Britain. A recent victory over the issue of allowing workers bottled water 'trackside' was attributed to using OS tactics of identifying workplace issues through surveys. This process facilitated stewards and organisers identifying workplace leaders and recruiting 200 more members. Both ROs and stewards spoke excitedly about the member-led logic of the OS: 'It's all about getting workers to get involved themselves... It is being promoted from the leadership of the union... but it only works when you do it bottom-up.' However, when considering the implications of such mobilisation for tackling employer intransigence over working hours, the ROs were more cautious: 'You manage... those expectations. You can't just go and say "Everybody out" – you may have done that thirty years ago but you'd be in breach of contract, it would be unlawful and it would be bloody stupid.' Another commented:

> *You do create a bit of a monster in some cases with what we're doing, especially if you get the wrong people... People who would think 'Oh yeah, we'd like a union in there because we can all go out on strike'... When identifying leaders you've sometimes got to have the right balanced approach.*

There was no mention of an unofficial walkout three years earlier which had been effective in forcing the company to back down over draconian overtime requirements (see Amicus 2005).

Outside the organising strategy

While many shop stewards and other activists expressed strong support for the OS in principle, interviews with workplace representatives in non-OS sectors revealed in practice difficulties with what were viewed as its neglect of 'actually existing' organisation and conflict. At the time of interview, the two leading activists concerned were themselves involved in a strike and emphasised the potency of the action in mobilising and building membership: 'People [had been] really scared... [Then] once they got outside the gates picketing it was out of [management's] hands and... as the control went from them you could see the empowerment of the workers building.' The action had also been 'a big recruiting tool... Once [management] start prodding you with a stick, people start fighting back and they think right, I've got to be in a union.' For this reason, one respondent was critical of the lack of orientation within the OS to existing sites of action and mobilisation: 'I think it's all well and good [that] they've got these organisers but... [if there's] an issue, a dispute, they should be recruiting there... The [Organising Department] should be available pretty much whenever people are having a dispute.' While striking contributed to the build-up of union organisation and membership participation at this site, these activists attributed earlier difficulties and an overall deterioration of union effectiveness to constraints on collective industrial action:

> *When we first started here trying to get a union in, it really was a case of people [feeling] let down by the union – they'd paid their membership for years…People…expect the union, once a problem comes up, to be able to solve it, and when you start saying that your hands are tied because of the law…their initial frustration is 'Well what's the point of being in a union?'*

Such constraints also explained some activists' hostility to the OS, whereby the desire to avoid the consequences of unlawful action seemed to take precedence over attempting to resolve members' grievances when they wish to deploy walkouts. Other activists similarly emphasised the importance of industrial action and the limits posed by the law. One car industry steward complained:

> *In the last three years we've had three repudiation letters when trying to strike against concessions. It's a huge danger for recruitment when people stand as stewards and then the full-time officer says: 'There's nothing you can do, you can't take action'. The danger then is 'Why be in the union? Why be a steward?' It's about what the union stands for.*

In bus transport, another activist argued: 'I think in about six to eight months all this "legal or not legal" [talk] on supporting a strike is going to be broken because of the weight of the people…Now, if the strikes don't go ahead people are going to be really pissed off.' A strike two years previously had put pressure on this local leadership: 'It gave a message – this is how the union should be.' But another car industry activist gave a different perspective: 'The whole Unite membership…now is upwards of two million. If they take them to court…It's a multi-million pound union now. They would never risk anything.'

Conclusion

A central theme of this chapter has been the contradiction and opposition between dynamic, more ambitious and conflictual trajectories of workplace-based resistance and the more cautious, institutionally structured perspectives of union leaderships formally embracing an 'organising' perspective. While incidents of major mobilisation remain relatively rare in current circumstances, it is worth recalling that the grassroots dynamic associated with previous periods of union strength – such as the 1968–74 'upsurge' – began not with formal unionism but with self-activity and workgroup organisation around concrete, highly specific issues of exploitation and work intensification. Such factors may impel union formation even 'before the union [comes] along' (Fink 2003: 135) or when 'a lot of [workers] didn't know what a union was yet' (Clawson 2003: 102). As de Turberville (2004: 788) pointed out: 'A genuine grassroots organizing model does not need modelling; it is, by definition, simply something people do *without* top-down influence' (emphasis in original). Yet this dynamic, historically associated even after unionisation with 'insurgencies from below' (Weir 2004: 294), fundamentally poses a challenge to the institutionalised preoccupations and priorities of union leaders.

The key to union renewal would, thus, appear to lie in a workplace-based process of self-activity and mobilisation based on the concrete impact of exploitation and intensification of labour. Such structural factors both spark action and resistance even among previously passive or intimidated workers and prompt union consciousness even in the face of pre-existing value systems (see Kirton 2005: 394; Redman and Snape 2006). The potential for union renewal of such mobilising factors lies in their independence from 'idealist' preconceptions of unionism and the influence of structural factors which may catapult even the most anti-union workers into confrontation with the employer (Cohen 2006). Yet such workplace-based resistance contains highly subversive implications for unions as institutions, as indicated by the T&G/T&G-Unite's purportedly mobilisation-oriented model of organising. In examining these contradictions and the dual-faceted nature of 'unions-as-institution' and 'unions-as-movement', attention to the underlying *politics* of unionism is essential. Such considerations have become more common in recent contributions to the continuing debate on the OM. Gall (2007: 105), for example, argued that 'one route to "squaring the circle"' between 'bureaucratic rationalist' and 'social movement' aspects of unionism might be 'for unions to engage not just in "organizing" renewal but also in "political" renewal'.

But what kind of politics should inform 'political renewal'? The reference to 'social movement' unionism is indicative, and indeed this characterises much of the recent response to the creeping bureaucratisation of the OM in the US (see Clawson 2003; Fletcher and Gapasin 2008).

Nevertheless, a recent British contribution (Holgate and Simms 2008) suggests, at least implicitly, a still more subversive dynamic. While 'social movement unionism' gains its meaning largely from factors extraneous to the workplace, these authors point out that the history of organising, particularly in the US, displays in some ways an 'anarcho-syndicalist' trajectory. The roots in the Industrial Workers of the World activity of one strand of 'organising' ideology are noted by these authors, while de Turberville (2004: 778) cites not only the 'Wobblies' but early Congress of Industrial Organisations (CIO) influences, along with British upsurges such as the First World War shop stewards' movement and 1968–74 workplace-based militancy, as evoking a (supposedly mythical) 'golden age of organising'.

While neither of these contributions can be construed as endorsing syndicalism, such analysis raises issues about the potentially anarchic, even revolutionary implications of 'ordinary' working-class resistance. As the aforementioned – non-revolutionary – strike leader described the frustrations of his members and fellow-stewards: 'It's almost becoming anarchistic where people are just going well sod the law, sod the unions, I've had enough…this situation's wrong and this is the only way I know how to deal with it.' While this may seem a rather melodramatic portrayal of the trajectory of standard 'economistic' worker activity, the research for this chapter is perhaps sufficient to assure us of the underlying paradox between institutionally based 'organising' rooted in formal structures and resources, and the essentially unstable, sometimes explosive dynamic of workplace-based resistance (see Gall 2005: 220). Despite its laudable aim of 'rebuilding the shop stewards' movement', policy stemming from the TGWU-Unite's OS indicated an emphasis on leverage campaigns funded by union resources well beyond the reach of lay activists, and sectoral organising choices based on head office research rather than on workplace-based resurgence. By contrast, the simpler logic of basing renewal on sites of already-existing activism was absent from the OS.

Perhaps as a result, while net gains in the Organising Department sectors have been considerable, the impact of the OS has not been to stem the overall fall in membership, let alone move unionism forward to a notably higher level of renewal and reinvigoration. The contradictions highlighted here between the institutional need for stability and the unpredictable 'movement' forces captured in the convenor's metaphor of a 'Pandora's Box' may, ultimately, be irresolvable (see also Gall 2009b). But, in the 'choice' posed between the two linked facets of the OM, those who see the fundamental potential of independent

workplace-based mobilisation and self-organisation for social and political change may opt for that route, whatever its implications.

Note

The help and support of Unite's Organising Department, organisers and
activists is gratefully acknowledged. My thanks are also to Gregor Gall
for his extensive help in revising this chapter.

1. By early 2009, the merger between Amicus and the TGWU to fully form Unite
   is incomplete. The TGWU identifies itself as 'the T&G section of Unite' on its
   website.

4
Social Partnership and Union Revitalisation: The Irish Case

Kieran Allen

Introduction

The Irish model of social partnership is sometimes hailed as a success story for unions. According to a familiar storyline, the unions avoided marginalisation and devised a strategy to balance competitiveness and equity (Hardiman 1988). They were given a political voice and were able to lessen the worst effects of neoliberalism. Unlike their British counterparts, who followed a path of confrontation and support for 'old Labour values', Irish trade unionism modernised and reaped the rewards. This, at least, is the storyline developed by its advocates. Paul Sweeney (2008: 125), of the Irish Congress of Trade Unions (ICTU), suggested that social partnership has brought about a fundamental change in the relationship between workers and employers, claiming that 'for unions and employers the biggest accomplishment has been getting into the heads of each other, to understand unambiguously what the deep concerns of the other side are'. Critics, however, might suggest that the communication traffic has mainly been one-way, with the unions taking on the employers' problems. Statistics on the distribution of wealth do not indicate that Irish workers benefited more than their counterparts elsewhere. Living standards certainly improved as a result of a long boom but the share of the economy distributed to wages declined. Table 4.1 presents data on the adjusted wage share of the total economy and indicates that the share distributed to wages declined faster in Ireland than in the original EU-15. More interestingly, the decline occurred as the number of employees increased dramatically. The figures indicate a significant shift in wealth and, thus, economic power within social groups in Ireland.

Nor can it be claimed that that the political exchange which was at the heart of social partnership – wage restraint for a say in policy-making – resulted in greater social protection. Ireland has the lowest level of spending on social protection in the EU-15 and is reducing it further, as Table 4.2 indicates. Means-testing rather than universal social insurance is more prevalent, with 29% of total expenditure on benefits being means-tested as against an EU average of 10% (European Commission 2001: 21). Ireland has also one of the lowest levels of spending on pensions, at only 3.7% of GDP as against, at the other extreme, 14.7% in Italy (Eurostat 2005: 138). One result is that Irish workers have longer working lives, with the average exit age at 64.4 as against an average of 61.0 across the EU (European Commission 2005: 59). In the private sector, pension coverage is very poor with only 38% of employees being covered for pensions (Pensions Board 2005: 38).

However, aside from these broader issues, social partnership has also coincided with a dramatic decline in union density and involvement by members (see Table 4.3). Absolute numbers of union members have increased but at a much slower rate than the expansion in jobs. In the decade between 1994 – which is conventionally taken as the start of the

Table 4.1   Adjusted wage share of total economy: Compensation per employee as percentage of GDP at factor cost per person employed

	EU-15	Ireland
1960–70	–	77.9
1971–80	74.5	75.9
1980–90	71.8	71.2
1991–2000	68.7	62.3
2001–7	67.3	54.0

Source: European Commission Statistical Annex of European Economy (2007), Table 32.

Table 4.2   Total expenditure on social protection as a proportion of GDP at current prices

	1991 (%)	1994 (%)	1997 (%)	2000 (%)	2002 (%)
EU-15	26.1	28.0	27.8	27.2	27.9
Ireland	19.6	19.7	16.6	14.3	16.0

Source: Eurostat (2005).

Table 4.3 Trends in union density in Ireland, 1975–2004

Year	Membership	Density (%)
1975	449,520	60
1985	485,050	61
1995	504,450	53
2004	534,300	36
2007	551,700	32

Source: Roche and Ashmore (2001), CSO (2008a).

Celtic Tiger – and 2004, total employment grew from 1.221 million to 1.836 million. But the figures for union membership showed a much slower growth.

These bald figures, however, hide an even more spectacular decline in key areas. Ten years ago, Dublin had one of the highest concentrations of union members but today it has one of the lowest regional densities, with only the West and Mid-West lower. Density is also declining even faster among younger people rather than older people. Only 15% of the age group 20–24 are union members and only 26% of the age group 25–34 are unionised. More surprisingly, union density tends to be falling faster among manual workers than among white-collar employees. Professionals have a 45% density but only 28% of craft workers and 36% of plant and machine operatives are members. The long boom, which swept along the economy after 2001 until its eventual crash in 2008, was sustained by the housing market. However, density in the traditionally strong area of construction declined to just 23% of the workforce. In hotels and restaurants, union density has slumped to a mere 8% (CSO 2008a: 7). The workforce in Ireland has undergone an extremely rapid transformation with the influx of migrant workers. Non-Irish workers account for 16% of the overall labour force and in particular sectors such as hotels and other production industries they represent 38% and 19% respectively (CSO 2008b: Annex 1 and 2). Yet union recruitment among migrant workers is lower than among Irish workers. Irish-born workers have a 35% density but only 13% of non-Irish nationals are members (CSO 2008a: 5). The failure to recruit migrant workers has been a major cause of union decline in sectors such as hotel and catering.

These overall figures also contain an important dichotomy that has developed. Union membership is now highly concentrated in the public sector, and in the private sector – and in the foreign direct investment sector in particular – it is a declining force. In 2005, it was estimated that union density was 20% in the overall private sector and only 11% in FDI companies. It remained, however, at over 85% in the public sector (*Industrial Relations News*, 3 March 2005). This new pattern was a direct result of a strategy by private sector employers to reduce union influence. Ironically, while the employers' organisation, Irish Business Employers Confederation, was claiming to be a partner with the ICTU, its members were simultaneously undermining a union presence at the workplace level. Employers in the FDI sector began a union reduction strategy in the late 1980s just after social partnership had begun. A University of Limerick study of 42 incoming transnationals arriving onto greenfield sites between 1987 and 1991 found that just 16 agreed to recognise unions (Gunnigle *et al.* 2005). However, the pattern accelerated in later years. The *Industrial Relations News*, 26 February 2004 magazine contacted 45 Industrial Development Authority-supported companies who had announced more than 100 new jobs between 2001 and 2004 – in effect, mainly in the FDI sector. Just one of the 17 new international companies setting up recognised a union while the existing companies, which were expanding jobs, were also staying 'union free' (*Industrial Relations News*, 26 February 2004). In some instances, they operated what was known as a 'double breasted policy' where they continued to deal with unions in long-established plants but refused to concede union recognition in more recent plants. An interesting study of the phenomenon concluded that this strategy was influenced by management's expectation that they would encounter little union opposition (Gunnigle *et al.* 2005).

That expectation was not entirely unfounded, because the unions failed to press the issue of union recognition on employers. Before 2001, unions could refer a recognition dispute to the Labour Court for adjudication if they agreed to be bound in advance by the decision. In the period 1985 to 1991, the Labour Court issued 67 recommendations relating to union recognition, of which 88% were in the unions' favour. Recognition, however, was given in only 16 firms – or in 27% of the cases (D'Art and Turner 2003). Yet, despite the failure of Labour Court rulings to compel employers to recognise unions, there was no pronounced upward trend in the strikes for union recognition in the 1980s and 1990s. Determination by companies to resist union recognition was accompanied by a human resource management strategy to individualise employment relationships and to promote performance appraisal-based pay structures (Gunnigle *et al.* 2002). Other mechanisms to corrode collectivist responses included sophisticated techniques to filter recruits, a stronger emphasis on individual development and upskilling, improved and targeted management communications and various forms of stakeholder consultation. The combination of an active managerial policy to marginalise unions in the private sector and the failure of union leaders to respond led to the dramatic decline in union density.

One dispute dramatised the battle over union recognition in the private sector. On 7 March 1998, clerical workers, loaders, mechanics, catering staff and even the airport police walked out of Dublin Airport in solidarity with 39 baggage handlers in Ryanair who had gone on strike for union recognition. The baggage handlers had taken part in short stoppages for nine weeks after their company refused to negotiate on pay, working conditions and safety matters. Instead of backing the escalation, however, the SIPTU leaders called the action off by agreeing to an inquiry into the dispute, chaired by a former union leader and a former employer leader. This dispute was the background against which a 'high-level group' consisting of government, union and employer representatives was established under the aegis of the social pact, Partnership 2000. The group recommended a statutory mechanism for dealing with disputes where there was no system of collective bargaining. But it explicitly ruled out any form of statutory union recognition because this would erode Ireland's voluntarist system of industrial relations. Instead, unions were to be given the right to refer claims for improvements in pay, conditions or procedures to the Labour Court, who would decide in the first instance if the referral was valid. In the event that it was, the Labour Court could make a legally binding recommendation. However, it could not force any company to engage in collective bargaining with a union. Many of these proposals were eventually embodied in the *Industrial Relations (Amendment) Act 2001*.

This limited form of union rights gave the unions considerably less than that which was offered to British workers by the Blair government. Under the British procedure, the Central Arbitration Committee could issue a declaration that a union could be recognised for bargaining if a majority of employees in a particular union wanted that. Irish union leaders failed to press for mandatory union recognition because they were convinced that the good working relationship they had with state agencies would deliver a form of limited recognition in the private sector. Two years after the promulgation of the *Industrial Relations (Amendment) Act 2001*, D'Art and Turner (2003) were already arguing that its procedures would prove a dismal failure and might even legitimise the exclusion of unions from the workplace.

The organising model

Even before hopes in the 2001 Act were dashed, some unions began to understand that a change of strategy was required. In 1997, an unknown factory worker, Carol Ann Duggan, took 42% of the vote in a bid to become SIPTU President. Although she was defeated, it was a strong indication that considerable disquiet existed at the base of the union. Much of that anger was directed at an old guard who had traditionally maintained a warm relationship with the Fianna Fail political party and had grown even closer during the years of social partnership. A new moderate left emerged around Des Geraghty and Jack O'Connor to take over the leadership. Both developed a rhetoric which denounced neoliberalism and inequality in Irish society while remaining ardent advocates of social partnership. The ascent of a new leadership in SIPTU coincided with a debate in the international union movement on the differences between a 'servicing' model and an 'organising' model (Heery *et al.* 2000). The former relied on the actions of union officials outside to deliver services to individual members, often on a rights-based agenda supported by legal mechanisms. The latter emphasised the need for membership involvement and a refocus on collective action.

The first union to adopt the organising model was the Amalgamated Transport and General Workers Union, the Irish section of the TGWU. In Britain, the TGWU were very much to the fore in the transition to the organising model and so the debates were familiar to their Irish activists. The ATGWU embarked on a major recruitment campaign, but no sooner had it started than it was engulfed in a major internal conflict. The London head office suspended the regional secretary, and the campaign to win his reinstatement – which was eventually successful – consumed most of the energies of the key activists. The internal difficulties that the ATGWU faced meant that SIPTU, which was the strongest supporter of social partnership, became the main advocate of the organising model in Ireland. There were a number of reasons why the new leadership of SIPTU embarked on this path.

First, the ethos of 'business unionism' that had accompanied the growth of Irish social partnership fed directly into a particularly negative version of a servicing model. Wage negotiation occurred nationally and many social partnership agreements ruled out any possibility of cost-increasing claims at local level. Social partnership agreements also contained clauses that allowed managements to implement 'normal, ongoing change' without union opposition. In return for pay rises workers were signed up to a host of productivity-enhancing clauses.

Given this particular context, the main focus of workplace unionism became 'casework'. Typically union representatives took up the initial individual cases and then referred them on to the professional full-time negotiator who processed them through the Labour Relations Commission or Labour Court. This servicing model led to a major decline in membership participation. SIPTU is organised into branches that average between 2,000 and 3,000 members. These, in turn, group together workplace sections that are represented by section committees. The decline in union participation was most dramatically illustrated in the erosion of the branch structure. Attendances at many annual general meetings of the branches declined to a tiny handful and often retired members came to play a more prominent role. Sections rarely held workplace meetings and so 'the union' often became a small number of core activists who formed the section committee.

Second, while the employers' organisation, IBEC, has supported social partnership in the past, it is not wedded to it forever. Irish union leaders became familiar with the Australian experience where a close alliance existed between the Australian Council of Trade Unions and the Federal Labour government from 1983 to 1996. During these partnership years, the unions were seen to have an influence on economic and social policymaking. But the very passivity which social partnership induced also led to their decline, with union membership falling by over 1% a year in this period. Then, in 1996, the Labour government was swept out of office and replaced by an anti-union Conservative government led by John Howard. The political victory of the right encouraged employers to adopt a 'union substitution' strategy that aimed to marginalise or remove a union presence (Hurd 1998). Thereafter, Australian unions faced major problems and were forced to embark on a revitalisation strategy. Concern about the Australian case grew among Irish union leaders even before the onset of a major recession in 2008. However, when the Celtic Tiger died, it rapidly became clear that the employers' support for partnership was even more tenuous. The more militant propagandists for employer interests argued that unions were merely a voice for public sector workers and had a limited involvement with private sector employees. The main employer organisation, IBEC, made virtually no concessions to the unions during national negotiations in 2008, raising the prospect that social partnership might formally end. The decision of the SIPTU leadership, particularly under Jack O'Connor, to move to an organising model resulted from these concerns and led to a number of developments. An organising unit was formed and a special commission was created to examine the wider implications of the organising model. It was chaired by Michael Crosby (see Chapter 9, this volume), a former director of the ACTU Organising Centre and an advocate of the organising model pioneered by the SEIU in the US.

The SEIU model

The SEIU is seen as a model for many unions across the world because it has bucked the trend of decline and almost doubled its numbers. It achieved fame through its Justice for Janitors campaign in 1989 and then went on to pioneer the organising model within the AFL-CIO. After failing to make headway, it split from the wider federation to form a new Change to Win grouping in 2005 and has placed an increased emphasis on global union alliances and exporting its organising model to other countries. Milkman and Voss (2004: 7) argued that the key to the SEIU's success was changing:

> *their internal organisational practices to shift staff resources to organising. This means shifting priorities away from servicing current members and towards unionising new ones – creating more organiser positions on the staff; developing programmes to teach current members how to handle the tasks involved in shop floor grievances so that existing staff are freed up to work on organising; and building programmes that train members to participate fully in the world of external organising.*

In order to effect this change, the SEIU argued that 30% of the union's dues had to be devoted to organising. It has systematically recruited ex-students with a track record of campaigning to take up posts in its professional organising unit. Alongside other unions such as UNITE-HERE, it has placed a major emphasis on recruiting migrant workers and changing its image so that it reflects the diversity of the modern workforce. The union has also pioneered a confrontational approach whereby a host of ruthless tactics are brought to bear on employers who refuse to accept unions. Alongside traditional tactics of taking industrial action, these include naming and shaming individual employers, demonstrations that have culminated in mass arrests, consumer boycotts and interventions at shareholder meetings. Instead of a haphazard approach to organising, the SEIU has systematically targeted particular industries where it seeks to have a high union density in order to gain leverage.

Alongside these innovative approaches, the SEIU model contains two major negative features that have caused it problems in recent years (see Moody 2007). There has, firstly, been a huge emphasis on central-isation and development of structures that minimise member involve-ment. The key agents for expanding the union membership are the professional organisers and the dynamic of change is seen to be driven from the top. Milkman and Voss (2004: 7), who are sympathetic to the SEIU's approach, argued that 'in unions that *have* been successfully transformed, the process has typically been orchestrated from the top, contrary to the rather romantic view that only the rank and file can be the fount of democratic change'. The result is a deep tension in the SEIU's approach. The union promotes a rhetoric of membership activ-ism and empowerment but organises those very members into ever-larger branch structures where leaderships are effectively appointed from the top. Membership involvement in union elections has been cut back and voting has been transferred to convention delegates who are more tightly controlled by a centralised leadership. Piore (1994: 528) has described the organisational ethos of the union's leadership:

> *The ideas that underline it were drawn from the business management literature. The staff read widely in the business press and the more schol-arly literature as well. Their single most important source was probably the Harvard Business Review. As noted, the union hired the American Management Association to do staff training.*

Secondly, the purpose of the confrontation tactics is to win union recognition in order to forge partnership with the employers. The SEIU argues that it can bring 'added value' to employers as well as improv-ing their members' conditions. In a recent interview, SEIU leader Andy Stern (cited in *Democracy Now* 2006) spelt this out:

> *Well, first of all, one strategy we're considering is actually to work with our employers to try to see if we can have a different kind of relationship, you know, where we don't start off assuming we're going to create problems, but we try to solve problems, and we're seeing a lot of good new results by try-ing to think about how do we help workers and how do we help companies at the same time.*

This partnership approach has meant that the union often tries to break into a particular industry and then offers a neutrality agree-ment to employers so that they facilitate union organisation. A recent celebrated dispute involving California nurses has helped shed some light on how these neutrality agreements work. In 2003, the SEIU and a chain of private nursing homes in California concluded a 'sweetheart' deal whereby the union agreed to lobby politicians on the employers' behalf, to oppose patient advocates who demanded more staffing levels, to adhere to template agreements which banned picketing or reporting of abuse to public authorities, and to accept management's exclusive right to manage the business. In return, they were to receive the employers' blessing to organise (*San Francisco Weekly* 11 April 2007). A similar agreement, revealed by the *Seattle Times* (5 March 2008), contained a 'negative rhetoric' clause whereby both the union and the employer agreed not to speak ill of each other and promised no strikes for ten years. Some neutrality agreements even give employers the power to decide which workers might be eligible for union membership and what proportion of their company can be organised.

The SEIU model has been embraced with some enthusiasm by the SIPTU as a ready-made template to the problem of declining density. Their support for social partnership and their long immersion in business unionism help to explain some of the affinities. The SEIU model allows Irish union leaders to put a greater focus on revitalisation of an activist base which has been eroded by the 21 years of existing social partnership. But it does so within the strictly prescribed limits. The aim of the new limited forms of confrontation is a wider and deeper partnership with employers in the future. So confrontation may need to be unleashed against hotel employers who have embarked on a deunionisation strategy, for example, but the aim is a renewal of a wider partnership process with employers nationally. SIPTU is also attracted to the SEIU's model of neutrality agreements because it too has a long history of doing 'sweetheart' deals. In the 1970s, the ITGWU – SIPTU's predecessor – was promoted by the Industrial Development Authority as the main union selected to organise workers in US transnationals. More recently, SIPTU has concluded recognition agreements with building firms, which have led to the signing up of members without any real shop floor structure. The GAMA scandal, where it was discovered that Turkish workers on SIPTU-organised sites were being paid less than the minimum wage, grew out of this practice.

The rhetoric of the SEIU is also sufficiently distant from the left and supportive of modern corporate organisational practices to appeal to the Irish union leaders. By embracing this model, they can deflect a discussion of the problems that have arisen out of social partnership into organisational solutions. The answer to declining union density is not to examine past policies but to make organisational changes. SIPTU has, therefore, agreed to move to a target of devoting 25% of its resources to organising. It is reorganising into larger, more industry-focused branches and divisions. It has also concluded pacts with other unions to avoid poaching from each other. The impetus from these pacts arose after hundreds of SIPTU cabin-crew members defected to IMPACT in 2000 because of dissatisfaction with the support they received. In a defensive move, SIPTU has concluded partnership agreements with both IMPACT and the ATGWU not to recruit each other's members but to focus on greenfield areas. It is hoped that these internal organisational changes and pacts will pave the way for more recruitment. But, like the SEIU, the aim of such recruitment has been to ensure that the union keeps its seat at the table of social partnership.

Partnership and union revitalisation

The shift to an organising model has already brought some progress in recruiting new members. But important questions remain about the viability of a strategy that promotes organising while also seeking to extend or deepen social partnership. It is, therefore, necessary to assess the extent to which the legacy of social partnership helps or hinders union revitalisation.

There has been considerable debate in the broader literature on how the choices that unions make influence their recruiting effectiveness. Some have played down the scope for union policy to influence recruitment while others argue that the organisational strategies of particular unions can have an impact (Mason and Bain 1993). This literature, however, tends to focus on the internal union environment and emphasises factors such as decision-making structures, scope for innovation or the degree of sophistication in the organisational structures themselves (Fiorito *et al.* 1995). These internal organisational structures will certainly have an impact on the effectiveness of professional organising teams. But the organiser–new member relationship can hardly be a sufficient basis for revitalising unions. Virtually all advocates of union revitalisation proclaim a support for grassroots involvement in organising. It is asserted that the core principle of organising must be a questioning of management legitimacy and a development of self-organisation of workers in opposition to them (Gall 2003). While organisational techniques such as mapping, person-to-person recruitment, advertisements to pressurise recalcitrant employers can be used by all unions and can lead to an increase in numbers, they do not guarantee member involvement or participation. It is, therefore, difficult to see how an organising model can be sustained without strong workplace unions that have the scope to challenge employers. Or, to put it more precisely, if the organis-ing model is about more than a mere quantitative growth in numbers, it will require the development of local workplace organisation that is capable of challenging employers and winning gains through bargain-ing. Yet this, in turn, runs up against limitations imposed by social partnership in three specific ways.

Legal obstacles

Unions can be organised in the most difficult of conditions but the legal framework can either help or hinder them. The close relationship that Irish unions have established with their state has brought a particularly ambiguous approach to laws, which makes grassroots unionism more difficult. One of the key laws is the *Industrial Relations Act 1990*, which outlaws strikes over an individual worker unless lengthy procedures are adhered to. It insists on a secret ballot of all workers who might be affected by solidarity action. Even when workers vote to support others, their actions only become legal after having been sanctioned by the ICTU. The act removes traditional immunities and places the onus on unions to follow narrowly prescribed procedures before establishing a legal right to take industrial action. Yet this act was a direct outcome of social partnership. In introducing the Bill, Bertie Ahern, the then Minister for Labour, indicated that it grew out of close consultation with the union movement. He stated that 'all I have to say is that if ever a Bill was discussed as much with the people concerned as this Bill has been, I would like to read the files on it' (Dail Debates 1990). Despite the fact that a recognition dispute in Pat the Baker's was defeated because the *Industrial Relations Act* effectively ruled out solidarity action in its shops, SIPTU has not made the repeal of this act a condition for enter-ing national partnership talks.

Similar problems attend the *Industrial Relations (Amendment) Act 2001*, as we have seen. However, matters have become even more unfavour-able for the unions as a result of a key judgement of the Supreme Court in favour of Ryanair in 2007. Here pilots invoked the above Act to estab-lish limited representational rights against the notorious anti-union company, Ryanair. But, after the Labour Court ruled in their favour, Ryanair appealed the judgement and the Supreme Court overturned it. It ruled that the Labour Court had not investigated whether there was internal machinery provided by the company to resolve disputes and further noted that it would be impossible for them to investigate that matter as none of the employees in dispute had identified them-selves. In effect, the Supreme Court ruled that workers in an anti-union

company had to first identify themselves before internal disputes resolution mechanisms. It is a bar that few non-unionised workers might
feel able to overcome – particularly if they are only to gain such limited
rights. The employers' organisation, IBEC, has made it perfectly clear
that it will oppose the overturning of the Supreme Court judgement
in the Ryanair case. A significant level of union mobilisation would,
therefore, be required to remove this legal obstacle to union activity.
But the very attempt to do so would make the continuation of social
partnership itself difficult.

Reluctance to organise the transnational sector

There has been a pronounced reluctance to target Ireland's transnational
sector for union recruitment. This sector employs 150,000 workers and
is, in the most part, union-free. Although it represents a comparatively
small part of the overall workforce, it contains some of the biggest
workplaces and plays a central role in Irish capitalism. The touchstone
for most political argument in the country – whether it is on war, the
environment, worker rights or taxation – is that Ireland must not do
anything to frighten away the transnationals. Social partnership has
ensnared the union in this discourse as it is premised on an economic
patriotism whereby unions, management and the state pull together
to 'help create jobs'. Given the prevalence of this discourse, the unions
are particularly vulnerable to the argument that any disruption to the
transnationals will damage Ireland's image. The result is that they have
made no serious effort to unionise this sector.

The SEIU model that has been imported into Ireland also leads to a
similar conclusion about avoiding the FDI sectors – but for different
reasons. The emphasis on 'strategic' organising whereby unions seek
to gain dominant 'market share' in one industry so as not to damage
pro-union employers leads to an avoidance of the more globalised sections of the economy. This strategy assumes that firms which cannot
relocate to other countries are easier targets for unionisation drives.
There is some truth in this but there is also a pessimism that flows from
a particular 'mythology' about globalisation. This cedes all initiative
and energy to global corporations and plays down workers' capacity to
inflict damage on them. Industrial action by, for example, Intel workers in Ireland would have a dramatic effect on the corporations supply
chain.

One of the greatest previous expansions in union membership arose
precisely out of battles in the FDI sector. In 1968, 380 union members
from a workforce in the EI plant in Shannon that was owned by General

Electric walked out on strike. What followed was a strike of extraordinary intensity that was only resolved when the comparatively conservative leadership of the Irish Transport and General Workers Union – the forerunners of SIPTU – threatened a national strike in support of their members. As a direct result, the Irish state eventually prevailed on EI to recognise the union and, more importantly, a precedent was set for the future. In 1971, the then Minister for Labour summarised Irish policy *vis-à-vis* transnationals and unions as follows:

> *The current policy of the [Irish Development Authority] is to approve grant applications only where there is an understanding that management, if approached, by trade union members employed in the factory, will negotiate with the union in relation to pay and working conditions of such members.* (Dail Debates 1971)

It is an extraordinary tribute to the impact of this strike that it took employers more than a decade and a half to undermine this policy. It also showed that it is not impossible to organise this sector – it is rather a matter of strategic choices. An attempt to unionise key US transnationals would involve the unions in a huge ideological battle against official Irish society. Unions, therefore, that seek a revival of national partnership arrangements will therefore avoid targeting this sector. But this only indicates that social partnership poses a further obstacle to union revitalisation.

Lay organising

An organising model needs to be based on a wide layer of local activists who take responsibility for identifying workplace issues around which members can collectively mobilise. Through such a process the organic recruitment of non-members becomes more possible. Of the many influences which affect the decision of non-union workers to join a union, the key one is 'union instrumentality' (Charlwood 2002). In other words, does the union appear to be making gains and will it make a difference? This means that the most effective strategy is the development of this layer of activists who can self-organise. Or, to put it differently, instead of having professional organisers engaged in constant 'in-fill' organising where there is already a union structure, these are enabled to concentrate on 'greenfield' sites (Heery *et al.* 2003). Revitalisation may start with limited and almost gesture mobilisations during an initial period of confidence building. But over the long term it requires democratic structures which encourage and facilitate membership activism (Fairbrother and Stewart 2003). Here, however, a contradiction develops with social partnership structures. Corporatist arrangements generally involve a growing together of the leadership of key economic interest groups so that over a period they develop a shared outlook. Panitch (1981: 24) summed up the inherent dialectic of such arrangements when he stated that they are based 'on mutual inter-action at leadership level and mobilisation and social control at mass level'. Writing from the German experience, Streeck (1982: 70) suggested that corporatism creates a growing professionalisation of unions where the numbers and influence of full-timers grow at the expense of the rank and file. The pressure to achieve a consensus with employers and government also leads to a 'sealing off' of key areas of decision-making from grassroots pressure.

All of these contradictions are exemplified in the Irish case. Far from growing membership involvement, the tendency is towards consolida-tion of union branches into ever greater units. Faced with declining membership, a defensive strategy of amalgamation has been adopted which does little to open the union structures to lay membership activ-ism. Within SIPTU, elections are increasingly seen as a troublesome and costly business. Elections to the National Executive Council by members have been abolished and replaced with elections by union delegates at the regional conferences. Moves are also afoot to remove membership involvement in the election for the three national officers of the union. Beyond the formal level, other more subtle mechanisms have developed in the social partnership period that discourage union activism. As discontent grew with union effectiveness, the leadership tended to rely on an older guard to maintain control over an ossified branch structure. This sometimes meant that tiny numbers of people who attended meetings outside workplaces often made decisions for many of the uninvolved. Despite protestations about gender equality or a desire to involve the new migrant workforce, the rhythms of union activity are more suited to middle-aged men. The culture of the union which has developed around this core – often based on the pub and over-formal speech codes – discouraged sections of the new workforce from active involvement. The new organising model, which SIPTU has adopted, promises to create more openings for younger, non-Irish and female activists. But opening the union up to new forces can also mean eroding the structures of support for the pro-partnership leadership. This danger can be avoided either by limiting the degree of change or by promoting greater centralisation. But the problem of membership involvement and participation will not entirely go away.

Beyond all this, there are a host of restrictions placed on workplace activism by the content of social partnership agreements. In these agreements, all union members vote periodically on detailed proposals for concessions to the employers that they themselves and, crucially, *other* workers have to give. Most have little idea what these concessions entail as they are not directly affected by the vast majority of clauses in the agreements. Moreover, the small pay rises that are granted under the social partnership agreements have become conditional on a process of verifiable adherence. A concrete example from the local authorities will help illustrate the process. In order to get the national pay rises, all union members were asked to vote on the following measures for local authority workers. The *Towards 2016* agreement specified that there had to be extended opening hours of offices and other facilities, greater flexibility in attendance patterns, staff deployment and reassignment, an acceptance of 'shared services' in a variety of areas ranging from water treatment plants to data capturing, and acceptance of public–private partnership schemes (Towards 2016: 134–41). The vast majority of unionists who voted on these concessions were non-local authority employees. But before local authority workers got their pay rises they had to submit reports to a verification body on how exactly they had implemented these provisions. If their relevant management did not add their signatures to these reports, local authority workers would not get the increase. If they dared engage in any form of industrial action on issues covered by this range of issues, they would also be denied the pay rise.

Conclusion

Given this multifaceted context, it is difficult to see how one can claim to promote a revival of workplace activism while also seeking to enter such detailed national partnership agreements that restrict the very scope of such activism. By its nature, social partnership promotes an ethos of class collaboration and a co-option of union leaders into the agenda of employers (Allen 2000). It demobilises workplace unionism by ensnaring it in a web of procedural agreements and detailed productivity concessions that have been dictated from above. In recent years, it has become the principal factor in encouraging a systematic demoralisation that justifies every retreat with the pithy comment: 'sure, but it could be worse'.

This is not to claim that a particularly weak form of an 'organising model' could not be imported to Ireland under conditions of social partnership. The SIPTU leadership is clearly intent on doing precisely this. But this form of organising will be primarily built around a professional cadre of EUOs who 'sell' the union to non-unionised workers and, sometimes, even to their employers. The focus will be on the raw accumulation of numbers rather than any real empowerment of the base of the union through workplace activism. As in many aspects of modern society, the more the rhetoric about 'membership activism' expands, the more centralised the union machine will become around an apparatus of employed officers. SIPTU and other unions will face a tangible danger of withdrawing from the 'servicing model' – which they cultivated during the two decades of social partnership – to an 'organising model' which is reliant on EUOs and which brings little concrete gains to existing unionised employees. A genuine organising model would quickly come up against the limits of social partnership because it would challenge employers constantly. It would assert the independence of working-class union organisation rather than carrying the burden of the problems posed by the employers' drive for either 'competitiveness' or 'sacrifices to overcome the recession'. Unlike the workplace militancy of the 1960s, it would most likely require a high level of politicisation. Such a politicisation would need to go beyond a rhetorical denunciation of neoliberalism that defines workers primarily as victims. Instead, it would need to draw its energy from a range of social movements that have shown a tremendous capacity to challenge the agenda of the Irish state. The most recent of these movements, for example, the over-70-year-olds' 'grey' or 'pensioners' movement was able to mobilise thousands to defeat a government that withdrew medical cards from its participants. If the Irish union movement developed even an ounce of the energy, dynamism and militancy of the over-70s, it might make manifest advances. But if it remains mired in social partnership, its leaders will want to engage only in limited battles to demonstrate to employers that they are still alive and have gained more union density. Once the battles are over, they will work equally hard to prove how trustworthy they are to any employer willing to take them on as a partner.

5

Union Organising in the Netherlands – a Combination of Organising and Servicing Strategies

Maarten van Klaveren and Wim Sprenger

Introduction

Several authors have recently analysed the Anglo-Saxon post-Thatcherite legal and industrial arena *vis-à-vis* union organising, sometimes comparing it with organising in continental European industrial relations systems (*cf.* Gall 2003, 2006b; Frege and Kelly 2003, 2004). In the Anglo-Saxon industrial relations systems, union power and influence seem more directly linked with union density and lay activism than in countries like the Netherlands and Germany. Frege and Kelly (2003: 16, 19) suggested that, while US and British union leaders have long regarded membership loss as an indicator of union decline, notably German union leaders have been less concerned with membership decline because of the institutional union protection, like mandatory extension (ME) of collective agreements. This assessment may also be relevant for the Netherlands, with its industrial relations system resembling that of Germany and an even stronger legal base for ME. In the same vein, Heery (2003) asked why 'union organising' the unorganised is central to attempts at union revitalisation in Britain and the US but is less of a priority in continental Europe. These differences in priorities may seem outdated. Actually, arguments for emphasising union organising efforts in countries like Germany and the Netherlands look convincing, especially as institutional union protection seems to be weakening here. Organising may be an effective lifebuoy for unions that are confronted with fundamental changes in the labour market and dramatic losses of membership.

In looking at the 'way forward' for unions, Heery (2003: 522) separated organising as a principal choice for labour unionism developing 'actionism and collective organisation' from servicing unionism that provides representation and other services for individual members. We enter two caveats here. First, it may be questioned whether these approaches are mutually exclusive. At least in the Netherlands, notably the growing proportion of more highly skilled employees in the labour market may be attracted by union policies concentrating on servicing. Second, concentration on (more effective) collective interest representation along the paths already developed extensively in the Netherlands at both national and sectoral levels – participation in advisory bodies, sectoral funds, collective bargaining at industry level – may still be another viable option. In this chapter, we evaluate the viability of these various options through an analysis of experiences and activities aimed at improving union power and union density in the Netherlands during the last two decades. We examine whether productive combinations of options may be possible. These tasks are carried out by analysing a number of projects that the FNV, the largest Dutch confederation, and some of its affiliated unions have initiated since 1988.[1] The data to analyse the projects was gained from project reports, both published and internal, and by additional interviews with eight EUOs involved in current projects.

Dutch industrial relations and union density

Dutch industrial relations have always been characterised by strong tendencies towards centralisation, and, thus, union representation at company level has been comparatively weak. Following the principles set out at the end of the nineteenth century by Henri Polak, leader of the Diamond Workers' Union and founder of the Social-Democratic Labour Party, the Socialist confederation and its unions and, later, their Catholic and Protestant counterparts, were based on strong internal discipline, EUOs, adequate central strike funds, and high membership subscriptions. After the Second World War, centralisation was further reinforced by the creation of machinery of the Dutch consultation economy which included the 'recognised' union confederations. The Foundation of Labour (StAr, bipartite, founded in 1945) and the Social-Economic Council (SER, tripartite, 1950) were and still are its peak institutions. In the 1970s, the union landscape was restructured. In 1976, the Social Democratic peak organisation, NVV, merged with the Catholic peak organisation, NKV, into FNV while the protestant CNV confederation attracted a number of independent Catholic unions, and MHP, a confederation of white-collar unions, was also formed. In this merging process, the last remainder of a craft union structure was abolished and now union structures are fully industrial (Van Klaveren and Sprenger 2004).

Shortly afterwards, union power was heavily tested by a comparatively early process of deindustrialisation, resulting in steeply rising unemployment (11% in 1983). In 1979, membership reached 1.792 million (36% density). In the next seven years, the unions suffered from a net loss of 0.24 million members, bringing density down to 24% in 1987. This demise had serious organisational consequences. Between 1985 and 1995, FNV and its affiliated unions reduced their staff levels by one-third. Their ranks of unpaid activists were even more heavily depleted. From 1986 on, the numbers of union members grew again, but it remained difficult to keep abreast of the growth of employment, after Ireland which was the EU's most rapid: the employment rate (percentage of population aged 15–64 in employment) grew by 11.8% annually from 1990 to 73.1% overall in 2004 (European Commission 2002, 2006). While union density recovered to 28% between 1993 and 1997, it gradually fell again to 24% in 2004. FNV unions' density fell from 22% in 1979 to 15% in 2004 (Van Cruchten and Kuijpers 2007: 16).[2] Yet, bargaining coverage remained high. In 2006, 81% of Dutch workers were covered by collective contracts (Ministerie van SZW 2006: 37). Although union leaderships highlight the latent support for unions that 70–80% of the Dutch wage earners express in surveys, for instance in a major 2004 survey (Harteveld 2006: 21), the 1937 Law on ME is the primary mainstay explanation. This law states that, if a collective agreement covers a substantial share of an industry's employees, the Minister of Social Affairs and Employment (MSAE) can extend the agreement to the entire industry.

Mainstream Dutch unionism continues to function through the national institutionalised partnership relations, and appears to have regained robustness after being heavily criticised for notably the exclusion of 'outsiders' like flexible workers (Vos 2006). Yet, after losing their seats on social insurance and labour market bodies in the 1990s, the formal positions of the union confederations are now more tied up in SER and StAR. The ME system puts considerable pressure on unions and employers to control and coordinate negotiations centrally. Politicians in the Netherlands have recurrently attacked this system as being rigid and frustrating the decentralisation of bargaining, though thorough analyses have demonstrated that ME has hardly had any upward wage effects (*cf.* Freeman *et al.* 1996). In 2004–6 cracks in the ME system began to appear when small unions negotiated industry agreements on lower terms, which the MSAE (of the then centre-right government coalition) extended. This has notably been the case in independent call centres and in hotels. These arrangements did not last, but they brought down the lowest wage scales in the collective agreements to just above the Statutory Minimum Wage (SMW) (Hermanussen 2008; Van Klaveren and Sprenger 2008). The ME system remains vulnerable – it may collapse if union density diminishes further and the representativeness of the large union confederations is broadly questioned. Moreover, there is no getting away from the fact that it is a major disadvantage for unions because it provides a disincentive for workers to join them. Although most Dutch workers have always been 'free riders', the declining union membership has now brought the union movement closer to the danger zone.

FNV 2000: A union density agenda from the 1980s

In 1986, the FNV confederation started a process of self-evaluation of its future position and representativeness. The resulting report (FNV 1987) highlighted a number of new challenges which required effective responses in order to guarantee survival. The report was based on research conducted by an academic, Jelle Visser, and concluded that the Dutch unions were losing ground in new sectors and among new groups of workers. While they maintained a strong position among public servants and in traditional manufacturing industries, the first signs of liberalisation and privatisation of public institutions, as well as the effects of global restructuring of traditional manufacturing, contained serious warnings. On the other hand, FNV showed major weaknesses in organising in the growing new service sectors, among women, young workers, contingent and, notably, temporary and part-time workers (both often being one and the same). Recognising the obvious difficulties of organising these 'outsiders', the report proposed a change in strategy which can be called 'field enlarging', whereby FNV would not only continue to focus on existing membership but would also strive to enter the 'greenfields' of new workers, and accordingly give organising priority to these groups (*cf.* Heery 2003). For these latter groups, the report concluded that new forms of collective and individual services had to be developed while concomitantly making union organisation more visible and active at shop-floor level, with lay activists playing a vital role in convincing co-workers to join and become active.

Projects stemming from the FNV 2000 programme were aiming at: (i) entering 'white spots' (rapidly growing sectors, corridors or regional clusters of new economic activities with very low density rates) with promotional, bargaining and service initiatives, at the same time trying to avoid duplication through coordinating organising activities from various unions in the same workplaces;[3] (ii) developing special programmes and new policies, attractive for the new groups in the labour market, with special attention to the qualification and training of younger workers, childcare and part-time issues in particular for women, and organising temporary workers within the service unions; and (iii) changing the public profile and image of unions as 'old boy' networks into more diversified, 'colourful' and multifaceted ones.

From 1990 until 2002, under FNV's aegis of FNV 2000, at least 14 projects at subsector and regional levels or aimed at specific groups of workers were implemented. These covered (in chronological order of start-up): retail trade (Dribbusch 2003; Meerman and Huppes 1993; Van Klaveren 2008; Wijmans 1993); wholesale trade (Van Halem and Wetzel 2001); audiovisual media (Van Klaveren *et al.* 1992); banking (Tijdens 1998; Van Klaveren and Van de Camp 1994; Wijmans 1993), Schiphol airport (Van Klaveren 2001: annex 2), industribution (Van Klaveren 2001: annex 1, Van Klaveren 2002); Rotterdam mainport (Van Klaveren 2001: annex 3); cleaning (Goedhard and Tijdens 1993); ICT (Bouwman *et al.* 1994; Tijdens *et al.* 1999); hospitality workers (Willemsen and Gründemann 1999); call centres (Van Klaveren and Sprenger 2008); self-employed workers (FNV 2007); homeworkers and teleworkers (Van Klaveren *et al.* 2002), and workers with occupational diseases. These initiatives in general combined a) research on, and analysis of, the salient issues (problems, attitudes and ideas of union members, employers' needs, chances for improvement) with b) 'organising activities' (tracing potential members, developing attractive longer-term union strategies) and c) attempts to recruit and retain members. Though these 14 projects were mainly ignored in a recent report on innovative union strategies published by the FNV (Kloosterboer 2007), they are worth evaluating. After examining two projects in greater depth, we present an indicative overview of processes, contents and target groups of the projects.

At first glance, it appears that the 'FNV 2000' efforts have yielded some substantial results in terms of organising. While care has to be taken in suggesting causal relationships, it is evident that FNV membership rose from 0.893 million in 1986 to 1.171 million by 2006 (30% increase). The share of FNV membership amongst all union members rose from 58% in 1986 to 63% in 2006 (Van Cruchten and Kuijpers 2007: 16). If FNV union density is the chosen yardstick, the projects in wholesale, retail, banking, and industribution were successful, with densities doubling at least. Yet densities in ICT, independent call centres and cleaning remained in the 5%–10% range, or only slightly above that (Hooiveld *et al.* 2002; Van Klaveren and Sprenger 2008). The proportion of women members grew from 13% in 1985 to 32% in 2006, although this still means women are 40% less likely to be organised than men (Visser 1990a; Van Cruchten and Kuijpers 2007: 8).

Yet, there seems no reason for obvious optimism concerning Dutch unions' organising potential. Though in the last decade the density rate of organised workers with permanent contracts versus those of flexible workers has shifted slightly in favour of the latter (from 30% versus 10% in 1995 to 26% versus 11% in 2006), the density rate of the first category is still two and a half times that of the latter. Moreover, the density rate of young workers between 15 and 24 years old has to be a major worry, for it fell from an already low 15% in 1995 to 10% in 2004. Concomitantly, the union constituency in the Netherlands is ageing. In 2004, the density rate of the 45–64-year-olds was 35%, against 21% for the 25–44-year-olds (all figures here, Van Cruchten and Kuijpers 2007: 17).

Previously in 1990, Visser (1990b) warned against too much optimism because of structural imbalances in FNV organisation. Then, he made a plea for a 'FNV project 2000-bis', notably taking into account that the union positions in services remained weak: 'To act resolutely, the union movement [simultaneously] has to centralise and to decentralise: centralise by allocating more strategic powers and means in a result-oriented way to the confederation level, decentralise by developing a stronger presence at workplace level' (Visser 1990b: 36). Nearly 20 years later, the level of centralisation has, indeed, moved somewhat in the direction Visser suggested. Thus, the two largest FNV unions (FNV Bondgenoten and AbvaKabo FNV) represent more than two-thirds of FNV membership.[4] Jointly with the FNV construction workers' union, the third largest in size, these large unions organise exactly 80% of FNV membership, with the remaining 13 unions being much smaller (based on FNV information as of 1 January 2008). Thus, the conditions to allocate powers and efforts more strategically have improved, although not at the confederation level but within the two or three major unions. As a consequence of the combination of these internal developments and the forced withdrawal from labour market and social insurance bodies, the confederation level has been weakened.

As mentioned earlier, latent support for unions exists amongst 70%–80% of the Dutch wage earners. Yet, most of these workers are hardly inclined to join unions. This historical paradox partly reflects the underlying 'free rider' problem. But the other part of the explanation has been that affiliated unions only ever undertook lukewarm efforts to combine the power and trust ascribed to FNV as a 'brand' at national level with visibility, proximity and decentralisation at local and work organisation level. Only now are a growing number of unions taking initiatives in order to bridge this gap. Symbolic – but rather important – in this respect is that from 2000 on nearly all FNV unions prefaced or suffixed their names with 'FNV'. Moreover, these unions, in particular the larger ones, split up into smaller target organisations, better responding to demands of proximity and identification. An example is the FNV construction workers' union, recently split up into five sections serving five specific subsectors (construction, finishing and maintenance, furniture and wood, waterworks, and housing services).

Organising the self-employed: Combining servicing, collective representation and organising principles

In 1995, a FNV conference on 'Renewal of Work Organisations' discussed the array of new challenges for unions, with the flexible work organisation as one of its key themes. Representatives of various unions reported a growing 'problem' in their respective labour markets, namely, new groups of workers as 'autonomous employer without employees' ('zzp-er' in Dutch). These self-employed workers used to be concentrated in agriculture and in some specialised services like media, newspapers and arts – mostly as freelancers. Yet, they increasingly showed up in construction, transport, HRM services, IT, barbershops ('renting a chair'), consultancy, engineering, and even in health care. The new phenomenon not only affected the 'reach' of collective contracting, but was also a potential threat to mobilising workers in industrial action. Some argued that it was time to organise these newcomers in their own interest and in that of the union movement as a whole. Consequently, it was decided to start researching the needs and ideas of the self-employed, and to evaluate whether FNV could offer them adequate collective and individual services. Unlike in other countries (Germany, Austria), it was not regarded as important whether or not the self-employed had chosen their employment status freely. The overarching argument was that various groups of self-employed workers had a lot in common with workers in permanent or non-permanent jobs. In its renewed foundation declaration, FNV stated it would be organising the self-employed from then on.

Yet, union practice was far more complicated than such a union declaration. The FNV construction workers' union congress blocked a proposal to start organising activities among the self-employed, as they were perceived as 'enemies' and 'traitors' (despite some former union activists having taken the step towards self-employment). In FNV Bondgenoten, the initiative met with more approval. Led by former service union president, Martin Spanjers, this union invited the confederation and other unions to join in an organising initiative. A common steering committee was charged with planning and monitoring the process, identifying common interests and union products to be advertised, while active organising was to take place at the level of the unions involved. The guiding principle was that many self-employed workers may first identify themselves with their trade, and less with their employment status. Nevertheless, both FNV unions chose to create a special sister organisation so as to avoid confusion for the existing membership. In a later stage, both FNV ZBO (self-employed in construction and wood) and FNV Zelfstandige Bondgenoten (self-employed in services, agriculture, trade, ICT, manufacturing, transport, and health care) have been recognised as autonomous unions with their own voice within the FNV confederation. It was agreed that after some years their mother organisation would stop their funding, and from then on they had to become self-supporting. Both new organisations experienced a steady growth in membership. In 2005, six years after creation, FNV ZBO had about 5,000 members, and FNV Zelfstandige Bondgenoten about 3,500. As per 1 January 2008, these numbers were over 10,000 and 8,700 respectively. The boards of both organisations expect a further rise in membership, given the high numbers of self-employed workers in their areas, and the growing recognition that they are representing these groups *vis-à-vis* industry and national institutions.

Both unions have contacted many self-employed workers (in person, in meetings, by email and the internet) to identify and analyse their needs: for instance, which insurances would they like to have the union offering to them; which other services could be offered which the market does not sufficiently provide, and under which categories (administrative services, tax information, information for starters)? Gradually, packages of services and information were developed, fitting the needs of individual members. This implied building collective services and collective agreements with external providers as well as developing collective bargaining and collective interest representation. For example, after a long political struggle a law concerning maternity leave for pregnant entrepreneurs was recently passed by parliament. The unions representing the self-employed also worked on long-term policymaking, resulting in the publication, 'The dynamic triangle' (FNV 2007). This imaginary triangle connects the self-employed (first pole) with the unemployed or disabled workers (second pole) and the workers with permanent contracts (third pole). The union movement sought to enable workers to move between poles, depending on their situation and needs while minimising risks. Thus, self-employed status does not have permanent status. Additionally, these unions offered opportunities for mutual help through the creation of members' networks. Union recruitment of the self-employed takes place in various ways. One very effective way has been the arrangement the new unions have with the Chambers of Commerce, whereby every three months the latter provide the names and addresses of starting self-employed to the former. Having been approached with 'starter packs' of union literature, one in four has joined a union. Surveys showed unions belonging to the strong FNV 'brand' constituted a major reason for joining. Thus, this successful project was based on both union power in the national arena and proximity (representation), in combination with a community structure and individually targeted services.

Improving union density in cleaning: A switch to 'organising strategies'

Since 1985, the cleaning industry in the Netherlands has shown rapid growth. Outsourcing of services changed the position of many cleaners, who used to be covered and protected by collective agreements in manufacturing industries, large service organisations and public institutions. In quite a number of cases, unions succeeded in preventing such outsourcing processes for some time, sometimes by legal means. Yet, the number of cleaners employed by specialised cleaning companies continued to grow. In the early 1990s, Goedhard and Tijdens (1993) analysed the position of these cleaners for the Industrial Union FNV (now part of FNV Bondgenoten), which continued to represent these mostly outsourced workers. They found 145,000 workers, 75% of whom were women, in 3,500 companies, of which only 14 were large firms. The preponderance of migrants among cleaners was rising and believed to be 20%–25%, and concentrated in the western urbanised regions. The skill levels of the workforce were relatively low. More than half of the workers had contracts for less than 15 hours per week. Turnover rates were in some years up to 60%. Workers quitting complained that cleaning jobs were boring, physically exhausting, too low-paid, and with an inferior work atmosphere. The choice to take a cleaning job was dictated by the need to earn income, lack of other jobs in the regional labour market, social contact at work and flexible working hours.

Beforehand, the Industrial Union FNV had already undertaken some organising activities with cleaners, like special 'cleaning days' and drop-in sessions to bring more attention to this growing 'white spot', where in 1993 only 5% were unionised. In 1991–2, the union monitored complaints received from cleaners, showing that 42% were about pay and 20% about dismissals. The union leadership concluded that existing collective agreements did not protect the workers effectively against exploitation and job insecurity. In 1992–3, the union campaigned in a number of companies, yet with rather disappointing results in terms of recruitment. Goedhard and Tijdens (1993) discovered a variety of reasons why potential members would not (want to) join despite the workplace problems they experienced; the union (name) remained unknown, as did its 'products' relating to membership fee (estimated as being much too high by many part-timers), relatively scarce contact with co-workers, and in some cases the mistaken idea that the husband's membership enabled use of union services. The researchers concluded that organising these workers on a larger scale would not be possible unless new methods, new forms of contacts and new forms of mobilisation were developed.

Subsequent to this, the cleaning industry went through further growth. The number of cleaners is an estimated 0.2 million, while the industry has remained one of the low-wage strongholds. Against this backdrop, since 2005 FNV Bondgenoten has developed a new organising strategy within the framework of international and public actions, notably the UNI campaign for a decent wage for cleaners. Meetings for cleaners on or near work sites like offices and other large buildings, well covered by television and newspaper media, have been organised. This new campaign has been launched and accompanied in cooperation with SEIU (see Crosby, this volume). Characteristics of organising activities in the US labour movement have, thus, been deployed in the Netherlands – focused campaigns, directed at leading employers and using a variety of tactics and means to persuade and mobilise workers, including coalition-building with other (community) organisations. A number of these tactics come close to the new forms of mobilisation that Goedhart and Tijdens (1993) recommended earlier. And a new element is the tactical use of the unions' relations and bargaining position with the large customers of cleaning companies, like Dutch Railways (NS) and Schiphol Airport, in order to put pressure on for higher wages and better working conditions for (outsourced) cleaners.

This instrument seems to have been successful. In 2008, the first substantial results have been gained in the new collective agreement, covering 135,000 cleaners with the minimum wage level of €10. NS agreed to renegotiate new service contracts, enabling cleaning companies to pay these wages. Moreover, the project has produced a group of about 200 new FNV union activists amongst the 14,000 cleaners that FNV Bondgenoten organises.

Union density projects in the Netherlands: Overview and discussion

Scope and patterns of organising, servicing and representation

In assessing the scope and patterns of organising, we partly derive criteria from Heery's (2003) categorisation and we add some yardsticks of our own. First, there is the level of commitment to organising which is apparent in formal organising policies and budgets and particularly earmarked budgets. The second dimension concerns the targeting of organising, with a basic distinction drawn between consolidation and expansion, the latter consisting of attempts to build membership in hitherto unorganised sectors. We previously mentioned 'field-enlarging' strategies as an intersecting dimension. And here we build on our earlier division between organising, defined as the activation of (new) members, encouraging their self-activity, and servicing and collective interest representation.

Processes of organising in 14 FNV projects

We have classified the main characteristics of organising processes in the 14 'FNV 2000' projects in Table 5.1, according to the aforementioned indicators.

Of these projects, 12 had earmarked budgets. All had rather clearly defined targets: 12 targeted at expansion, and only two at consolidation. A quite striking feature is that there was hardly any overlap between projects directed to activation of members (eight) and servicing members and collective interest representation (six). The combination of activation and servicing was only found in one of the projects (self-employed) with these elements coming out with alternating presence in the rest of the projects. The more recent projects showed a substantial servicing content, with the latest three including a high level of individual arrangements. Table 5.1 also shows that in the three most outspoken 'high skilled target groups' (audiovisual media, banking, ICT) servicing was dominant.

Table 5.1 Processes in 14 FNV projects

Section/issue	Budget	Targets	Activation members	Servicing/collective representation	Research
Retail trade	y	e	y	n	y
Wholesale trade	y	e	y	n	n
Audiovisual media	y	e	n	y	y
Banking	y	e	n	y	y
Schiphol Airport	y	e	y	n	y
Industribution	y	e	y	n	y
Rotterdam Mainport	n	c	y	n	y
Cleaning	y	e	y	n	y
ICT	n	e	n	y	y
Hospitality workers	y	e	y	n	y
Call centres	y	e	n	y	y
Self-employed	y	e	y	y	y
Homeworkers, teleworkers	y	e	n	y	y
Workers with occupational diseases	y	c	n	y	y

Note: 'y' denotes yes, 'n' no, 'c' consolidation and 'e' expansion.

In retail, wholesale, cleaning and hospitality the scope was the other way round, namely, activation without much servicing. The same held for the more regionally oriented projects (Schiphol, industribution, Rotterdam Mainport), though servicing and developing collective representation structures played a somewhat larger role here. Finally, it was of note that nearly all projects were supported by research.

Contents of FNV projects

We have grouped the main characteristics of the contents of the projects in Table 5.2 according to the fields of workers' interests mainly touched upon: wages, job quality and working time, job security, labour market arrangements, and the building of a social infrastructure (representative industry structures, works councils, other negotiating bodies).

In a large majority of the projects, job quality and working times were central themes (11 of 13), followed by wages, job security and

Table 5.2   Contents of FNV projects

Section/issue	Wages	Job quality/ working time	Job security	Labour market arrangements	Social infra structure
Retail trade	y	y	n	n	n
Wholesale trade	y	y	n	n	n
Audiovisual media	y	n	y	y	y
Banking	n	y	n	y	y
Schiphol Airport	n	y	y	y	y
Industribution	y	y	y	y	y
Rotterdam Mainport	n	n	y	y	n
Cleaning	y	y	y	n	y
ICT	n	y	n	y	y
Hospitality workers	y	y	n	n	y
Call centres	n	y	y	y	y
Self-employed	y	y	y	n	n
Homeworkers, teleworkers	y	y	y	n	n

Note: 'Workers with occupational diseases' was not included on the grounds of irrelevancy.

building social infrastructures (all eight), and labour market arrangements (seven). Nearly half of the projects (six) showed a combination consisting of four out of the five topics. Another four combined three of them while the rest (three) focused on two. We found no project limiting itself to just one of the five variables.

Target groups in FNV projects

We have classified the main target groups of the 'FNV 2000' projects in Table 5.3. This shows that most projects were targeted at three different labour market groups. Six had two special target groups; three targeted just one of the five categories. Three projects had no specified target group as such, for Rotterdam Mainport concentrated on all workers connected with mainport activities, the self-employed project directed itself to the self-employed in general, and one project was targeted at the group of workers confronted with occupational diseases. Temporary workers have been the dominant target group (eight projects), followed by young workers (four). Women, migrants and highly skilled workers were a target group in three projects.

Table 5.3 Target groups in FNV projects

Section/issue	Young	Women	Migrants	Temps	High-skilled
Retail trade	y	n	n	y	n
Wholesale trade	n	n	n	y	n
Audiovisual media	y	n	n	n	y
Banking	n	y	n	n	y
Schiphol Airport	n	n	y	y	n
Industribution	y	n	y	y	n
Rotterdam Mainport	n	n	n	n	n
Cleaning	n	y	y	y	n
ICT	n	n	n	n	y
Hospitality workers	y	n	n	y	n
Call centres	n	n	n	y	n
Self-employed	n	n	n	n	n
Homeworkers, teleworkers	n	y	n	y	n

Note: 'y' denotes yes and 'n' no. 'Workers with occupational diseases' was not included on the grounds of irrelevancy.

Conclusion

Within largely comparable institutional contexts, Dutch unions – notably those grouped in the FNV confederation – seem to have undertaken organising efforts earlier and on a relatively larger scale than their German colleagues in response to loss of power and density (*cf.* Dribbusch 2003). Since 1988 in the Netherlands, projects aimed at entering 'white spots' (i.e., expansion) and at diversifying recruitment practices were initiated. Here, early and massive deindustrialisation, mass unemployment and the early fall of the density rate have acted as 'wake-up' calls. It has to be recognised that the timing of constraints differed between the two countries. While in the Netherlands – as in the UK – the largest part of the fall in union density could be located in the 1980s (from 1980 to 1990 by 10.5%, against 3.7% for Germany), the major fall in Germany happened after the reunification in 1989, with a fall in density rate between 1990 and 2003 of 8.6 percentage points, against 2.0 percentage points in the Netherlands in the same period of time (adjusted data from Visser 2006: 47). Moreover, though nowadays density rates in both countries are about equal, Germany, unlike the Netherlands, is recently confronted with a substantial loss in collective bargaining coverage (Bosch and Weinkopf 2008: 66–8; Dribbusch *et al.* 2007).

However, there is no reason for complacency on the part of Dutch unionists. Indeed, a number of characteristics of the projects that we examined looked positive. The majority had a special budget and were targeted at expansion. Moreover, all but one were supported by research. This did not, however, guarantee further development once the project had to be transformed into everyday union activities. Tentative updates on membership figures from our interviews suggest widespread problems with the retention of newly won members at that stage. As in the evaluation for UK union organising efforts, the resource inputs have been large but the longer-term outcomes relatively meagre, with the unions in danger of 'running very fast merely to stand still' (Gall 2007: 102). On the other hand, our cleaning 'story' showed that further development after the official project period is feasible, provided renewed union attention and facilitation are made available.

Opportunities for strengthening the union movement may remain underutilised. Most remarkable in this respect is our finding that the combination of activation and servicing was only developed in one of the FNV projects, be it a rather successful one – of the self-employed. This project was rather special as the new unions started from scratch, with considerably fewer constraints than in existing unions to combine activation and servicing and to select capable EUOs and other staff for that purpose. Start-up investments were linked with performance targets and aimed at self-sustenance after the project period. The other projects comprised either 'activation' or 'servicing/representation', with this being influenced by the nature of the target groups: services dominant for highly skilled and higher-paid, activation for lower-paid. Until now the first category seems to display a higher need for servicing and collective representation. Servicing may well take root here, as for them a number of collective arrangements at national or industry level (for instance, on health costs) have already been privatised and an often bewildering number of options are offered in the marketplace – a situation which is actually developing for the Dutch workforce in general.

We traced two Achilles' heels of union organising in the Netherlands. The first is the lack of using servicing and activation as combined, mutually enforcing or reliant concepts. This may look odd as the Dutch union movement seems well placed in this respect. Adding to older forms of servicing, like the widespread FNV tax service (volunteers' support in filling in income tax forms of members), since 1990 Dutch unions have developed quite a number of servicing tools, like employability and career services (Sprenger and Van Klaveren 2004). The staffing of projects played a major role here. Projects nearly always relied heavily either on EUOs or, as was the case in most FNV 2000 projects, on temporarily engaged project assistants. Reliance on EUOs is already a disadvantage if one looks at the high transaction costs because of investment in EUOs' time (*cf.* for Britain, see Gall 2007). Moreover, in the Dutch industrial relations context, the competencies of many EUOs are heavily formed through their tasks concerning formal representation in many consultative bodies, and these are prone to hampering the advance of organising efforts. On the other hand, project assistants were mostly rather exclusively oriented on organising. When leaving at the end of the project, they took most of the knowledge and experience with them.

A second weak point to be distinguished, though related to the first one, concerns the transition of project activities to day-to-day union work. It may be true for the Netherlands that a direct connection between the existing and rather dominant institutional frameworks and the success or failure of organising projects cannot simply be constructed. Yet, indirectly, the strong influence of the consultative economy on Dutch unionism is hampering the embedding of activation efforts in more traditional union practice, notably through the dominant position of EUOs, their competencies largely focused on formal consultation, and the weak position of organising projects within union hierarchies (*cf.* Van Klaveren 2002).

Thus, we argue that new paths should be explored more intensively, such as initiatives at industry level, including new facilities and services for individual workers, linked with collective interest representation. In the Netherlands that representation can still be closely linked with that main and still rather effective union instrument, the industry-based collective agreement. Our evaluation of recent union projects indicates the viability of approaches in the Netherlands that allow for the interaction of activating and servicing concepts, resulting in stronger union positions in collective bargaining processes. In the most successful projects the interplay of EUOs and lay activists, but also coalition-building outside the classical union ranks, already has shown the potential of enlarging the attractiveness of the unions and recruiting members. Yet, union decision-makers should structurally give more attention to safeguarding the position of organising projects in union decision-making and union structures, as well as to related HR policies, notably to the development of competencies of EUOs and other union staff aiming at combining activation and servicing tasks.

Notes

1. In a smaller number of cases CNV, the second largest confederation, with about 30% 'of' FNV membership, followed FNV initiatives and started up projects of its own. We did not trace projects run by MHP, the third confederation (with about 15% 'of' FNV members).
2. All figures used in this section are net rates, based on the numbers of union members younger than 65 and employed as wage earners for at least 12 hours per week. In 2004, this group included 84% of all union members (Van Cruchten and Kuijpers 2007: 10).
3. The Netherlands has no substantial tradition of inter-union demarcation conflicts, and within FNV a set of agreements concerning the division of (new) members according to subsector has long been in place. However, with the developments of new sectors and clusters, demarcation conflicts started to arise between FNV-affiliated unions. In the early 1990s, such demarcation conflicts took place in 'industribution', the physical part of Value Added Logistics (VAL) which grew rapidly in the Netherlands, and their incidence was one of the reasons for initiating a joint-union project in this new industry, aimed at organising and, to a lesser degree, servicing (Van Klaveren 2001, 2002).
4. The formation, in 1998, of FNV Bondgenoten ('Allies') through the merging of manufacturing, food, transport and commercial service unions 'reflected' FNV's displeasure that the process started by the FNV 2000 report did not amend its structure. By amalgamating unions representing both declining and growing sectors, the founders of Bondgenoten hoped to provide the organisational conditions to allow sufficient investment in the service sectors by facilitating reallocation of funds and efforts within one decision-making structure.

6
Reinvention of Activism: A Chance for Union Renewal in New Market Economies? The Case of Poland

Adam Mrozowicki, Valeria Pulignano and Geert van Hootegem

Introduction

While the diagnosis of the crisis of labour unionism is common to both the old capitalist countries in the West and the new market economies in Central and Eastern Europe (CEE), the question of union renewal in CEE has attracted significantly less attention from industrial relations scholars. In contrast to a growing body of literature devoted to the strategies of labour's revitalisation in the West (*cf.* Frege and Kelly 2004, Murray and Waddington 2005), the majority of analyses of the CEE have dealt with factors of unions' weakness rather than their possible empowerment (*cf.* Phelan 2006). The weakness of organised labour tends to be explained either by the structural properties of new capitalist regimes (Bohle and Greskovits 2007) or by the durable cultural legacies of past unionism, which impeded the redefinition of collective interests and supported the hegemonic market ideologies (Ost 2005). Despite a straightforward logic offered by the 'labour weakness' thesis, its limitations become clear if we try to account for the recent signs of reinvigoration of labour unions' activities in the region. For example, Meardi (2007: 503) noted 'the resurgent "voice" from below, through strikes, organising campaigns, informal collective protests and collective bargaining innovations' in most CEE countries. If structural and cultural contexts are as rigid as the labour weakness thesis suggests, it is legitimate to ask whether, and under what conditions, labour unions and/or workers are able to challenge these systemic constraints and what the effects are for organised labour in CEE.

Examining the sources, the processes and the outcomes of union renewal in post-socialist conditions, this chapter takes the case of Poland. The chapter argues that the first signs of union renewal in the country have been underpinned not only by macrostructural forces and more active union politics but also by the evolution of union commitments among union activists and a creative 'reinvention' of old union traditions (Hobsbawm 1992). In contrast to deterministic culturalist and/or structuralist approaches, we suggest union renewal can be better understood by focusing on the interplay between the evolving structural and cultural properties of the social system and the changing reflexivity of labour unionists themselves. We set out this argument by analysis of our interviews with long-standing and new union activists, following discussion of the historical contexts and the theoretical and methodological framework of the research.

Polish union movement: From marginalisation into reinvigoration

Polish unionism is a good example of an internal transformation of a labour movement from an initial found strength followed by marginalisation and then transmogrification into slow but visible revitalisation at the beginning of the new millennium. Despite the militant traditions of Solidarność (Touraine *et al.* 1983) and relatively well-developed structures of workers' representation at the beginning of the 1990s, systemic change led to the diminution of unions' collective strength (Gardawski 2001). From a structuralist point of view, union power diminished due to the accelerated privatisation, introduction of anti-union management styles in the private sector, high unemployment and increased segmentation of workforces. From the culturalist perspective, Poland constitutes a good illustration of the thesis of the crucial role of past legacies hindering union renewal (Ost 2005). The rationale for union passivity towards market reforms was stated by the historical leader of Solidarność, Lech Wałęsa, who assured people in 1989 that 'we cannot have a strong trade union until we have a strong economy' (Ost 2005: 53). Union-hostile media discourse (Kozek 2003), withdrawal into private life (Mrozowicki and Van Hootegem 2008) and the consent to market economy among Polish workers (Gardawski 1997) are other cultural factors underpinning labour unionism's weakness. Sharp decline in union membership, underdeveloped sectoral-level collective bargaining and atrophic corporatism at the national level (Pollert 1999) were typical indications of Polish labour unionism's decline in the 1990s.

However, the beginning of the millennium brought about new developments. In contrast to the initial reluctance to unionise private workplaces, by the end of the 1990s Solidarność established a Union Development Unit (DRZ), and the second biggest union – formerly the 'official' socialist confederation, OPZZ – founded the Confederation of Labour, with the explicit aim of organising non-unionised workers. DRZ representatives interviewed in Lower Silesia region in 2007 indicated three main directions for union renewal: a) reinvigorating union commitment through training, promoting membership growth, and monitoring union development; b) organising new membership in non-unionised companies through approaching employees face-to-face at companies, offering legal advice on work-related issues, and advertising in local press; and c) union restructuring in the form of creating 'local union organisations' at subregional divisions of the union (Billewicz *et al.* 2007). Greater focus on organising coincided with other indicators of unionism's revitalisation. They included increase in the intensity of pay disputes (Meardi 2007), union mergers (with the third largest confederation, the Forum of Trade Unions established in 2002), and the first signs of international East–West solidarity (e.g. joint protests against the EU service directive).

The effects of these recent trends are still difficult to evaluate. In particular, it is hard to estimate the scope of union-organising campaigns in Poland due to the lack of systematic quantitative research on this. Data collected in Lower Silesia (one of 38 regions within the organisational structure of Solidarność) suggests that 50 firms were unionised in the years 2005–7 (Billewicz *et al.* 2007). By early 2007, the Confederation of Labour established 220 new union organisations across the country.[1] On a national scale, density has not grown, even though its decline has halted at 14% between 2002 and 2007 (Wenzel 2007). No significant progress in collective bargaining coverage and national-level social dialogue has been observed either (Sroka 2007). However, it would be misleading to suggest that nothing has changed. In particular, union organising – whose intensity and institutionalisation seem to exceed those observed in other CEE countries (*cf.* chapters in Phelan 2006) – has brought about tangible, qualitative change in Polish industrial relations. It not only led to an increased vibrancy in the dynamics of unionisation of workplaces (e.g. hypermarket chains) and sectors (e.g. security services), which were previously established as 'union-free' by private owners, but also reintroduced unions as active players at the workplace level. How was it possible? What have been the effects on the emerging model of unionism in Poland?

Union activism reinvented? Union organising and bottom-up revitalisation

In accounting for the recent reinvigoration of unions in Poland, a range of exogenous and indigenous factors are salient. First, economic growth and decreased unemployment (after 2005), as well as a massive migration abroad after the EU enlargement, reduced the fear of job loss and reinforced the bargaining position of workers. Second, the violation of Labour Code by private employees encountered some grassroots worker resistance, widely reported by the media. Changing media discourse legitimised, if not supported, union organising campaigns. Additionally, concrete expert and financial support from the western trade unions (such as the help of ALF-CIO in establishing DRZ in the 1990s, or more recent support of UNI Global Union in organising campaigns in the security sector) furnished Polish unions with resources, ideas and reference models which supported their search for innovation.

While all the abovementioned factors were certainly advantageous for union revitalisation, it would be misleading to assume that they acted in any mechanical way. The dominating view in the debate on labour unionism in CEE adopts a deterministic perspective typical of most research on post-socialist transformation. According to this perspective, criticised by Burawoy and Verdery (1999: 1), the strategies of social actors are considered 'the expression of structures, policies, and ideologies of a macro character'. Our theoretical position is different. We adopt the critical realist approach developed, among others, by Archer (2003). What mediates between 'social structures' and 'agency' is individual reflexivity, defined as an 'internal conversation' through which social agents define their place in society, their interests and their schemes for future actions (Archer 2003: 9). Contrary to an approach centred on the negative effects of the cultural legacy of past unionism, we assume that union ethos, underlying 'schemes of perception, thought and action' in social reality (Bourdieu 1990: 54), can be both constraint and resource for union renewal. In this context, the question of union renewal is intrinsically linked with the redefinition of unions' role by workers themselves and cannot be explained merely by the evolution of social systems and the strategies of unions as institutions.

There are several reasons which motivate our interests in the role played in union renewal by union activists themselves. The first is historical. In the Polish context, it is impossible to overlook the role of the committed women and men who in 1980 devoted themselves to the Solidarność fight for their rights as workers, citizens and the members of a national community (Touraine *et al.* 1983). Yet, we still know little about the evolution of their union commitments after systemic change. Had the 'working-class' aspect of union ethos been transformed into consent to hegemonic market logic (Ost 2005) or just 'hibernated' (Meardi 2000: 275) during the initial shock of transition? The second follows from the scarce studies on union revitalisation in Poland. If the renewal of union strategies was not only top-down directed, but also motivated by bottom-up pressures (Meardi 2007), involving 'changing subjectivity' of labour unionists themselves (Ost 2006), we then need a better understanding of the potential of grassroots transformations of unions, often *despite* their fossilised union structures (Moody 1997b). Finally, the question of activism and commitment is central in the organising model of unionism, in which the two biggest Polish union confederations became engaged. If union organising is defined as a proactive bottom-up model of collective organisation, centred on the issues of workers' empowerment (see Carter 2006), it is crucial to know how and with what consequences such a model could have been implemented in Poland, given the dominant claim in industrial relations literature about local unions' passivity and weakness.

Despite growing interest in the role played by union commitments in the process of union renewal, there is a disagreement about the consequences of such microchanges for the model of unionism that is emerging. On the one hand, Ost (2005: 177) argued that union renewal in Poland indicated 'a move away from broad civic and political concerns' and implied 'the continuing importance of old-fashioned economic unionism ... defending the short term economic interests of their members'. Developing an argument about the central role of 'producer-ist' identities within the Solidarność union movement, the same author suggested that union revitalisation will lead to the development of the small unions of skilled, male, elite workers – 'a kind of unionism for a new labour aristocracy' (Ost 2006). On the other hand, Meardi (1996: 294) criticised analysis which portrayed labour unionism there as 'a simple "Polish business unionism"'. He emphasised the continuous relevance of broader social commitments embedded in the Solidarność ethos and involving universal values, such as defence of human prerogatives at work and in society (Meardi 2000: 268). Similarly, Stenning (2003) considered the Solidarność traditions 'an opportunity for a community-based renaissance of worker influence'. Remarkably, existing accounts implicitly refer to a potential of union renewal included in the 'reinvented traditions', defined as 'responses to novel situations which take the form of reference to old situations' (Hobsbawm 1992: 1), but they see the institutional consequences of such process differently. This chapter demonstrates that the recombining of these seemingly opposed stances is not only possible, but also necessary for a viable model of union renewal under post-socialism.

Polish union activists in empirical research: Methodology and analysis

Given the centrality of the proposed theoretical framework vis-à-vis reflexivity, union commitments and life strategies within unionisation, biographical narrative interview was chosen as the main method of data collection. The biographical method aided an understanding of the interplay of structures and agency in the processes of becoming a union activist. Reflecting the processes of subjective mediation of the properties of social and cultural action contexts (*cf.* Ferrarotti 2002: 26), it focuses on reflexive 'internal conversations' accompanying the formation and reformulation of union commitments. Even though the biographical method has rarely been used in industrial relations research, it affords another useful way to interrogate the issues associated with bottom-up union renewal.

The empirical data encompasses 45 biographical narrative interviews with company-level union representatives of Solidarność (29), OPZZ (12) and smaller unions, collected in traditional industrial companies (constituting the old 'core' of unionism) and new private companies in industry and retail services (chosen due to their relevance as targets for union organising campaigns). Data was gathered between 2002 and 2004 in south-western Poland (in Lower Silesia, Opole Silesia, and Upper Silesia). In line with Schütze's (1983) method, each interview included a complete life story followed by the additional substantive questions (including personal experiences with unionism). The informants were women and men of different ages employed as manual and semi-manual workers in private enterprises, privatised firms, and 'commercialised' companies (i.e. prepared for privatisation). This data was supplemented by two group interviews with the representatives of DRZ Solidarność in Upper Silesia and Lower Silesia (in 2007).

The methodological framework was determined by the methodology of grounded theory, including the intertwined process of data collection and data analysis (Glaser and Strauss 1967). Data analysis consisted of open coding (separating data into analytical categories) and selective coding (focused on the integration of categories with the core concepts of the study 'accounting for patterns of behaviours which [are both] relevant and problematic for those involved' (Glaser 1978: 93)). We applied the strategy of theoretical sampling from a larger sample of workers' narratives, based on the maximisation and minimisation of differences between comparison groups, representing the different patterns of commitment to unions. Data coding allowed us to draw a typological distinction between the 'transitional' pattern of union activism, mostly observed among the activists engaged in unions both before and after systemic change, and the 'renewed' pattern, most typical of new union activists, i.e. those who became involved in unions from the 1990s onwards.

Table 6.1 includes a schematic description of the two reconstructed patterns. Transitional union activism, embedded in durable commitments both to company and unions, is likely to coexist with a consensual stance towards employers, occasional sectional mobilisation, and the endorsement of historical union identities. Union activists tend to focus on mitigating the social costs of organisational changes and convincing grassroots unionists to sacrifice a part of their economic benefits for the sake of the survival of their firms in the market reality – this is termed 'disciplining'. Reinvented union activism, grounded

Table 6.1 Types of union activism in a post-socialist context: A summary of propositions

	Transitional union activism	**Reinvented union activism**
Biographical background	anchoring in a company and/or craft	fragmented/blocked occupational careers
	community-centred reflexivity lasting union commitments	individual-centred reflexivity (re)discovery of unions
Strategies towards employers	modernisational cooperation self-limitation of economic claims sectional mobilisation	civilising employment relations focus on economic interests fluid solidarities
Strategies towards union centrals	endorsing historical union identities centrals as the loci of traditions	reconfiguration of historical traditions centrals as reinforcement's agencies
Strategies towards members	integrating and servicing combined with disciplining and mitigating the costs of organisational changes	integrating and servicing combined with promoting an active membership and the democratisation of unions

in discontinuous or blocked occupational careers, generates a 'recombinant' model of unionisation, linking the morally oriented defence of workers' rights with focus on economic interests, and an efficient servicing to members with the promotion of 'active membership' and union democracy.[2] Since the patterns form a continuum rather than a dichotomy, some of the aspects of the old pattern are also endorsed by some 'new' union activists (and *vice versa*), and in the text we specify further some conditions for such 'reversals'. In subsequent sections, the types of union activism are discussed on the basis of selected quotations from biographical interviews. The quotes have been chosen in order to accurately reflect the various manifestations of action logics implied by two discussed patterns. Consequently, the quotations represent properly the variety of union activism observed in our fieldwork interviews.

It should be noted that typology does not include the multiple options of withdrawal from unions which were present in our data and analysed elsewhere (Mrozowicki and van Hootegem 2008). The focus on the cases in which unionism remained meaningful limits the generalisability of obtained results, but it remains coherent with the aim of making sense of the recent positive changes in the Polish labour movement.

Transitional activism: Cultural legacies and the changing patterns of commitments

The transitional pattern of activism indicates the forms of commitment to unionism. Its main features derive from long-standing union experiences under state socialism, within either official unions or the anti-communist union movement. Participation in unions and life projects are tightly interconnected via community-centred reflexivity, which rests on establishing the meaningful relationship between an individual biography and workers' collective history. In the typical cases, biographical experiences include long-term employment in one firm and advancement up the union organisational ladder. The logic of biographical presentation is characterised by strong embedding in history, which depicts a tendency to locate biographical experiences within a framework of historical events reinterpreted in ideological terms. Ideological cleavages, internalised via participation in anti-communist opposition and engagement in union organisations controlled by the Communist Party, tend to be translated into cleavages between the people, involving the criticism both of historical antagonists and of those disinterested and withdrawn. The process of becoming a unionist is connected not only (and sometimes to a very limited extent) with a utilitarian definition of interests, but also with the internalisation of broader ethos within family, locality, religious communities and national community. A good example can be found in the narrative of a Solidarność activist, Sergiusz:

> *Concerning my union activism ... I'm glad that after so many years I can still serve Solidarność, to which I became intimate virtually from scratch [in 1980]... Our union activity, well, at this moment we first of all help union-ists, who are in difficult family situations, we give financial aids. Naturally, we're going to different meetings, pilgrimages, with this flag, because we've our flag, we've our monument of Saint Catherine on company's premises. We also have to care about all this things, all these issues of history, so that noth-ing is squandered, because this will be inherited by the next generation... As far as my professional work is concerned... we'd risked to work here, because we'd counted on that we would go on early retirement... but, unfortunately, the government changed everything... And this is precisely the domain of a union and union activity to restore all these rights.* [W-125/2004] M, 48, foreman in machine industry, large privatised firm[3]

In Sergiusz's story, the strong interconnections of union commitments and community-centred reflexivity come into view. He was born into a working-class family and employed for all his life in the same firm as his father; his motivation stemmed from his engagement in unions through his family's anti-communist ethos and his personal opposition to communist management and bad working conditions in the firm. This ethos–stance was transformed into a pragmatic and company-centred approach after organisational changes in the firm. In this and similar cases, relations with grassroots members were dominated by the 'servicing' model, indicated by focusing upon distributing financial aid, and 'integration', characterised by attempts to bind together work com-munities and to protect the union ethos for further generations. The pattern of collective mobilisation was defensive and sectional, based on reclaiming the rights guaranteed to a particular occupational group in the past. Responses to changing conditions revealed some degree of ritualism. The main adversary of union action remains the state and not a new private employer, while the focus is on the cultivation of trad-itions and the union role is limited to mitigating the negative effects of economic transition.

While the 'transitional pattern' resembles the arguments of propon-ents of the thesis of the constraining role of past legacies for union development, it also reveals the complex character of the ethos shaped

through long-standing activism in unions (which the former analyses underestimate). On the one hand, in most of the interviews with
Solidarność and OPZZ reps, support for organisational changes follows
from the assumption that 'belt-tightening' – encompassing reductions
in 'excess' workers, disciplining them, and convincing them to post-
pone economic gratification – has been necessary for company survival
in the new market reality. Long-lasting anchoring in one firm supports
the redefinition of union activity as a means to protect company integ-
rity, in which both significant social resources and collective identities
are embedded. On the other hand, the repertoire of motives established
in workers' struggles in socialism is not forgotten and can nourish the
hope of grassroots union renewal. An illustration of the continuity of
this positive side of the union ethos is the approach of Wojciech:

*Nobody feels drawn to [union] work at this moment... It's true, he'll join,
because if he's in union, they'll protect him or so. But he doesn't feel like
getting down to any activism on his own... which means that when this
generation [dies off], everything will wither. Or else, it's going to be so
bad... that once more, another union emerges. That these people will unite
in all these firms, which exploit [them] at this moment, in these big firms,
in supermarkets. And that they'll create a new union... We should have
been powerful, strong union, to build strong union central... But they went
into politics and passed these men in the street over. At least... here, in the
factory, the role of unions is really big. They defend employees. But in the
country... it went the wrong way.* [W-21/2002] M, 51, pump controller,
large privatised company

As with many other informants, Wojciech elaborated on the process of decomposition of the transitional pattern of union activism,
which he saw as challenged both from above, by the emergence of a
deregulated private sector, and from the bottom up, by the decomposition of an ethos of selfless, universal engagement. Importantly, it
is not a unionism for a new labour aristocracy (*cf.* Ost 2006), which
skilled workers like Wojciech appeal to but a chance for union renewal
consisting of unity of the underprivileged workers in the peripheral
sections of labour markets. In other words, a plea to reinvent unions on
the basis of grassroots mobilisation, distance from high-level politics
and the defence of the *human* against exploitation recalls the founda-
tional values of Solidarność (Touraine *et al.* 1983). But it is a long way
from the discursive repertoires of resistance to collective mobilisation,
and most of the activists revealed a great scepticism with regard to

the real possibility of union renewal on a national scale. However, the point should be clear. Contrary to the dominant view in the literature on the weakness of labour unionism in Poland, the legacies of the anti-communist union movement are multiple and often contradictory, including not only support for modernisation changes, but also, as recently argued by Kurczewski (2006: 125), 'a strong socialist component, which...is an effect of the previous struggle of Polish labour with the Communist ruling class'. This component of union ethos can also be founded on the 'reinvented traditions' of official unions in state socialism. A good example of the reflexive reintroduction of old motives into a new social and political situation is Edward, a former communist party activist in a chemical company:

> *I worked on a voluntary basis here, in a head office, still in the Party's organisation at that time ... Until now, I'm still trying to do something in this company, there's still our organisation, which somehow counts in this country. I've been going to Warsaw to different rallies and other things...But I'm afraid that, nowadays, all our successes can be squandered.... They're clipping our wings too harshly. This is dangerous. Even recently, I was in such training, we're in D-city, there was an MP, people from the Federation [OPZZ] came...I'm asking [them] all the time, what when we enter the EU? Why don't we do something, why don't we lead these people out of factories? Because they die away...A capitalist won't show any consideration [for workers], if he hadn't trade unions over him...At this moment, people should talk with each other, unionists cannot look [at] 'us' and 'them'. If there's 'us' and 'them', it will be always like that.* [W-11/2003] M, 56, a pump controller in chemical industry, large privatised plant

Edward's argument highlights the process of reinterpretation of some of the main properties of transitional unionism. There is a reflexive redefinition of the union role, marked by the call for challenging historical boundaries, building a 'strong centralised union' and reinterpreting the union role in terms of class conflict. In this negotiation process, socialist discourse, which in the past system supported the cooperation of unions with Party and management, becomes a foundation of resistance against new disempowering conditions which emerged in the process of economic globalisation (identified with the EU enlargement). Likewise, however, in the majority of the cases of Solidarność activists, this call for collective mobilisation clashes not only with the inertia of centralised unionism ('clipping our wings'), but also with the durably embedded identities and ethos of unionists themselves.

New unionists in the private sector: Towards the renewal of activism?

Although the evolution of the patterns of union commitment was already evident in the interviews with long-standing unionists, it took its most coherent forms among those who can be labelled 'new union activists'.[4] Sharing limited union experiences from socialist times, they joined or established unions in previously non-unionised companies or took part in the revitalisation of unions in the firms after union atrophy there. Differing from long-standing activists, whose collective commitments were shaped by participation in (or opposition to) anti-communist unionism and the relative stability of their occupational careers, the forms of reflexivity of new unionists are less historically embedded, much more focused on individual and family projects, and affected by the discontinuity of occupational experiences. Although they emphasise their relatively strong position in their workplaces, their patterns of professional careers are often marked by ruptures and involuntary dead-ends, following constraining labour market and work conditions. In this context, engagement in unions presents an attempt to regain the sense of control over individual life both at work and in a broader societal context.

In non-unionised organisational contexts, unionisation means challenging multiple structural boundaries. New union activism starts with a limited agenda of raising wages, counteracting the unlimited power of managers, and introducing employee rights guaranteed by the Labour Code. The main pathways to unions include an instrumental approach and an ethos-centred path. From an instrumental perspective, strong unions are necessary to reinforce workers' rights at shop-floor level, but the identification with their collective traditions is weak. The development of broader collective commitments depends on linking personal life projects with resources provided by unions. Such evolution is documented by a story of an activist of the Free Trade Union Sierpień '80, Robert:

> *Generally in this firm, it's like that there're good and bad times. And, well, time came, when there was wife, the kids ... I felt threatened, didn't I? ... My family is the most important, so ... I found that, well, I've to start to be active. ... So I joined Sierpień '80. I don't know, why? Just happened ... Later on, it appeared that this is exactly a union, which ... fights non-stop, all the time, doesn't it? I even started to like it, because ... in general, we're fighting for workers' issues, aren't we? ... Because they repeatedly violate*

the law. At this moment, for instance, there's a problem, because [new car model] sells like hot cakes ... and there's problem with holidays and child-care ... There're such managers, who claim that ... they cannot give it, 'cause there's demand, isn't there? There's nothing to be done, because there's a ban. ... So I call here [the union office], or I come here in my working hours. And there's immediate reaction! And I like it! [W-85/2004] M, 30, a car assembler in automotive industry, large privatised plant

The biography of Robert reminds us of that of many young workers. Disappointed with low wages, deskilling of jobs and the lack of other perspectives on the labour market, he locates his main concerns outside the disempowering work conditions – in family and private life. Classic research on 'privatised workers' (Goldthorpe *et al.* 1968) suggested that home-centred life strategies will lead to disinterest or instrumental attitudes to unions, but Robert's example proves the possibility of a reverse process. Activism in Sierpień '80, a radical breakaway from Solidarność known for promoting a radical class discourse, is redefined by Robert as a chance to reclaim the balance between working life and family life, which, in turn, encouraged him to support a broader union agenda. A similar pattern of union commitment can be observed among the second category of new activists who followed an ethos path to unions, motivated by values and ideologies represented by union traditions. A good example is Szymon, a Solidarność rep in an automotive plant established by a transnational corporation in Upper Silesia:

[In a mine], I joined Solidarność ... just to belong to it ... It gave me a sort of ... inner pride to be in Solidarność ... [Afterwards] I was employed in a [vehicle manufacturer], together with the [future] president of the union ... Already during preparatory trainings, he has asked me if I wouldn't like to join a union. I answered that sure, I would join Solidarność ... There's a lot of [issues employees have to demand], starting with ... earnings ... Well, it's clear that an employer doesn't have to [pay you more] of his good-will ... [if] he doesn't allow you to earn, you've to demand it ... I'm a trade unionist, so, for sure, I'll defend unions. The name of unions is not import-ant, Solidarność or OPZZ, the principles of this union are important ... that it defends these employees' rights. [W-63/2003] M, 33, a car assembler, large 'greenfield' company

Szymon, a former miner in Upper Silesia, had many intrinsic reasons to join Solidarność: his grandfather was deprived of farmland by communist authorities; his father, as a son of *kulak*, was sentenced to work in a 'penal brigade'; and Szymon himself was forced to work in the 'penal shift' after rejecting joining the Communist Party in the mine. While his union participation in the mine did not involve strong engagement, the internalisation of the Solidarność ethos motivated his decision to join the union established from new in a large automotive plant. Disillusioned with the course of transformation and overburdened by intensified work, new union activists reshaped an inherited ethos into new forms. The self-limitation of claims in line with a general discourse of 'belt-tightening' is thus replaced by an emphasis on the economic interests of workers. The historical cleavages between unions are rejected and democratic procedures at grass roots are promoted.

The importance of a 'reflexive belonging', which replaces mechanical solidarity imposed from above (Hyman 1999), emerged even more clearly from the interviews with new women unionists. Deteriorating positions of women after 1989, their growing aspirations and outflow of male craftsmen from unions opened a space for the emergence of a new wave of women activists. According to a regional Solidarność leader, women made '7 out of each 10 founders of unions' in Lower Silesia in the years 2006 to 2007. Biographical interviews suggest that women activists can bring new subjectivity into play, which transcends the boundaries of old, predominantly male, industrial unionism. A good example is the story of Katarzyna:

> *My soul is rebellious, so I noticed some irregularities [in the firm], and I started also to fight [on my own]... We've been exploited, they've been notoriously breaking the Labour Code, no respect for dignity of an employee. And, as I said, out of employees' needs, an idea emerged to join unions ... To be in a union, to be active in an organisation ... this gives you, that you aren't idle, you don't stay aside, but you're all the time active, let's say, you're always in control, you've this control over the employer and over this what happens in the firm ... My life's got more interesting, since I've been in this firm and I've joined the union. Before it was only, you know: work-home-kids, work-home-kids ... Now, since 2001 ... I feel that something's going on around me, that I have an influence on something' [W-50/2004]*
> *F, 50, a checkout assistant, a private supermarket chain*

Katarzyna's story documents the process of surmounting structural and cultural constraints, imposed by the routine of domestic life and exhausting work, by means of engagement in labour unionism which was defined as a biographical turning point. Union activism increases the sense of agency both at work and beyond it, by challenging boundaries formed by lowly occupational position, older age and traditional ascription of women to family roles. In this sense, new union commitments transcend traditionally understood industrial democracy and refer to the issues of empowerment in society. The new sensitivity to gender has grassroots character, since the leadership of national unions in Poland is still dominated by men (Pollert 2003: 344–5). At the workplace level, women combine attempts to 'seek for positive solutions' (Billewicz *et al.* 2007) with abilities no lesser than men's to survive anti-union management's pressures. Katarzyna, who in 2006 won a trial brought by employers accusing her of the defamation of the company, extended her union involvement to other 'repressed unionists', motivated by mutual help and solidarity received from trade unions during her trial.

The development of fluid solidarities activated in emerging situations is only one consequence of the embedding of unions in private firms. Although new union commitments bring about courageous involvement in reclaiming basic rights in the workplace, they can also reproduce the patterns of self-limitation, since activism increases not only union commitments, but also attachment to companies. A good illustration is the case of Marcelina, a Solidarność leader in a large hypermarket, who combines strong criticism of management's misbehaviour with the readiness to accept intensified work under the assumption that 'we're all in the same boat' [W-166/2007]. Such discourse strikingly recalls the transitional pattern, and might lead to similar consequences, including the discrepancy between unionists' strategies and workers' criticism of worsening work conditions. While the situation of conflict sharpens the cleavages between workers' and management's goals, a test for their long-term grounding, which is a necessary condition for full social dialogue, would be the further embedding of unionism in private firms.

Conclusions

The need to account for the recent signs of union renewal in the new market economies in CEE, exemplified, *inter alia*, by the union-organising drive in the private sector in Poland, has been the focus of this chapter. Contrary to the more deterministic, structure- and culture-centred approaches, our findings illustrate how the interaction of old cultural motives, new unionists' reflexivity and changing institutional context creates the conditions for the new forms of union activism in Poland, in which the legacies of the past start to be 'reinvented' as resources for the new forms of commitment and resistance. Long-standing unionists, protecting their social identities durably embedded in union traditions and work milieus, were likely to refer to their union ethos to justify their consent to 'modernisation changes'. New activists, sharing the experiences of severe constraints on pursuing life projects in an actually existing capitalism, redefined this ethos in an innovative way. The active definition of economic interests, the reflexive work on historical legacies, and the rediscovery of the relevance of the unions' project to individual life strategies indicated the change in the level of unionists' subjectivity, which underlay a favourable bottom-up response to the recent union organising campaigns.

In accordance with Ost (2005: 177), this study suggests that it was neither political activism, nor the rhetoric of broad social change, but a more efficient representation of economic interests in the workplace which attracted new membership. However, this economic agenda was built on an ethos which transcends 'bread-and-butter' unionism, involving the issues of civilising workplace relations and defending human dignity, deeply embedded in local union traditions, Catholic national culture and socialist past. Because of this local cultural context, new unionism in Poland is unlikely to evolve into a 'business unionism' or an 'aristocratic unionism' of skilled, male, core craftsmen (*cf.* Ost 2006). Grassroots pressure on unions is not 'elitist', but it involves the voices of those structurally and culturally marginalised (including women) employees in greenfield private companies, and amongst young people. Their concerns encompass not only higher pay, but also reconfiguring the balance between work and family life, reclaiming the stability of occupational careers and increasing the sense of agency in a broader societal context. Yet, new union commitments do not resemble social movement unionism either. In comparison to the former, demanding 'broad social and economic change' (Moody 1997b), new Polish unionism is quite distant from grand ideologies and high politics.

What emerges from the biographical data is the recombinant unionism, which links local union traditions with the elements of market discourse. Even though activists themselves do not interpret their union work as political action, their actual praxis 'reinvents politics' (Beck 1994) on a grassroots level, by changing employers' assumptions about the weak, cheap and permissive labour in the new capitalist economy of Poland. However, this new unionism, at least in its current stage, remains also market-oriented. Union organisers from DRZ Solidarność defined their union as a 'firm, which needs to adapt to changing conditions' (Billewicz *et al.* 2007) and, like company-level union reps, they did not question the capitalist system itself, but the variety of it that has emerged in Poland. This recombinant character of union renewal can be detected also at the workplace level with the connection of the proactive 'organising model' of unionism to a model based on rendering services to members. Establishing social funds in the private firms and new incentives to join unions (such as additional health insurance or discounts at stores cooperating with unions) are only two examples of the continuous relevance of 'servicing' in the Polish union movement (*cf.* Gardawski 2001).

Even though we can see qualitatively new elements emerging within the union movement in Poland, some 'realism' is needed. The 'reinvention of activism', especially if limited to a motivated leadership, is not enough to achieve a far-reaching transformation of the industrial landscape in the long run. Although the socialist and post-socialist legacies can be overcome, structural constraints on the unionisation of private sector are likely to persist. Under conditions marked by a sharply uneven distribution of power resources between unions and employers, managers can effectively oppose union organising by improving contractual terms, by adopting paternalist practices, and, which is most often the case in Poland, by persecuting activists (see Carter 2006: 420). In this context, the potential of bottom-up unionisation needs to be supplemented by both stronger union structures at national level and the greater democratisation of unions. The politics of 'clipping the wings' – of suppressing bottom-up pressure in line with national-level 'real politics' – and the situation of women unionists, who despite their commitments to union renewal are still poorly represented at the higher levels of union structures, are only two illustrations of the broader problems of union democracy. While the 'reinvention of activism' creates a positive potential for union renewal, this grassroots transformation can be easily squandered if it is not supplemented by the reinforcing of the institutional position of unions in post-socialist economies and their internal democratisation.

Notes

1. Email exchange with the union officer (14 March 2007).
2. The concept 'recombinant' is borrowed from the neo-institutionalist studies on post-socialism (Stark 1997: 38), which used the term to describe how 'actors respond to uncertainty in the organizational environment by diversifying their assets, redefining and recombining resources' accumulated by them in the past.

3. Brackets include the code number of interview/year of interview. Label contains: [a code number] (age, sex, occupation, the type of company). All names have been changed.
4. We refer to 9 out of 12 core cases of Solidarność and Sierpień '80 activists employed in the automotive industry and large hypermarkets. Three remaining cases exemplified the initial defeat of unions within the firm.

7
The 'Servicing–Organising–Community Continuum': Where Are Australian Unions Today?

Marjorie Jerrard, Sandra Cockfield and Donna Buttigieg

Introduction

In countries such as Australia where the state offers reduced support for union activities and also may be openly antagonistic towards them, unions have been seeking alternative strategies to retain their relevance as industrial relations actors, especially as the 'servicing model' – which has been practised widely in many western countries – is no longer seen to be a viable long-term option. As a consequence, Australian unions have been seeking to move from the servicing model, which arose largely out of union dependence upon the traditional arbitral system of conciliation and arbitration for rights and relevancy, towards a model of organising that has been widely promulgated in both British and North American writing and research on union renewal strategies. Under the auspices of the Australian Council of Unions (ACTU), Australian unions have been encouraged to adopt at least some of the elements of organising. It can be argued that some Australian unions have always pursued such an approach with extensive workplace delegate structures, organisers being responsible for information sharing, communicating, and establishing ongoing contact with the members for whom they are responsible, while also practising elements of a servicing approach. This accords with Fiorito's (2004) findings that the models of servicing and organising are not mutually exclusive. In this chapter, it is argued that there is a continuum through which Australian unions are moving strategically (the continuum ranges from servicing through to organising and, finally, community unionism) and that, while different unions are predisposed to take certain approaches due to their histories and nature, organising is a necessary precursor to community unionism as it provides an organisational shift upon which sustainable community unionism is based.

This chapter uses a series of 22 interviews with elected and appointed union officials and representatives from community groups in Australia, to develop case studies of six unions which may be regarded as moving along a continuum, with their position on the continuum still largely determined by their historical strategies. This qualitative data set is extended by content analysis of union and community group websites and an analysis of union–community campaign media coverage. The unions selected are the Australasian Meat Industry Employees' Union (AMIEU), the Construction Forestry, Mining and Energy Union (CFMEU), the Maritime Union of Australia (MUA), the Australian Workers' Union (AWU), the Australian Nursing Federation (ANF) and The Police Association of Victoria (TPAV). Each union is at a different stage of progression towards community unionism because of a range of factors that inhibit progress, sectoral differences that impact upon the strategic behaviour of a union, the availability of community group partners, and the internal structure and regulations of each union, which may handicap resourcing of organising and community unionism. The chapter proceeds with a discussion of the origins of organising through to community unionism. This is followed by six case studies of unions, each at a different stage in terms of the continuum. The chapter finishes with some concluding comments on the concept of a servicing to community unionism continuum.

Origins of the organising model

The organising model was developed in the US as part of a renewal strategy for unionism. The organising model is the ' "empowerment" of workers, in the sense of stimulating activism and strengthening unionism in the workplace in order that workers can resolve their own problems without recourse to external representation' (Heery 2002: 27). It involves various techniques such as mapping of the workforce, the use of committees to involve people in campaigns and person-to-person recruitment (Heery 2002). It is set in contrast to the servicing model of unionism where union members are dependent on union staff to deal with grievances (Fiorito 2004; Fletcher and Hurd 1998). Over time, variants and extensions of the organising model have developed. Fletcher and Hurd (1998) distinguished between internal organising and external organising. The former occurs where unions seek to consolidate membership growth in existing areas, while the latter refers to expansion into areas where union membership is low or non-existent. The latter also involves targeting non-traditional members such as women, part-time and casual workers and youth. Attracting this new membership requires not just new techniques but also a rethink of the issues around which a union should organise. Significantly, this involves organising workers in their communities, whether defined spatially or by interests or identity, through coalition-building, public campaigns and similar techniques. For Danford *et al.* (2003), the organising model would have maximum effect if unions engaged in internal, external and community organising simultaneously, although they recognise a staged movement is more likely due to internal political constraints. It is from this staged movement that the concept of a continuum arises.

Union movements in several countries, such as Britain, Australia and New Zealand, have adopted the organising model as the ideal. In Britain, the 'Organising Academy' of the TUC was established to train organisers. Similarly, in Australia, 'Organising Works' was established in 1994 to train organisers to organise in a manner consistent with the organising model (Carter and Cooper 2002).

Evidence in Britain indicated that almost half (45%) of respondents to a survey undertaken in 2000/2001 among British unions indicated that they were adopting the organising model (Fiorito 2004). Another study undertaken by Heery *et al.* (2000) found that there was an uneven application of organising techniques in British unions. The techniques were more frequently used by larger unions and those associated with the Academy. In Australia, Cooper (2001) argued that the objectives of the organising model have been mainstreamed and that every significant union has had some association with training programmes to encourage the organising approach. However, Burchielli and Bartram (2007) argued that Australian unions have only adopted the early stages of organising, with many still maintaining a servicing role. Their findings assume a dichotomy between organising and servicing, rather than a union moving from servicing to organising and retaining many elements of servicing. These are then combined with organising elements, giving rise to a continuum along which unions move, retaining elements of previous models. The fact that the models are not dichotomous is further supported by Fletcher and Hurd (1998) and Fiorito (2004), whose study found that 36% of respondents to his study stated that there is a false dichotomy because servicing is still expected by members. Further, Fiorito (2004) argued in Britain that poor leadership, rather than the use of the servicing model, is a frequently cited reason for problems with unions. Poor leadership would also pose difficulties for unions seeking to engage in community alliances.

From organising to community unionism?

Moving beyond the debate between servicing and organising, a number of authors see the main limitation of the organising model as the absence of a political agenda. While the model advocates a range of new tactics which may halt membership decline or contribute to growth, critics argue this signals union resilience rather than union renewal (see Fairbrother 2000). For these critics, union renewal requires a fundamental shift in union purpose and strategy away from business unionism, which relies on cooperation and accommodation with capital in return for workplace entitlements. Business unionism is argued to be unsustainable in the changing political economy where neoliberal policies have seen the state withdraw support for the incorporation of unions into the sphere of regulation. While the changing political economy creates a crisis of representation and repertoire for unions, it also opens up opportunities both inside and outside the workplace. For unions, this translates into opportunities to work with and alongside others in civil society, and has manifested in growing awareness of the need to engage with 'the community' (see Upchurch *et al.* 2009). However, for unions to be able to take advantage of these opportunities, they need to operate in an institutional framework that enables them to act in different ways and they need also to be able to resource community engagement through member activists, elected officials, and employed officers.

Community unionism is one concept attached to this new model of unionism (Tattersall 2007a; Wills and Simms 2004). Others include social movement unionism (Clawson 2003; Lopez 2004), social capital unionism (Jarley 2005) and citizenship movement unionism (Johnston 2002). All approaches stress the need for unions to move beyond traditional practices and methods, and develop a community-orientated approach, but there is no consensus around the form and character of these relationships. Attention has focused on coalitions and alliances between unions and community groups (Frege *et al.* 2004; Nissen 2004; Tattersall 2007a), but community also may refer to the broader public (Lipsig-Mumme 2003) or the formation of independent organisations (Fine 2006; Turner 2006). The issue is whether, or to what extent, these various practices represent a shift in union purpose and strategy or are simply new tactics to promote traditional goals. Ross (2007) provides a useful framework to assess this.

Borrowing from social movement studies, Ross (2007) identified three axes along which different models of 'social unionism' can be understood and compared. First, in social unionism models the *collective action frame* identifies and defines workers' interests broadly, eschewing narrow sectional interests in favour of social justice struggles reaching beyond the workplace and into the daily lives of workers. Consequently, public sector unions are seen as having an advantage because their work relates directly to the provision of services to the community (Cockfield *et al.* 2009; Johnston 2002). While union–community initiatives of necessity are framed broadly, they do not necessarily mean the union is moving toward a social unionism collective action frame. Key questions concern the centrality of social justice issues to the union's purpose, how they relate to more traditional union goals associated with bargaining, and the extent to which they serve the broader community – and not just members' – interests.

Second, social unionism is characterised by methods and practices that go beyond the workplace and traditional bargaining processes. Within this repertoire, union–community initiatives are central. However, the presence of this repertoire is not enough to signify social unionism (Ross 2007) because it must be understood within the collective action frame. For example, coalitions with community groups may be formed for instrumental purposes and sectional interests may remain dominant (Cockfield *et al.* 2009). Any analysis of community initiatives should explore the power dynamics within the relationship and the longer-term goals and outcomes for all parties involved. Internal organisational practices of unions form the third axis along which union–community relationships can vary. At the heart of both the organising model and more radical approaches to union renewal are drives to foster members' activism, engagement and participation (Clawson 2003; Fairbrother 2000; Lopez 2004). Therefore, the scale at which community unionism initiatives occur is important in shaping the level and type of union participation (Tattersall 2007a). Whether these initiatives derive from and are driven by the leadership or membership is also significant. Mobilising members through organising tactics is insufficient for union renewal because unions need to strengthen membership control over decision-making by improving participative and direct democracy within unions (Schenk 2003; Wishart 1992). Similarly, Clawson (2003) argued that top-down, community-driven campaigns, such as the living wage campaigns in the US, are beneficial in the short term but have the potential to remove responsibility and control from people most concerned – the workers – and hence have an anti-democratic element.

Many practices associated with organising are central to social unionism but lack the social agenda and internal political change that are required to transcend business unionism. When assessed against Ross's (2007) framework, many of the initiatives labelled community unionism lack the political change necessary to stimulate union renewal and are just an extension of a narrow organising approach. However, the framework offers insights into the possible transformation of unions beyond business unionism and how this might occur. Thus, as servicing exists alongside organising, business unionism may coexist alongside more progressive models of unionism, particularly in the short term. The organising model provides the seeds for organisational and political change within unions but still recognises traditional union purposes. The organising model is a stage through which unions may pass and it is most likely that those unions reaching out into the community will be those who have most actively and successfully adopted an organising approach. This is demonstrated in the following case studies.

Community–union alliances: Case studies

The case studies are selected from a larger sample collected since 2004, primarily from within Victoria but including some other Australian states. The six cases represent different types of unions operating across different industries and work types. The unions self-identified themselves during the interviews as to their utilisation of the organising model and presented evidence of various campaigns around enterprise bargaining and occupational health and safety issues, in particular, to support their position on the servicing–organising continuum. The campaigns involved organisers supporting members to take control of the issue at their work site and their actions surrounding it. The unions, represented by members of their executives and some organisers, were asked about existing and planned community alliances and the benefits and outcomes of such alliances – the quotes in the case studies come from interviewee comments. The alliances reflect different stages of development from mature in the case of TPAV and Neighbourhood Watch to developing in the case of the ANF and its aged-care sector partner to temporary in the case of the AWU and CWA. The alliances represent the political spectrum of the Australian union movement, from conservative to left-wing. The alliances are analysed to ascertain the degree to which they are practising social unionism, including their ability to foster member engagement, participation and activism, all elements judged to be central to the organising model.

AMIEU – Stop Live Exports

AMIEU covers the meat-processing industry in Australia. It has a delegate structure based on categories of work carried out in an abattoir. For decades, it has engaged in membership participation in decision-making as a means of strengthening the union and has utilised aspects of the organising model (Jerrard 2000) to ensure membership identification with the union. Its executive, organisers, and delegates are elected from the shop floor. AMIEU regards itself as an organising union operating on participatory democratic principles which the federal Executive believe has made it easier for state branches to work effectively for over three decades with different animal rights groups (Jerrard 2007). This case study examines one more recently formed alliance between AMIEU and the independent community group, Stop Live Exports.

AMIEU's Western Australian (WA) branch began working with Stop Live Exports, formerly known as PACAT (People against Cruelty to Animals in Transport), a decade ago, to organise rallies and meetings (Stop Live Export 2008) in Freemantle, the port from which live animal ships leave that state. The alliance sees Stop Live Exports taking the leading role as the dominant partner because it was formed as an organisation independent from AMIEU (WA) and has as its mission the replacement of export of live animals for slaughter overseas with the lucrative chilled and frozen meat trade (Stop Live Export 2008). This mission supports the industrial objective of AMIEU to save jobs in the industry but belongs to an independent organisation. AMIEU has worked with Stop Live Exports to publicly present the argument in respect to the cruelty of the live shipping trade, which is also destroying jobs in the meat-processing industry (AMIEU (WA) 2003). AMIEU successfully lobbied other unions to pass a resolution at the 2004 Australian Labor Party state conference to form a Meat Industry Task Force under the responsibility of the State Minister for Primary Industry, Kim Chance. The alliance partners have on their respective websites information about reporting cruelty to animals in transport, as well as anti-live export petitions, and research about the live export industry practices to raise public awareness and to encourage lobbying of Parliamentarians to halt the trade.

Stop Live Exports, like other animal welfare groups, cuts across the traditional class divides underpinning social movements by including middle-class and working-class animal rights activists (Bagguley 1997) allied with members of a militant, left-wing, blue-collar, organising union. It has a diverse membership, representing men and women (Munro 2001) and various cultures and age groups:

> *Stop Live Export's members come from all walks of life ... Some are vegetar-*
> *ians and some are meat-eaters. Some ... are local residents disgusted with*
> *the stench, road noise and dust from the trucks, as well as the sight of dis-*
> *tressed animals. Others are former meat workers who have lost their jobs to*
> *the live export trade, or current meat workers, [and some are] farmers who*
> *are concerned about how their animals are treated once they have left their*
> *care.* (Stop Live Export 2008)

The alliances between animal welfare groups and AMIEU have a polit-ical perspective, focusing on achieving an industry reform which neces-sitates legislative change at both federal and state levels (Jenkins 1995). A common goal – stopping all live animal exports – unites diverse par-ties and allows centrally planned cooperation and deliberate resource allocation within and between the alliance partners (Jenkins 1983). The campaign relies on AMIEU members and Stop Live Export members jointly participating in rallies and protests to gain public support and utilises elements of the organising model to gain member commitment to and control over the campaign. This alleviates resourcing issues for the union because the alliance is not dependent upon a small number of activist members and union officials for its momentum. The alli-ance is, therefore, sustainable because of widespread AMIEU grassroots involvement supported by the AMIEU Executive. This indicates AMIEU is utilising organising alongside community unionism as part of its strategy. However, the alliance is also a tactic to promote traditional goals, which does not necessarily mean AMIEU is moving towards Ross's (2007) social unionism collective action frame. This is because the objective for the union is still protecting members' job security and it is just coincidental that this objective can be achieved by halting live animal transport, the aim of the community partner. However, this alliance goes beyond narrow organising and therefore has potential to stimulate union renewal, but has not yet done so.

CFMEU – Perth Indigenous Community (Swan Brewery Site)

The CFMEU's construction division relies on a combination of pattern bargaining in agreement-making and organising for day-to-day issues at work sites. The division has sent organisers to the ACTU's Organising

Works training (Crosby 2002) and has an extensive delegate structure supporting members' rights on all large urban building sites. The Executive and organisers are elected by the membership. The union uses integrated recruitment and organising, an ongoing sustained strategy to retain membership, and strong membership identification with the union – 'touch one touch all' being the motto. It also retains elements of the servicing culture, primarily to provide a range of services and insurance protection and because of industrial relations legislation which ensures union organisers must enter workplaces through the employer and hold a valid entry permit.

From the late 1980s into the 1990s, the Construction Division of the CFMEU in Western Australia spearheaded a Perth-based campaign to protect the sacred Goonininup site, also known as the Waugyl Dreaming Track, on which the former Swan Brewery stood. The land title was held by the Western Australian Government but the brewery buildings remained on the site (Churches 1992). A Brewery Preservation Society was formed by local Perth residents to preserve the buildings, but the local Indigenous people wanted the site returned to nature to form a park that could be used by all. With the support of the Executive, CFMEU members established pickets at the site and refused to work to either preserve the buildings or develop them, stalling development until the late 1990s. This industrial action occurred despite breaching tough State anti-strike laws and costing members jobs on the proposed site. The Indigenous community also supported the pickets. The union's Executive provided financial support for Aboriginal campaigner, Robert Bropho, in his unsuccessful four-year legal campaign to save the site for indigenous people. The site has since become a commercial operation and function centre fronting the Swan River and desecrates the sacred nature of the site for Indigenous people. While the campaign did not succeed in creating an Aboriginal heritage park, it demonstrated that the union and the Indigenous community working together had power enough to delay development for several years on heritage listed and sacred sites, thus forcing developers to carefully plan to allow for community and special interest groups' concerns. Further, it provided a basis for the CFMEU Executive and membership to continue working with Indigenous groups on issues of common concern, cementing a relationship that continues.

The campaign achieved little in the way of bringing direct economic, political, or industrial advantages to the union's members, apart from its few Indigenous members, but did fulfil human rights and welfare objectives that locate the union as an important part of society. The campaign, while not achieving its objective, also demonstrated that joint Executive and membership involvement could sustain a campaign for a much longer time frame, despite legal obstacles, and thus raise the issue in the public consciousness for a sustained period of time. This campaign is also indicative of current Indigenous–CFMEU alliances which draw on CFMEU members who are supported by the union's leaders. This alliance to save the Swan Brewery site was based on a social justice issue that placed it into Ross's (2007) collective action frame because its objective reached beyond the workplace and a narrow industrial agenda focused on traditional bargaining processes. Indeed, the coalition resulted in the application of collective principles and traditional union tactics to a developing social issue in Australia. The CFMEU continues to utilise organising alongside community unionism, as does AMIEU, but has moved further toward a social unionism collective frame than has AMIEU. The CFMEU does not regard community unionism as a strategy for revitalisation but as 'part of the union's role in the community' because 'the union is part of the community'.

MUA – Stella Maris Seafarers' Centre

The MUA, like the CFMEU and AMIEU, is a militant union that has traditionally been positioned on the labour movement's political far left. Executive and organisers are elected from the shop floor and the union's rules prohibit coverage of supervisors and those above this level. The MUA has a strong delegate structure and an effective delegates' committee which meets regularly and involves members in decision-making. Delegates represent members on day-to-day issues as well as in formal enterprise-bargaining. Organisers have attended formal ACTU organising training but, according to the Victorian secretary, the union was already utilising aspects of an organising model prior to the ACTU's programme: 'this is why the members identify with their union.' The MUA also has a long history of engaging in community-based and welfare-oriented campaigns, which was repaid with public support for the union's 1998 campaign against Patrick Stevedores when the company, urged on by the Federal Minister for Workplace Relations, sacked its entire unionised workforce. According to the Victorian secretary: 'humanity is at the forefront [of the MUA agenda] and that's what it should all be about…people'. The fact that the union has organised its membership effectively and is able to work with different groups and people outside the union movement has probably made it easier for it to engage in a number of community partnerships. This has also made the people resourcing of these partnerships easier for the MUA because it is not reliant upon officials and activists to drive them but on members and the community partners.

One MUA–community alliance that benefits seafarers when on shore is with the Stella Maris Seafarers' Centre in Melbourne. Stella Maris falls under the auspices of the Catholic Church's official missionary work with seafarers and the St Vincent de Paul Society. The Centre was first opened in 1973 to provide a range of services for seafarers whose ships were docked in Melbourne. These services have extended from food and entertainment to offering a wireless-networked communication centre so seafarers can communicate with family and friends anywhere world-wide. Funding comes from the Catholic Church, government, and fund raising and donations from the MUA – the most recent donation being a bus to transport seafarers between the port and the Centre, which is also used for transporting MUA members to rallies and meetings. The Centre is largely staffed by volunteers, some of whom are MUA members. The MUA's Port Welfare Committee and Officer cooperate with Stella Maris on a range of seafaring issues from protecting seafarers' employment rights through to occupational health and safety (OHS) issues, including the state of the vessels on which seafarers are sailing. The latter is particularly important where 'ships of shame' or 'flags of convenience' ships are concerned because of both the poor work conditions and the state of the ships in general. The alliance partners cooperate to raise public and political awareness of seafaring issues, but can run into disagreement as Stella Maris adopts a church-sanctioned line while the union may adopt more vocal, militant and left-wing positions on issues. However, on welfare issues, the partners tend to work together effectively. The alliance involves Stella Maris Committee of Management representatives and community volunteers working with MUA Executive and members, especially in fundraising campaigns. To date, the alliance has been successful and its continuation is assured because the union accepts that the alliance partner may have 'different priorities' and 'disagreements sometimes' but these can be overcome.

This alliance draws on business unionism because there is an emphasis upon charity and fundraising by the MUA but it is a reciprocal alliance when it comes to seafarers' welfare and rights. The latter are social justice concerns and place this alliance in Ross's (2007) collective action frame. In essence, the MUA is drawing on its collective resources to provide support and representation, albeit limited, to a group of workers who fall outside the jurisdiction of Australian labour law. The campaign around 'flags of convenience' shipping utilised methods and practices that go beyond the MUA's usual industrial tactics but allow direct membership involvement. The MUA, like AMIEU and CFMEU, is utilising an organising model with community unionism to achieve a broader social justice objective. For the MUA, membership growth and revitalisation are not the key concern. Rather, the union's engagement with the community reflects its political identity and progressive ideology. This engagement with progressive community issues has been reciprocated through support for the union against Government attacks, most notably the 1998 maritime dispute. Like the CFMEU, the MUA is moving closer to a social unionism collective action frame with its community alliances and its broad social agenda, though the core activity of both unions remains collective bargaining.

AWU – Country Women's Association (CWA) – WorkSafe Victoria

The AWU traditionally relies upon third party intervention through conciliation and arbitration and political strategies, fitting within the right wing of the Australian Labor Party. Its executive is elected but organisers may be appointed. The AWU is not readily regarded as an organising union, particularly in rural industries where workers are isolated from each other and reliant upon an organiser to provide services and advice. Despite organisers being trained in organising techniques, the AWU, in certain industries at least, remains heavily oriented towards servicing. This has proven a challenge when issues such as OHS are on the agenda because members need to take responsibility for their own safety, particularly on farms.

The alliance aimed to improve OHS and involved the AWU with the CWA, supported by WorkSafe Victoria, the government agency which oversees Victoria's OHS system. The CWA is a politically and socially conservative rural women's association that is an influential lobbying body to state and federal governments and to rural employer bodies: 'it might be conservative but it's got a lot of political clout'. The AWU wanted to reduce Victorian farm-related deaths and injuries and needed access to farm workers, the farmers themselves, and their children, who often work alongside their parents. The AWU's National Director of OHS and the state secretary identified the CWA as best placed to provide two-way information between the farmers and the union. WorkSafe Victoria provided 'do-it-yourself' safety kits and training for CWA members so they could teach farmers and workers about major agricultural hazards. The kits were launched in 2002 at the CWA's annual Victorian conference and three AWU-sponsored scholarships enabled country women to further their education in areas related to OHS and the general health of men. The biggest challenge for the alliance partners was overcoming their initial distrust of each other. This required several meetings between the National Director of OHS and representatives from the CWA Executive to establish personal relationships and build on mutual understanding and respect before any progress could be made. The CWA Executive then invited members to participate in the project. As both the CWA and AWU were membership-based organisations, this allowed for greater understanding of possible issues regarding interactions between their respective Executives and members.

This alliance, unlike the previous three case studies, was temporary and very much leadership-driven. While CWA members were relied upon to act as farm safety officers, there was no grassroots involvement by AWU members, their role restricted to being recipients of OHS information and training if they worked on farms. Instead, the campaign was driven by the Director of OHS, which was time-consuming and exhausting for him. The campaign achieved its objective of reducing farm accidents and deaths, but by the end of 2003 it was over and the union had moved onto other issues, leaving the alliance to die. This reflected an attitude typical in unions, namely: 'the campaign has achieved its objective, so let's move on.' Without membership involvement, the union lacked the resources to sustain the alliance and build a long-term relationship. The alliance was developed to achieve an industrial objective for the union. It does not indicate a move towards a social unionism, even though it served broader community interests by reducing accidents and deaths on farms, because it has no AWU membership involvement and retained elements of instrumentality on the part of the union. The AWU, traditionally a servicing union, lags behind the previous three unions in terms of applying the organising model and moving towards community unionism. Unless AWU can develop an organising approach for its membership, it will not be able to sustain long-term community alliances and will not be able to use these as part of a revitalisation strategy.

ANF – aged-care sector

The ANF identified itself as using the organising model to increase membership and achieve successful outcomes from enterprise-bargaining campaigns in both public and private hospitals across Victoria. However, its campaigns in aged care have been less successful, failing to increase membership in this area. Aged care has the lowest union membership in the health sector as well as the worst working conditions and pay, and highest staff turnover. For the next round of bargaining, a targeted advertising campaign was planned in 2007/2008 by ANF

Executive to raise public awareness about employee and patient conditions in aged care. This strategy had previously worked for ANF in other areas of public health because the community readily identifies with nurses (Cockfield and Lazaris 2007). An underlying assumption with community unionism is that a community partner already exists. In the case of aged care, there are no such groups and the challenge for the ANF is to build pressure groups around aged-care issues to attract political and media attention. A recently appointed aged-care organiser has taken up this challenge. The difficulties confronting her are many, including high employee turnover, which makes it difficult to recruit members, let alone build a relationship between organiser and member. High turnover also contributes to difficulties in building a relationship between nurses and patients' families, making it difficult to encourage family members to form alliances and lobby on behalf of patients (and many patients do not have families, or else their family members visit rarely). The 'out of sight out of mind attitude' means that aged care is not noteworthy in the public's mind. The ANF provides the organiser with resources to attempt to develop some community groups to take on a political and lobbying role. This raises the question of where unions should focus their resources – on existing members and alliances or on creating a community partner to ultimately share the workload. If the attempt to build the partner is successful, it will be resources well invested for the community and the union. However, active grassroots involvement from those members working in aged care will be needed. Further, the Executive and organiser must effectively utilise the next round of enterprise-bargaining as a membership drive.

In this case study, the union utilised organising but it has not yet been effective in aged care, which may then limit the success of this attempt to engage in community unionism. The campaign currently relies on a top-down approach and the danger is that, when members are recruited to ANF, they may not feel part of the campaign and may not become workplace and community activists. If a community organisation is formed, it will need to be representative of the community, drawing widely for its membership base, as in the Stop Live Export case, but still include some ANF members to strengthen the alliance with the union. As ANF has demonstrated in other areas of health care, the benefits of organising combined with community-based campaigns may well give rise to another success in the aged-care area with an increase in membership and activism, but at the moment it relies heavily on a sole union organiser. Further, as was shown in the AWU–CWA alliance, a campaign relying heavily upon one person within a union is unlikely to lead to long-term partnerships and sustained outcomes.

TPAV – Neighbourhood Watch

TPAV does not have organisers, but does have over 70 delegates for approximately 9,800 members in Victoria. TPAV, therefore, did not identify itself as an organising union. However, its delegates fulfil many of the roles of organisers in other unions, including promoting membership involvement and control over campaigns. The Executive is appointed, not elected, and is the strategy-making body. TPAV's main role is to provide services to members, primarily insurance and other professional services. It also collectively bargains for its members. It has been regarded as a conservative union, but over the last decade its members have engaged in industrial action during enterprise-bargaining campaigns, indicating an increased militancy and commitment to campaigning, arguably elements of an organising model. In terms of gaining public support for its industrial campaigns, TPAV has proven itself to be effective at engaging in media campaigns and liaising with various community groups. TPAV, like the ANF, has the advantage of having members who interact regularly with the community, thereby making it easier to attract public support. The 2008 'Save Our Streets (SOS)' campaign is such an example.

The purpose of the campaign from TPAV's perspective was to increase police numbers and police presence on the streets to deter crime. By increasing police numbers, it is hoped that police can work more reasonable hours and at a single location, rather than being seconded to different stations outside their designated geographic area to fill staff shortages. The community partner supporting TPAV is Neighbourhood Watch, a community organisation formed over thirty years ago with the aim of 'reduc[ing] residential crime'. The alliance is long-term, reciprocal and mutually beneficial for the partners, even though TPAV retains most of the power in the relationship. The way the alliance is working during the SOS campaign is indicative of the importance of grassroots involvement of members in a campaign, because it is police officers in local stations who build a relationship with individuals who are Neighbourhood Watch members. However, grassroots relationships, while able to effect a stable alliance, can also have the opposite result as police officers are transferred between regions and as the level of commitment to Neighbourhood Watch activities by members of the community fluctuates at any given time. For the SOS campaign, the local-level relationships are reinforced by speaking at Neighbourhood

Watch meetings and providing advice and other support to these groups. From these relationships between individuals comes the capacity for TPAV to utilise Neighbourhood Watch members to publicly distribute SOS leaflets and stickers, which include requests for the public to lobby Victorian politicians and write letters of support for the campaign to newspaper editors. Campaign details are published in Neighbourhood Watch newsletters distributed in the local community. TPAV has used this same strategy in previous enterprise-bargaining campaigns to gain public support for its industrial objectives because these objectives, it argues, would also bring a benefit to the community.

The SOS campaign retains an instrumental objective for TPAV, namely, to increase police numbers to bring about better conditions and an increased likelihood of achieving work–family balance (but it will also be supported by industrial action if necessary). In many ways, the campaign and its objectives are typical of a narrow industrial agenda, rather than of social unionism. Despite this, TPAV has shown that it combines elements of organising with the ability to build long-term community alliances, placing it ahead of the AWU in terms of a possible continuum. TPAV, unlike the other unions discussed, has 98% coverage and does not need to use community alliances as a means of revitalisation but as a means of gaining mutually beneficial outcomes for its members and the community from enterprise-bargaining campaigns.

Conclusion

This chapter has examined the relationship between organising and community unionism, in particular the presence of a continuum through which unions may move strategically from servicing to organising and, finally, to community unionism. It was argued that unions that adopt an organising approach are more able to build sustainable alliances with community groups. Unions with a history of strong delegate structures and member participation are further along the continuum of servicing–organising–community and are using organising strategies alongside community alliances. Of the cases presented, the CFMEU and the MUA are to date the most successful at utilising organising alongside community alliances and both have a long history of community partnerships for social justice objectives, establishing them more closely to the social unionism collective action frame. For these unions, the objective of community unionism is not to increase membership and union power. Instead, these unions seek to organise and empower the community. Reciprocity is a not a condition of continued alliance support. This is in sharp contrast to the alliances formed by the AMIEU and TPAV. These unions have been able to build and sustain successful alliances because they are able to tie their industrial needs to broader social justice terms and their organisational structure encourages member involvement and participation. However, these alliances are driven by instrumental goals and their continuation is subject to the strategic needs of the unions. Nevertheless, these AMEIU and TPAV forms of community unionism do provide the potential for the development of a social unionism collective action frame. The AWU and ANF cases illustrate the difficulties in building sustainable alliances in the absence of prior member organising. The AWU appears to have the most distance to travel in terms of adopting the organising model, actively engaging the membership in campaigns and building permanent community alliances because of its historical reliance on arbitration and servicing and its commitment to political representation. This union's approach to community unionism does not reflect any move toward a more democratic or progressive form of unionism. In contrast, the ANF successfully utilises the organising model in other areas of health care, as it does community alliances, which suggests the aged-care campaign may develop into a successful campaign over time. Those Australian unions that have adopted at least some elements of organising, particularly with regard to mobilising members, have been shown to be more able to effect long-term community alliances to achieve both industrial and social justice objectives, combining organising and servicing with more radical forms. Future research should therefore examine whether these findings from Australia are generalisable to other cultural contexts.

8
Labour Union Strategies in the European Union Steel Sector

Dean Stroud and Peter Fairbrother

Introduction

Labour unions need to develop policies and demands appropriate to the changing political economy in which they operate. Thus, for example, it is important for unions to seek to place members at an advantage within the extant processes of 'modernisation' and restructuring. It would seem, however, that on a range of different issues it is management that dictates the shape of change, with union leaders and activists failing to engage employers (or their own members) in ways that challenge policy and practice that disadvantage workers. The evident danger is that workplace union influence is marginalised. In this chapter, we identify how unions have failed to respond in effective ways to the restructuring that is occurring across the European steel sector. We suggest that unions have found it difficult to address the shift in corporate form within the sector, from nation-based and focused corporations to both multinational (and increasingly transnational) ones – a key development that is at the base of the sector's restructuring activity. The specific contention is that unions have maintained an approach to interest representation that focuses on the state and/or supra-state, rather than the emerging corporate form that is beginning to characterise the sector. We suggest that one initial issue for unions to focus on is the articulation of alternative perspectives to prevailing corporate practice, as part of union strategy development (see Hyman 2007). Such an articulation takes the form of an active engagement by union leaders with members about possible futures and developing capacities to challenge corporate practice.

Recent debates about labour unionism address a number of themes. Of particular note are analyses of union organising and associated discussions about union renewal and revitalisation (Frege and Kelly 2003; Voss and Sherman 2003). Accompanying these studies, and focusing principally on national union movements, there is also a growing literature about ways international union bodies address international policies and practices (see, for example, Croucher and Cotton 2009; Tørres and Gunnes 2003; Müller *et al.* 2003; Wills 2002b). Running parallel to such debates are those concerned with union strategy, particularly in relation to corporate processes of workplace restructuring. However, what remains unclear is how unions might begin to address new uncertainties in a proactive manner and what difficulties they might face in the process. While unions are beginning to appreciate the complexities of corporate and sector restructuring, initiatives by unions are dependent on their capacities (developed in Hyman 2007: 198). Complementing these analyses is an argument about the continued saliency of labour unionism in advanced capitalist societies. Often implicit in analysis, the argument is that unions often remain rooted in their past and old ways of doing things, although the political economy of particular sectors is changing and evolving, in unexpected ways. The outcome is a disjunction between forms of union organisation and practice and the institutional and related changes that are taking place (Dufour and Hege 2002). In addressing these themes, our analysis rests on a distinction between 'business unionism', that form of unionism associated with the narrow pursuit of economic interests and objectives, and 'social democratic' unionism, where union purpose is defined in relation to both economic and political interests. The latter is designated by Hyman (2001: 55) as 'political economism' and defined as 'a synthesis between pragmatic collective bargaining and a politics of state directed social reform and economic management'. Taking this as a starting point, we aim to explore the limits of political economism in relation to a sector where 'social-democratic trade unionism' is based on bargaining (or partnership) with governments and employers, and which now struggles to deliver positive outcomes (Hyman 2001: 56). Although until relatively recently beneficial for memberships – albeit in relation to the regulation of labour markets and the social wage – subsequent developments within the emerging political economy have rendered such approaches largely redundant, bringing about the need for new approaches.

With the limitations of social-democratic unionism now evident, it is necessary to consider alternatives. Our approach rests on a view that campaigning unionism (Tattersall 2007b), as a dimension of union organisation and action, is for the most part absent from the steel sector. This type of unionism is member-focused, characterised by delegates and leaders committed to developing active forms of trade union collectivity (Stephenson and Stewart 2001), where leaders reach out to each other via network relations and where attention is focused on both companies and legislatures. It is a qualification of a form of unionism predicated on partnership and pressure for state-based solutions to workplace-generated problems. There clearly is a place for political economism, but there is an inadequacy to this form of unionism when dealing with multinational companies with internationally focused agendas. It is our contention that more active and collectively based forms of organisation and action will lead to approaches that can more readily challenge these companies in ways that recognise both the specificity of work and employment in a sector and the wider set of sector developments that take place at an international and global level.

Research methods

We employ data from a programme of research conducted across the EU steel sector that began in 2000, and is ongoing and is collectively referred to as the Cardiff Steel Research Programme (CSRP, www.cf.ac.uk/socsi/research/researchcentres/CGLR/events/steelresearch.html). The focus is on a number of different but interrelated sector issues, including processes of restructuring and redundancy, workforce reconfiguration and subsequent equal opportunities implications, and, skills and training needs. The principal research methodology was case study research of selected companies (and steel plants) and communities within Britain and across the EU (augmented with aggregate data wherever possible). The case studies involved semi-structured interviews with production workers, team leaders, apprentices, training staff and section/production managers, union officials or officers, HRM and company directors or senior managers (150 one-hour or longer interviews with 209 respondents). Further interviews were conducted with local politicians and other key actors. Steel companies/communities in eight countries were visited between 2001 and 2006 (Britain, Czech Republic, France, Germany, Netherlands, Italy, Poland, and Spain).

Steel sector developments

The modern EU steel sector is one of the best examples of the regional blocks that characterise the sector worldwide. Companies are organised principally in relation to the region and trade outside this is limited.

This is, however, a sector that is undergoing a transition from nationally based companies operating within a region to a more outward-looking and sectorally focused global sector. In particular, the emergence of supra-European steel companies presents a number of challenges for European institutions and social partners. Indeed, this wider restructuring and merger activity, which has been foreshadowed and paralleled by a diversification of the activities of steel companies and a shift towards the production of higher-value-added steel products, has impacted upon the steel sector workforce in a number of different ways.

Through several waves of restructuring and rationalisation activity, workforce numbers across the EU have fallen drastically. The EU-15 experienced particularly large cuts in its steel workforce between 1980 and 1990, with numbers dropping from 0.637 million in 1980 to 0.386 million in 1990 or by 39% (ILO 1992). This restructuring continues, being exemplified by redundancy programmes of Corus in 2001, 2003 and 2008. The reduction in the international steel workforce has coincided with the demand for a more diverse, highly qualified, multi-skilled, flexible and differently organised workforce (Bacon and Blyton 2000, 2004; ILO 1992; Stroud and Fairbrother 2006). Massive investment in training and retraining has, moreover, become a necessary feature of the European steel sector's continuing process of change and restructuring, as it struggles to meet its skill needs (Hertog and Mari 1999). The problem the sector now faces is that its workforce has more complex and diverse needs (and expectations and aspirations) to which both employers and unions must respond, particularly if the sector is to attract and retain the calibre of person it now seeks to recruit.

These changes and the outcomes of long-term restructuring have been the focus of much union activity. From the foundation of the EU in 1952, steel unions have played a part in the way the sector has been shaped at policy level (e.g. European Coal and Steel Community – ECSC) as well as dealing with the outcomes of the changes engineered. Concomitantly, the way in which the EU has evolved over its 50-year history has set the scene for union activity and concern. Of note, the 1993 Maastricht Treaty transformed the European Community into the 'European Union'. The Treaty placed an increased emphasis on 'social dialogue', although national unions were unevenly involved. However, unions face two contradictory developments, one concerned with the internationalisation of steel corporations and the other located in the increasing political and economic integration of the EU, with its associated political fora. The contradiction arises from the focus of the EU on regional development and the increasing involvement of corporations outside the EU, promoting a regional (EU) set of arrangements that do not necessarily dovetail with an international (corporate) perspective. Unions are nationally 'embedded' and the tension for unions is how to extend their national interests in ways that create synergies with unions elsewhere, as well as in relation to the sector as a whole (see, for example, Traxler *et al.* (2008) on cross-border bargaining coordination).

Most recently, with the end of the ECSC in 2002, the Steel Sector Social Dialogue Committee (SSSDC) was established in 2006, providing a platform for dialogue at the European level, and involving the major European-based steel companies and the labour unions, including the peak body, the European Metalworkers' Federation (EMF). Such fora provide European steel unions with the opportunity to address the implications and outcomes of extant changes. The question is, what are the implications of the developments described above for the workforce (and steel communities) and what is the role of unions and other forms of worker representation as these developments play themselves out? In what follows, we draw on the CSRP research to highlight specific examples of sector developments and the strategies adopted by unions.

Union responses and strategies

Union activity over the salient developments has involved a dual strategy, involving the EMF, on the one hand, and the affiliate unions on the other. Until recently, the EMF was a lead player in the ECSC, articulating its affiliates concerns and preoccupations on steel policy and practice. The confederation has taken up policies relating to employment development, competitiveness, working conditions, salaries and working time. It was a lead partner in establishing the SSSDC, bringing together major employers and unions in the steel sector, and creating policy on the development of, for example, training and skills, and environmental policy and sustainability. Our focus is on the tasks facing affiliate unions if they are to address the challenges of a changing steel sector (see Table 8.1 for the union federations and affiliate unions).

The developments we describe are interrelated and are part of the broader processes of sector restructuring and 'modernisation'. First, we discuss the bargaining agenda, illustrating this with reference to the need to recruit a more diverse and highly qualified staff. Then, we discuss some of the equal opportunities implications that flow from such developments. Second, we detail labour union-organising strategies with regard to training and learning, and the particular ways in which

Table 8.1   Case study federations and affiliate unions by country

Country of origin	Labour union/Union federation
Britain	1. Community
	2. Amicus (now Unite – the union)
Czech Republic	1. Odborový svaz KOVO – OS KOVO
France	1. Confédération Générale du Travail – CGT
	2. Confédération Française Démocratique du Travail – CFTD
Germany	1. Industriegewerkschaft Metall – IG Metall
Italy	1. Federazione impiegati operai metallurgica – FIOM
	2. Federazione Italiana Metalmeccanici – FIM
	3. Unione Italiana Lavaratori Metal meccanici – UILM
Netherlands	1. Federatie Nederlandse Vakbeweging – FNV
Poland	1. Solidarność
	2. Ogólnopolskie Porozumienie Związków Zawodowych – OPZZ
Spain	1. Confederación Sindical de Comisiones Obreras – CC.OO
	2. Union General de Trabajadores – UGT

they are developing in relation to recruitment and retention. Third, we look at the mobilising strategies pursued by unions in the steel sector, focusing particularly on two separate events in Britain and Italy, and union responses to threats of plant closure. Our claim is that these three sets of activities illustrate the ways unions are 'locked' into understandings and approaches that may have had a salience in the past but no longer in the current period.

Addressing workforce recomposition and equal opportunities

Steel sector workforces have traditionally comprised men recruited from stable, working-class communities in close geographical proximity to plants, and skilled by experience. Now, it is increasingly evident that recruitment strategies focus upon younger and more highly qualified workers, and upward movement through the occupational hierarchy is less based on time served, with merit and qualifications taking pre-eminence. Consequently, there is much greater potential for employment of 'non-traditional' groups and individuals. Indeed, recruitment of women to production is much more likely than previously, and in places such as Corus (Netherlands), it has been actively encouraged. Concomitantly, some groups are now being marginalised from the sector. Thus, migrant workers, who have been relied on heavily in some countries, like Germany and the Netherlands, particularly for low-skilled manual labour, are now less evident than previously. Unions have addressed these developments in a variety of ways, generating bargaining programmes in distinctive ways, shaped in relation to the workforce recomposition that is underway and the bargaining fora in each country.

The unions have sought standardised bargaining objectives. For example, in the Netherlands, the FNV confederation has the largest (about 75%) membership at the Ijmuiden plant, and an EUO based there, leading the negotiations and union relations with the plant management. The union's leadership stress the importance of negotiation, under the auspices of works council arrangements, and usually within the framework set by the management. In negotiations, it has long supported skills training for workers in general, promoted language programmes for migrant workers (so that they are better placed to up skill and avoid redundancy), and negotiated wage and related concerns. Strikes are relatively unusual, with the longest most recent strike being a ten-day stoppage in 1973, although shorter strikes do occur from time to time, involving specific sections for relatively limited objectives.

In Germany, IG Metall encouraged migrant worker involvement in representative structures, meaning that migrant worker issues are more likely to have been engaged with directly. Some of these initiatives date back to the mid-1990s, when unions in the steel sector (and elsewhere) pursued equality agreements. These agreements recognised the link between qualifications and language, with non-German speakers missing out as the companies began to emphasise credentialism in relation to employability in plants. Many of these concerns were dealt with via works councils and these initiatives very much depended upon the range of representation, in terms of ethnicity as well as gender on these councils. However, other developments in the workforce profile have not been so well addressed by unions – or employers. This is particularly the case with regard to the equal opportunities implications that emerge from new recruitment strategies, focusing on young highly qualified staff, adopted by most companies.

Indeed, paralleling the developments described has been the emergence of equal opportunities issues, which, although always existing, have become increasingly visible. For example, pressure for better work–life balance arrangements is coming to the fore as workforce composition moves beyond its traditional profile. More highly educated, younger (and often female) workers carry different expectations of work–life boundaries than 'traditional' parts of the workforce, and press for change (see Huldi 2002). These pressures are, we contend, being individually rather than collectively expressed and addressed at present, underlining the instrumentality of corporate approaches, rather than the effectiveness of European 'law' (Room 2005: 118). Relative union passivity on these matters is exemplified by union stances involving, for example, CGT and CFDT, which only began to focus on promoting equal treatment (rather than opportunity) in 2006. More typical was Solidarność, which had no specific policy and simply made reference to the labour code. Such developments raise issues concerning the capacity to manage and respond to transformations in workforce composition, and deal with the equal opportunities implications that flow from such developments.

The way in which steel sector work is organised, and the relation between this and employment relations, is a crucial dimension in any assessment of union bargaining agendas. As workforces recomposed, so did patterns of representation and salient issues. In Germany, for instance, between 20% and 30% of workers either were born outside Germany or come from minority ethnic communities. By 2000, the composition of both union leadership and works councils began to reflect this. Nonetheless, despite an emphasis on recruiting more women into the steel workforce in the Netherlands, only five of the 120 works councillors in 2002 were women. So, there is evidence that inequalities are built into critical aspects of the employment structure, and, by implication, the unions.

Organising in relation to training and learning

The current profile of the workforce is rooted in the redundancies of the early 1980s, when large numbers were shed in a relatively planned and orderly way (Beguin 2005). This process involved unions, and was broadly supported by them, articulating a social-democratic approach to workforce change. However, the labour shedding also was accompanied by an agreed block on recruitment. Towards the end of the 1990s, steel companies began to recruit again, with the result that workforces across much of Europe became polarised by age. Against this backdrop, steel sector employers have tended to operate in rather instrumental ways, in practice at least, if not in terms of training policy development, with the emphasis on organising training and learning to meet a company's most pressing skill deficiencies. Specifically, the sector's training and learning strategy derives from a traditional reliance on informal practices, such as learning-by-doing, to skill workers. However, at the same time, the companies active within the Steel Sector Social Dialogue Committee are aware that a more highly sophisticated training strategy is necessary. They are working towards this end – in some countries, in partnership with unions (see, for example, Bacon *et al.* 1996). The outcome is that parallel strategies can be observed – regardless of the vocational education and training (VET) structures, social-partnership relationships or collective bargaining arrangements that exist in relation to training and learning in any particular country, such as those developed by IG Metall and FNV (see Stroud and Fairbrother 2006, 2008a). A premium is placed on *regressive* learning strategies for some sections of the workforce, such as learning-by-doing, which provide limited opportunities to acquire qualifications and enhance skills and employability profiles. Others, mainly newer, more highly qualified recruits, benefit from *progressive* strategies, defined by multiple opportunities to achieve credentials, enhance skills levels and facilitate career opportunities within organisations (Stroud and Fairbrother 2006).

Workforce recomposition signified by this history draws attention to VET policies. Via social dialogue practices, unions have addressed issues of training and qualifications, particularly for traditional industries, such as steel, where employers have typically relied on poorly educated and specifically skilled workforces (see Heyes 2007). The form of VET in each member state is distinct, often sector-specific, shaped by specific histories that reflect both established social partner cooperation and distinct forms of work organisation (Bosch and Charest 2008; see also Maurice *et al.* 1986). With the restructuring of work and employment relations, coupled with the changes in ownership, and the emergence of transnationals from the former state-based companies, two sets of relations are at work. Thus, VET arrangements are nationally specific, and, as steel corporations develop as transnationals, they end up dealing with different sets of VET arrangements. It is the intersection between national and sector arrangements that enables these corporations to reshape and train their workforces more or less as they see fit (see Stroud and Fairbrother 2008b).

As this corporate strategy on skills enhancement has emerged, the place of unions has largely been one of servicing an existing membership (see Stroud and Fairbrother 2008b), and 'servicing' debate (see Carter 2006 and Forrester 2005: 258). Union leaders have defined members' concerns in restricted and narrowly work-related ways, often in terms of pay and conditions (including job security), and not in terms of more ill-defined questions relating to job development and alternatives. Consequently, for the most part, unions have not addressed important issues of employability, especially through workplace learning and life-long learning agendas. Indeed, steel union leaderships tend to view workplace learning as an additional and narrowly defined objective rather than as core to members' interests and concerns, so failing to articulate members' interests and express their worries about their future. The ways in which companies on the one hand, and unions on the other, develop approaches to skills needs and enhancement, it is contended, derive from historically embedded recruitment, retention, training, and learning practices within the sector, with which unions and their membership are complicit (Stroud and Fairbrother 2006).

Mobilising strategies

The focus here is on union capacity with reference to the closure/partial closure of Corus plants in south Wales (Ebbw Vale and Llanwern) and the partial closure of the ThyssenKrupp AG (TKS) owned plant in Terni, Italy. The results of mergers in the 1990s, both Corus and TKS have been involved in ongoing and extensive programmes of restructuring and rationalisation. In both Italy and Britain, the steel sector is privately owned, increasingly dominated by transnationals and much-reduced workforces, very much reflecting the general picture of restructuring across the EU steel sector. The response to the closure announcements was quite different at each site, but both illustrate the uncertainties associated with social-democratic unionism. The announcement of redundancies by Corus was followed by a limited and narrowly focused response by unions, whereas the TKS announcement was challenged in much more solidaristic and collective ways.

The Corus closures derive from the merger in 1999 of British Steel and Koninklijke Hoogovens, the Dutch steel producer, to create Corus. Following the merger, Corus reviewed its corporate strategy, part of which has involved the review of British operations, especially in relation to carbon steel production. One outcome was that Corus announced a wide range of closures and staff reductions in 2001 across Britain and the Netherlands. This programme included the complete closure of the Ebbw Vale plant, with the loss of about 900 jobs, and cessation of steel making at Llanwern, with the loss of 1,300 jobs (the hot and cold rolling mills remain in operation at Llanwern, employing about 1,600). Ebbw Vale is the main town in the county of Blaenau Gwent, situated in the south Wales valleys. Llanwern is located in Newport, the third largest city in Wales and the hub of a much larger area. The closure of the Ebbw Vale plant was in two stages, with half the workforce leaving just a few weeks after confirmation of the closure. The remainder departed when the plant finally closed in July 2002, with a small number remaining on site until February 2003 to organise and carry out its decommissioning. Steelmaking at Llanwern ended in mid-2001, with the majority of redundant workers going then and others following as the close-down proceeded.

The redundancy announcements wrong-footed the unions, for they (and their members) were taken by surprise at their extent. But the manner in which they were announced, and the way they were to be implemented, left the unions reeling too. Many union officials (and members) learned of the closure announcements in ways other than through formal contact with the company (such as by radio on the local news). When it came to dealing with the announcement, each level of union representation dealt with one aspect of the redundancy proposal and programme and not with the event as a whole. Indeed, with other redundancies announced across Britain, each plant 'union' operated independently of the others. Significantly, each plant 'union' maintained a site-wide coherence of response (see also Danford *et al.* 2003: 49–54, who showed how the maintenance of a site-wide form of union accountability ensured a unity of response to managerial decisions). Local representatives sought agreements on the orderly departure of redundant workers, while the regional representatives tried to coordinate the responses of the different plants, playing their part in the All-Wales Task Force and petitioning the Wales Assembly Government. Meanwhile, the national leadership dealt with the corporate management and the government. This form of representation 'proved highly amenable to the pursuit of a managerially-defined agenda for change' (Blyton and Turnbull 2004: 223), facilitating the redundancy process. Principally, the unions became involved in two main levels of activity, at a national level, via the National Steel Co-ordinating Committee (NSCC), and at a plant level, with a more discursive involvement by national and regional officers in the All-Wales Task Force. The NSCC secured a moratorium on implementation of the proposals so that it could draw up alternative plans, nationally and plant-by-plant, but these interventions were to no avail and plant closure became inevitable. Critically, there was little engagement between unions in Britain and the Netherlands regarding these corporate decisions.

In Italy, there was a more 'militant' response to the partial closure, but, as in Britain, much of this was to no avail. TKS was formed by the merging of German companies, Krupp-Hoesch AG and Thyssen Stahl AG, in 1997. In 2000, TKS embarked on a Europe-wide reorganisation, establishing a divisional structure, and promoting production according to an assessment of each plant within each business unit. As part of this, TKS in 2003 proposed transferring production of 150,000 tons p.a. of low-grade electrical steel from Terni to other steelworks, as well as ending the production of specified high-grade steels. In 2002, over 4,000 employees worked at the plant, each with an average age of 48 years. In the early 2000s, increasing numbers of older workers left, following the application of legislation relating to the employment of workers who had been exposed to asbestos. By 2004, 650 young replacement workers were employed on fixed-term contracts, with the workforce comprising just fewer than 3,000 employees by 2005.

Most of the workers belonged to one of the local branches of the three main union confederations in the sector, FIOM, FIM and UILM. At the plant level, a joint-union committee dealt with management, having had close and long-standing relations with the city and regional levels of the union organisation as well as the relevant political administrations. With the announcement of partial closure in early 2004, the plant unions initiated a strike, accompanied by road blockades, demonstrations and rallies. Almost a month later, a temporary settlement was achieved, with an agreement to retain production of electrical steels and promote investment within the plant and by public authorities. However, nine months later TKS withdrew from further negotiations. The Joint Union Works Committee recommenced its campaign against closure, with limited success. In early 2005, timed to coincide with a meeting of the Supervisory Board of the company in Germany, the unions organised a four-hour strike, including a blockade of the motorway and the central railway station.

The Supervisory Board, however, confirmed the end of electrical steel production (with workers' representatives voting against). In response, the unions organised strikes covering each shift, with continued blockade of the railway station. With the failure of national negotiations, the plant unions escalated their campaign and after another extended period of blockades, strikes, and rallies, a settlement was reached a month later. The settlement included cessation of electrical steel production, relocation of 350 threatened workers (unless they wanted to take voluntary redundancy) and the conversion of 650 temporary contracts to permanent ones. The aftermath of the dispute lingered on in the plant and community, and there remains a general unease that TKS may eventually close down the plant or at least severely curtail production. Here too, there was room for engagement beyond national structures of representation, and the Italian labour unions did try to engage with IG Metall and the EMF, but neither the Federation nor IG Metal took a particularly firm stance against TKS here.

In both cases, the approach to the prospect of closure was rooted in a past set of relations that were increasingly obsolescent (see Hyman 2001: 56–7).

In each case, rather than develop an active locally based alliance of interests, linking the work and community together, and proposing alternative strategies to both corporate leaders and local political bodies, the unions in each case sought a national political solution and a changed corporate decision. While the latter focus was understandable, it would appear that a more engaged and locally focused campaign would serve to question these policies in ways that at least starkly highlight the outcomes of these types of corporate decisions, if not lead to an alternative outcome. Nonetheless, in the case of Italy, the local unions were more engaged than was the case in Wales. These unions engaged with policy-makers at each level, local, national and occasionally internationally, but they did this in a disaggregated way.

Indeed, in both cases, the unions failed to create an integrated union approach to the events that took place. Instead, each level of the union hierarchy responded in a distinctly layered way, with local officials dealing with plant management, regional union officials addressing regional political bodies and national union officials addressing national political bodies and the national corporate management, with some *ad hoc* engagement at the multinational level. Again, the Italian engagement at the multinational level was more focused and textured than in the case of the British unions. We suggest, however, that in the changed circumstances of the 1990s and 2000s, such challenges to corporate decisions and policies by unions are no longer effective; bargained solutions via forms of political economism no longer have the salience of the past. Unions can challenge transnational corporations, but in this process, unions may find it necessary to look beyond the wage relationship to a broader range of policies, including the impact of workforce recomposition and training and learning within the changed context of the steel sector – as discussed above.

Discussion

The EU steel sector has restructured in significant ways, raising a number of issues that unions need to address. The programmes of redundancy and rationalisation implemented by major steel corporations were designed to respond to market conditions (and at the same time maximise profit margins for shareholders). In the plants that do not close, smaller, more diverse and highly skilled and qualified workforces must now work differently to be more productive and efficient. This necessitates change in recruitment and retention strategies and, in parallel with this, the development of more highly sophisticated training and learning strategies. Such developments are priorities for the EMF and the Sector Social Dialogue Committee, which comprise the affiliate unions that formed part of the CSRP research. The contention is whether or not unions (and federations and confederations) are well placed (or sufficiently organised) to counter what are supra-sector-wide issues in effective ways, and engage with processes of restructuring and 'modernisation' to the benefit of their memberships.

One focus here has been on the ability of unions to 'frame coherent policies' (Hyman 2007: 198), coupled with the implications of maintaining long established forms of organisation and representation, indicated by the continued adherence to political economism in these types of unions. The difficulty faced by unions and the associated confederations is that the language of bargaining and representation is infused by a 'social dialogue' rhetoric, the accompaniment to social-democratic forms of unionism. Thus, bargaining agenda and organising approaches are often presented by union leaders in terms of the potentialities of partnership, rather than in terms of more adversarial relations. This discourse is reinforced by the experience of works councils, various consultative arrangements, and the language of the European Commission and associated institutions. In a number of countries, particularly the coordinated market economies, such as Germany and the Netherlands, the institutions associated with training and learning are part of the firmament of macro-cooperation and consultation (Bosch and Charest 2008).

However, the paradox is that while the EU has become more prominent, corporations are beginning to reposition themselves both within and beyond the EU as a region. At present, it would seem that unions are failing to address transnational corporate policy effectively. The EU steel sector is experiencing change in a number of ways, shaped by corporations responding, in very general terms, to market demands and to meet market interest. What we have tried to show is that there are distinct parallels (and a synchronicity) across the sector in the way it is restructuring and developing. In this sense, unions within individual nation states across Europe need to address the same issues in alliance with each other, although at present they are not doing so. This was dramatically illustrated by the different approaches from the Netherlands and Britain (see above). Here, each union was bound by the particular legislation and practices that applied in both countries and the cross-border approach to 'rationalisation' by the corporation was not accompanied by a cross-border union response. Indeed, the embrace of neoliberal policies by governments (and supranational bodies) in the context of an increasingly internationalised sector, exemplified in the increasing fluidity of capital and corporations, compromises the ability of unions to challenge supra-sectoral change to the benefit of nationally based union memberships (see Hyman 2007: 195).

The union form of organisation is critical, and in many cases decisive, bringing us back to discussions about union form and the analysis by Hyman (2001). While companies set the context for decision-making and associated responses to workplace restructuring and reorganisation, unions take this context as given. Thus, while perhaps unsurprising, unions dealt with the proposals for reorganisation and restructuring in trifurcated ways – at an international level (via the EMF), at national levels (in terms of the specificity of states), and at the plant level (dealing with the practicalities of an orderly change). Reliance on the cross-border confederations, such as the EMF, raises questions about capacity, which may lead to an overestimation of what is possible. To address policy initiatives collectively requires an active form of union organisation, where members and their leaders actively attempt to address corporate decisions (for an appreciation of the difficulties associated with such an approach, see Bronfenbrenner 2007b). It also means that the relationships between affiliate unions and cross-border confederations should be re-forged in ways that give both affiliate unions and the confederations the capacity to question transnational corporate policies and practices. However, this requires attention to the form union organisation takes (see Danford *et al.* 2003).

Some labour unions are responding to these developments by identifying synergies with foreign counterparts and forming cross-border links and relationships, with the aim of tackling the 'international' repositioning of the employers with which they must negotiate (Tattersall 2007b). It is not that such forms of merger and cooperation represent a new alternative for regional and global union federations are a response to globalisation and the international movement of capital. What such forms of union organisation represent is a recognition that forms of union 'political economism' cannot provide an adequate response to the repositioned corporations of the European steel sector. Thus, the problem under debate is not unionism *per se* but the capacity that unions have to develop an appropriate set of policies for the changing circumstances of work and employment, particularly in traditional industrial sectors, with their long established routines and practices. For unions, a tension develops between the long-standing pursuit of state-focused strategies and policies (for example, bargaining agendas, organising agendas and mobilisation strategies) and addressing the implications of corporate restructuring. The contention is that these unions have been too reliant upon political exchange. In the emerging circumstances of multinational corporate entities, pressures on state bodies, at a national or European level no longer suffice. These private multinational corporations respond to different pressures than the past state-based entities and work under complex new market relations that place new and distinctive pressures on unions. In this respect, the starting point is workers, their leaders and the multilayered features of unionism – locally, regionally, nationally, and increasingly internationally. The first task is to realise union capacity from the workplace and worksite upwards. Only then will the institutional reorganisation underway begin to be addressed in ways that enable the realisation of mobilising capacities. Our contention is that this requires the enhancement and development of union collectivity (Stephenson and Stewart 2001). Second, unions must begin reaching out to each other, not so much in the context of the established fora, such as the social dialogue committee for the sector (albeit an important initial step), but from affiliate union to affiliate union. Only then will union memberships be able to share experiences, plan joint actions, and shadow each other in addressing the challenges posed by the increasingly globalised corporations that have begun to characterise the sector. It is in this respect that political economism belongs to the past and unions increasingly will be pressured into developing forms of democratised and participative representation and engagement.

Conclusion

The European steel sector has become increasingly consolidated into fewer hands, although it remains some distance from the levels of concentration in, for example, the automobile sector. At the same time, aided by neoliberal de-regulation, employers have become increasingly assertive, if not hostile. Thus, it is in relation to the ways in which the scene was set by corporate policies that unions in the steel sector negotiate and represent their members. Complementing these contextual developments, union organisation may take centralised or decentralised forms. These are not participative and engaged unions. Nonetheless, they operate in increasingly decentralised contexts, with limited capacities to mount unified and coherent resistance to managerial proposals at the corporate (and sector) level. Unions are struggling to meet the challenge of comprehensive and widespread restructuring. The outcome is a tension between state-based policies and practices and the specificities of corporate initiatives and structures. How unions address these developments and the complications associated with them, is a pressing task. While the principal focus here has been on the limitations of union policy development in the steel sector, it is also necessary to consider how union capacity may be realised in these changing circumstances. However, for unions to address the varieties of restructuring that are taking place in sectors such as steel, it is necessary to break with the limitations of 'political economism'. In the context of neoliberalism, albeit in the specific form embraced by the EU, with its hybrid form of social democracy and neoliberalism, unions face challenges that mean they must look beyond the verities of 'political economism'. In this respect, unions need to look again at the policies and objectives they pursue at both local and national levels.

9
CleanStart – Fighting for a Fair Deal for Cleaners

Michael Crosby

Introduction

In every country, no matter how strong the recent economic upswing, workers are routinely ripped off and disrespected. They lack the power to stand up to their employers. In Hong Kong, steel erectors on construction sites marched in protest at the fact that they have suffered a savage decline in wages every year for six years – despite a booming construction sector. In Malawi, security guards employed by the world's biggest security transnational have received not a day off in seven years – not weekends, not public holidays. In Britain, a giant insurance company demands that cleaners campaigning for a living wage be removed from their jobs – on the grounds that they pose a security risk. In the US, the service sector is built on minimum wage immigrant workers who are incapable of providing a decent standard of living for their families. In Germany, security workers in some parts of the country earn less than five Euros an hour. In Australia, the land of the 'fair go', cleaners see penalty rates – the payments made to cleaners for work after normal hours, on weekends and public holidays – disappear, workloads increase and wages fall. The proceeds of the 'good times' go to those with power – while those without it sit trapped at the bottom of the labour market. All this happens because unions in virtually every country are in retreat. Density is falling and there are very few signs that these trends will be reversed any time soon.

Unions in many countries are increasingly aware of the problem and in recent years have tried to do something to address it. The solutions outlined by Hyman (2001) in relation to British unions seem to be universally relevant:

> *Faced with marked decline, [they] tried six options; these were, the develop-*
> *ment of individual services, the promotion of employment rights not con-*
> *ditional on union membership, partnership with employers, active social*
> *campaigning on non-traditional but work related issues, raised organisa-*
> *tional efforts and increased communication with members.* (summary
> cited in Willman 2004: 77)

Willman (2004) is right to characterise these as a conservative response.
Such a systemic failure of unionism in a time of economic growth is
surely a sign that there is something wrong with the fundamental
model of unionism. We need to look for a far more radical response to
systemic union decline and in Australia we have looked – perhaps to
our own surprise – to a North American union, the Service Employees
International Union (SEIU) (see Woodruff 2007). North American
unionism has rarely been seen as a model to be imitated in Australia
(or New Zealand). With our higher historical density and better outcomes for workers, we are entitled to have been sceptical about 'US solutions'. The cultural fit is also difficult. We have difficulty in relating to
American levels of aggression in campaigning. We respond negatively
to the high levels of evangelical enthusiasm in everyday US union practice. The legislative framework that applies in large parts of the US and
Canada with its recognition system and reliance on either closed shop
union security or the chance to negotiate 'Fair Share' payments from
non-members has no echo in our part of the world.

But in Australia our decline has been so savage, so catastrophic that
most of us have had to overcome any inhibitions we might have had
about learning from our comrades in the US. The fact is that a union
like the SEIU has doubled its numbers over a period when we have
been losing huge swathes of membership. Our learning has not been
uncritical. We like to think that in a few areas we have picked up the
union change agenda and taken it a bit further. We have tried to work
out how to apply organising principles to an 'open shop' environment.
But we are also very clear that tacking a few organising tactics onto an
unreformed union structure simply will not work. We tried that – some
unions still do it – but it has manifestly failed and simply dispirited
some of our most courageous trailblazers.

Successful organising depends on a remaking of the vision of what a
successful union looks like. It demands a scale of organising not seen
in our country since the turn of the nineteenth century. It remakes

the relationship of members with their unions. It takes a fundamental reorientation of every part of the union organisation to the pursuit of power for its members. It makes necessary leadership courage as organising strategies test the boundaries of anti-union laws. At times, it requires leaders to 'bet the farm'. It requires the adoption of internal processes that guarantee strong national leadership in contrast to 'warlordism', which afflicts too many state branches. It requires a shift in the reward systems for staff. It ensures that the union has to relate to the community and the political system in ways not tried in our country for generations. Above all, union success depends on a complete restructuring of the union's financial system. Waste must be driven out, tight financial management of limited resources is crucial and members generally need to be prepared to spend more money to be represented by a union organisation that exercises manifest power in their industry or sector.

The case study that follows is an application of the union change agenda pioneered by the SEIU in another environment. It describes how two unions have gone about organising Central Business District (CBD) cleaners across ten markets in two countries – Australia and New Zealand. The campaign – CleanStart – represents some of the early fruit of the process of union transformation. It is not yet complete and the jury is still out as to its success. But, in its scale, reach and single-minded determination to win no matter what the cost, it marks a radical shift in the way in which the Australian union, in particular, proposes to organise. It could never have happened without the union undertaking a process of root-and-branch reform at every level of its operations over the last ten years.

CleanStart

In 2005, the Liquor Hospitality and Miscellaneous Workers Union (LHMU) – along with New Zealand's Service and Food Workers Union (SFWU) – faced the total collapse of their cleaner membership. In Australia, in particular, with the introduction into parliament of the Howard government's *Workchoices* law – the *Workplace Relations Amendment Act 2005* – the default setting for industrial relations would become individual non-union contracts for every worker. In labour-intensive, contracted-out industries like cleaning, the result was likely to be catastrophic. When similar legislation was introduced in Western Australia (WA), a downward wages and hours spiral in the cleaning industry began and the sector was almost entirely deunionised. After five years of individual contracting, the WA Branch of the LHMU had just six cleaner members in the whole of the Central Business District, workloads had grown to three times that of a typical US cleaner, penalty and holiday loadings had been stripped out of contracts and cleaner incomes were at an all-time low. The decision needed to be made as to whether the union could save its cleaner membership from exposure to a market that was regulated almost entirely in favour of the employers.

The development of strategy

Over ten years, LHMU had developed a close relationship with the SEIU. The union had been inspired by the organising success of SEIU and by its willingness to do whatever it took to build the power of those it represented. Equally, the SEIU leadership felt an affinity for an Australian movement battling to survive in an environment of increasing hostility. On his first visit to Australia, Jay Hessey, an adviser to the campaign from SEIU, asked the LHMU's Executive: 'Why cleaners? It's tough organising. You have to put in a lot of resources and maybe you'll get more members in other areas.' The response was very clear. One Secretary said: 'Cleaners formed this union. The day we give up on them, we cut out our heart.' Another said: 'We cover the missos [miscellaneous workers] – the people no one else wants. That's where cleaners are and that's why they're our business.' The campaign was a question of principle rather than the application of a cost–benefit analysis.

Traditional methods of organising cleaners

The existing coverage of cleaners was, in fact, a product of the traditional Australian closed shop arrangements (which are now unlawful). Indeed, in the days of a strong award system, providing legally enforceable minimum standards at a high level across the whole workforce, there was little reason for an employer to want to go non-union. The law prevented employers from competing with each other on the basis of the cost of labour. Membership stood at probably 20%–30% without any great controversy and without a huge amount of activity on the part of the union. With the demise of the closed shop and the gradual destruction of the award system of minimum rates, this whole settlement began to unravel. Employers found that they could cut corners and the union lacked the power to do much about it. Pressure built on all contractors to start looking very carefully at how labour costs could be cut. Individual agreements and subcontracting started to appear at the margins of the industry. Reports of cash-in-hand payments surfaced. Overwork became standard. With the cutting of hours, many cleaners were forced to take two and three jobs just to be able to cobble together a living wage. Injuries at work became more frequent with cleaners rushing to finish their allocated areas. Turnover increased as long-term cleaners left the industry. Buildings were increasingly being cleaned by a constantly shifting workforce of foreign language students. Membership began dropping as old members left and new members – particularly when they were students – were not signed up.

In the face of these developments, individual branches of the union attempted to stem the tide. Organisers were either hired or redeployed to the largest buildings and went from building to building – where they could get access – trying to sign members up. All the techniques of organising were used. Organisers tried to build committees, develop activists. They used the organising frameworks to get workers angry about the way they were treated. They tried to build hope in the prospect of acting together. They tried to get workers to take action, join and demand a better deal. Some benefit was seen. The organisers in the buildings targeted could see increases in membership. But at no time could they manage to get contractors to improve the situation of cleaners – lest they lose the contract. And at no time was the inflow of members sufficient to overcome the steady turnover of cleaners as workers left the industry.

The new strategy

The strategy developed by the LHMU was based on the following: (i) our vision was of a cleaning industry that provided good jobs to cleaners which were worth doing well. That could only happen if cleaners were organised; (ii) contractors had to be persuaded to be neutral – to grant real freedom of association to those they employed. To get neutrality required us to make it safe for contractors to allow their workers to organise; (iii) that meant that those letting the contracts – the owners – needed to focus on the standard of cleaning as much as its price. It required them to recognise that competition on price alone had brought about a failure in the labour market which could only damage levels of tenant satisfaction.

Four researchers were hired and SEIU loaned LHMU a lead researcher from their Property Services Division, Carol Tyson. She trained the researchers in US research techniques and together they developed their own techniques and a database that would record who cleaned, managed, secured, owned and occupied every major CBD building. They dug into the issue of cleaning rates and used the research that had been done by academics such as Ryan (2001), which set out the problems facing cleaners. What quickly became clear was that the 'theory' was right. A strategy aimed at contractors alone was doomed to failure. They simply lacked the power to improve the treatment of cleaners given their dependence on building owners. Unilateral improvement by one contractor would ensure that the contractor lost market share to lower-priced competitors. The key shift that had to be achieved was to get owners to understand the crisis in the contract cleaning industry. They needed to understand that this was not just a crisis for cleaners. It had an impact on tenant satisfaction and that ultimately was sure to affect their occupancy rate and rental income. At cleaning rates of 1,000 square metres per hour, it was crystal clear that buildings were simply not being cleaned. At best, spot cleaning was practised, where cleaners only cleaned the most obvious dirt and refuse. Horrific stories about the standard of cleaning in toilets and kitchens – and the cross-contamination of both – were collected. And case studies were developed showing how important a trained cleaner workforce was for the achievement of green targets in the management of buildings. The researchers enabled LHMU to make the business case for a well-trained, fairly paid, stable workforce with the time to do their job properly. The researchers were able to tell LHMU how many of the owners had to be moved to action if we were to have a significant impact on the industry as a whole. We needed engagement from the 14 owners who owned more than 50% of the large buildings in each of the markets. All of them were at least national players and some were present in both the Australian and New Zealand markets. About half were global players with a presence outside the two countries.

The organising

While this research was going on, around 25 organisers across the cities had been allocated exclusively to the campaign. This was almost revolutionary. Australian unions have scarcely ever organised on this scale or sought to ensure that a nationwide campaign was coordinated and managed centrally. The organisers were brought together and trained in the skills required to engage workers. They understood the strategy and they developed the tactics that would be used as part of the campaign. Central to CleanStart was the idea that we were organising the whole industry all at the one time. That is, we had enough organisers and would develop enough activists to be able to bring pressure to bear on the whole industry as we defined it, in every market in which we were organising. Typical of the concern to ensure that this was seen as an industry-wide campaign was the use of common branding – the name

CleanStart, the logo and associated artwork, shared campaign materials, a campaign website – right down to the finer details of shared T-shirts and banners. The organisers even spent time in working together to develop their chants and songs to be used in demonstrations across the two countries. Organisers were asked to look for workers who were prepared to take action. Their job at this stage was not to sign members up – we wanted to do that at a time in the campaign when members could join the union without fear. Instead, we were looking for a group of workers who were prepared to form an activist minority.

Jay Hessey encouraged us to schedule a year-long programme of action in the streets. He made sure we understood that big spectacular demonstrations were fine but the thing that would really get the industry's attention was a 'steady drum beat' of activity. Every day the industry needed to see that we were there, we would be there tomorrow and we would never go away until the cleaners got justice. Each month branches arranged 'National Days of Action'. The same action was planned across all ten cities – wherever possible against common targets. In between those actions smaller actions were scheduled by each branch against local or national targets. Every day something was due to happen – even if it only consisted of a couple of organisers or activists outside a building leafleting during lunchtime. The actions were specifically required not to cause any owner or contractor economic harm. Rather, they were designed to draw attention to an invisible workforce and its problems. We aimed to educate the public and enlist public opinion in our cause. Australian union demonstrations until then could largely be described as a 'nice walk in the sun'. Unless there are a thousand people turning out in a march, the demonstration is seen as a failure – unnoticed. In CleanStart, with just 30 people, we could have an overwhelming impact – if every one of them wore the CleanStart shirt, had a drum or noisemaker, and if they were all trained to sing out the funny chants and songs developed earlier.

Communications strategy

Communication was our means of magnifying the union's work so that as many people as possible understood what was happening to cleaners, that there was a problem and that something needed to be done about it. We approached two senior journalists with our story – Adele Horin at the *Sydney Morning Herald* and Elizabeth Wynhausen at *The Australian*. Both wrote large sympathetic features in the highest-circulation Saturday editions spotlighting what was happening to these workers at the bottom of the labour market. Wherever we could we encouraged workers to tell their own stories, why they needed to organise, what was wrong with the way they were treated, the importance to the community of their job, their inability to provide for their families, and why they were demonstrating. We wanted the members and workers to speak for themselves as much as possible. We also staged our demonstrations with a view to their media impact. Our chants made it into the most read part of the *Sydney Morning Herald* – the 'Stay In Touch' column on the back page. The piece got in not because of the justice of our cause but because our chants were funny and got bystanders in the city laughing as we marched past. We held a 'Golden Toilet Brush Award' and presented a gigantic toilet brush to the owner who failed to meet with us. He came on board by 5 p.m. that day. A campaign website recorded every step in the progress of the campaign. Employers and owners were assiduous in tracking our campaign and noting our successes. This helped us build a sense of momentum and inevitability.

The community

Cleaners are a largely immigrant workforce and we wanted to enlist the support of the community for our cause. This needed to be something more than a union-organising campaign. We wanted society to see it as the whole community coming together endorsing traditional Australian values of fairness and equity. The union in Australia had little in the way of reciprocal relationships with community organisations and this part of the campaign was difficult. Two state branches of the union employed community organisers during the campaign and they set about building long-term relationships with the community. Community organisations were prepared to send letters of support and sometimes speak at our rallies but they were not able to turn out groups of their own members. The commitment to community organisers has continued, however, and the hope is that, in the next major campaign, community organisations will see the welfare of their constituencies tied up in the success of the union's campaign. One group was unwavering in their support of cleaners: the churches were happy to lend their considerable credibility to the defence of low-paid workers. Sister Libby Rogerson was a frequent speaker at our rallies and Bishop Pat Power prayed the 'Cleaner's Prayer' at demonstrations in Canberra – to the delight of the cleaners. Clearly, a number of the churches – particularly the Anglican and Uniting Churches – also used their influence as property owners to ask questions of their contractors, making sure that the churches' opposition to worker oppression was being lived out in the behaviour of their own contractors.

The position in New Zealand was different. A very high proportion of the SFWU's members are of Maori or Pacific Island background. The union has long been seen to be an effective representative of these communities and enjoyed very close and long-standing links with the various Maori and Pacific Island organisations. The union could only allocate two organisers and a half-time lead. They made up for this dearth of resources by mobilising community support for the campaign. SFWU demonstrations for CleanStart were notable for the involvement of literally hundreds of community activists on the streets of the two cities. The campaign became as much a campaign for respect for Maori and Pacific Island workers as it was a campaign for cleaners.

Politics

Throughout the campaign – until November 2007 – Australia had been ruled by a virulently anti-union government. There was no point in trying to engage the federal government or any of its regulatory authorities in support of the cleaners. Indeed, the fear was that they would only obstruct the efforts of the union. Every state government, however, was a Labor government and considerable work went into trying to get their support. In places like Queensland and Tasmania, state governments were very significant property owners in their own right. In every state, governments were highly significant tenants. Politicians, when we were able to get access to them, proved highly sympathetic. Each of the state premiers, for example, signed a full-page advertisement placed in the *Australian Financial Review* by the union in support of the campaign. Individual members of parliament were very happy to make statements in parliament, appear at our demonstrations and generally take a very prominent place in the public campaign.

Getting that political buy-in with the public servants actually administering contracts was much more difficult. Government, in fact, has the reputation of being focused on cost to the exclusion of performance and so contractors felt extremely pressured by government to compete on price and nothing else. With hindsight, we needed to be much clearer in our engagement with all levels of government, so that politicians were asked not just to declare support but to ensure that public servants both understood our concerns and reflected in practice the policy of the government. At the same time, senior politicians were very helpful in putting their *imprimatur* on the campaign so that all parties understood that CleanStart was both thoroughly respectable and reasonable. The deputy premier in NSW went so far as to host a reception for the industry in Parliament House in Sydney and spoke warmly in support of the campaign and the union itself. In New Zealand, the government has been crucial in bringing the parties together and hammering out an agreement that will deliver what CleanStart seeks. Again, it is a significant owner and tenant in its own right, and that clout means that contractors need to ensure that they are compliant with government policy. The Labor government for its part was anxious to help, given its ideological commitment to low-paid workers and no doubt also in light of the importance of the Maori and Pacific Island community to any party hoping to win elections.

Reaching out to owners

We attempted to arrange meetings with the owners. Most refused to see us. They had never had a relationship with the union before and did not understand why they should engage with us. After all, they had contracted out the cleaning workforce and it was someone else's problem to solve – either the contractor or the building manager. Whenever owners refused to meet with us, a demonstration arrived outside their building. In many cases this happened outside every one of their buildings on the same day across all ten cities. In almost every case, owners quickly agreed to meet. At those meetings, we made our case and presented the business case for owners to play their part in fixing these problems. Interestingly, in at least half these cases, owners responded instantly to the plight of cleaners. They accepted their responsibility to ensure that people working in their buildings be treated fairly and in a non-exploitative fashion. It would be nice to think they were motivated solely by respect for the power of the union. In fact, in many cases, the motivating force appeared to be their genuine ethical concern about the treatment of cleaners. To that extent at least, I am sure that they differ from their American counterparts.

Our 'ask' was that they agree in principle to the CleanStart Principles. These were quite general principles which sought to address the crisis that was clearly apparent in the industry's labour market. They proposed that the industry work together to settle its problems on a cooperative basis. In tendering cleaning contracts, owners would ensure that tenderers adhered to labour norms, applied principles of Freedom of Association, directly employed cleaners and took care to limit the incidence of occupational health and safety injuries. The principles also proposed measures designed to limit excessive workloads and ensure that cleaners received training. In a very short space of time, a majority of owners agreed to give in principle support to the principles – although some of these insisted that the details of the principles needed to be worked out under the auspices of the Property Council. A very few owners refused to deal with us in relation to support for the principles. In these cases, our demonstrations aimed to alert the tenants in buildings owned by these owners to the abuses that were going on each night when the buildings were being cleaned. Notably, tenants were almost universally supportive. They complained about the standard of cleaning and they too thought that cleaners should be treated fairly and given time to do a good job. Those who were irritated by our demonstrations were asked to contact the owner and complain.

The breakthrough with the owners came once the Property Council became involved as a spokesperson for the owner community. Talks between unions and the leaders of the Council were opened. They were not a negotiation. We were not seeking an agreement in the traditional sense. Rather, we were advocating our position to the owners and encouraging them to take action in their own commercial self-interest to ensure that buildings were cleaned properly and tenants kept happy. The result was that the Council very quickly adopted their own Principles of Fair Contracting, which gave us most of what we wanted in our own CleanStart Principles. The one issue that they refused to move on was the concept of establishing a cleaning ratio for the whole industry. We understood – and so did the Property Council – that workload would have to be the subject of continuing campaigning as each cleaning tender was let building-by-building. The relationship between Property Council and union has matured to the point where both sides respect each other's expertise and dialogue occurs to the mutual benefit of both parties.

The contractors

With the owners alert to the need to do something about the way cleaners were treated, we then moved the focus of our campaign to the cleaning contractors. Our aim here was not to start negotiating wages and working conditions with them. The key aim first was to secure their neutrality so that workers could make up their own minds about whether they wanted to be part of the union campaign. Only workers could decide what they wanted in a collective agreement. We needed high density to deliver what they wanted and to fund continuing activity. We asked each of the major contractors to sign a document called a Responsible Contractor Policy (RCP). This was not a legally binding agreement. It could not be. *Workchoices* (in Australia) provided for heavy fines for unions who even asked for a union security provision in a registered – and therefore legally binding – agreement. Rather, this was a written acknowledgement by both sides that we would work together to the common benefit of the industry. The union would at all times try to resolve disputes on a cooperative basis. The employers agreed that they would do the following: (a) allow the union in work time to meet for 30 minutes with every worker they employed; (b) provide a letter to each worker which explained that it was entirely their choice as to whether they wished to join the union and bargain collectively; (c) provide access for the union to the induction training of any new worker; and (d) provide delegates' rights and work release for training.

Most contractors resisted this phase of the campaign. Many had grown used to being able to exercise total authority over their workforce and were extremely reluctant to allow union organisers to get anywhere near their workers. Despite our best efforts, they simply could not accept the logic of our strategy and believed that our campaign would fizzle out if they held together in opposition. The exception to this view was ISS – a major global player with head offices in Denmark. They were the biggest cleaning company in Australia and identified very quickly that the crisis identified by the union was a crisis that undermined their ability to make money in the market. Tenders were continually undercut by contractors cutting labour costs. They were conscious that in some markets the only way to stay competitive was to indulge in exploitative practices that were contrary to the ethos of the company and its managers in Australia. To the consternation of other contractors, they signed the RCP quickly.

Member action was then brought to bear on one contractor after another. Owners – who had used their influence to get the Property Council to address the issue – were dismayed to find the demonstrators reappearing outside their buildings. One by one, the contractors signed on until gradually some 60% of contractors in our targeted contractor group were signatory. A few resisted to the bitter end – notably, one of the bigger contractors in Melbourne. The pressure from the Victorian branch and its team of organisers and members was absolutely unremitting and gradually escalated in intensity. Finally, the employer took proceedings in the Victorian Supreme Court for injunctive relief against the branch's actions. Their claim was met with a dossier from the union listing hundreds of violations of cleaning practice across the whole of the employer's cleaning portfolio. These reports had been meticulously collected and filed by the branch organisers. The union clearly had an arguable case that it was entitled to defend the interests of workers against an employer doing what it perceived to be the wrong thing. The judge in the case was persuaded to accept binding undertakings from the union that were very closely drawn and would have little effect on the union's ability to pursue its campaign. After some toing and fro-ing, the company settled with the union, signed the RCP and has ever since been a strong advocate of the aims of the campaign.

Building density

Some membership was built as the campaign went on through work-ers joining after taking action. But worker meetings held as part of the RCP settlement with contractors were the place where density really grew. The LHMU adapted a form of induction meeting first developed in its Western Australian branch. The results exceeded all expectations. While the inductions were time-consuming to set up – liaising with the owner and the contractor, finding a venue, arranging a time and get-ting organisers to attend – the fact was that, when cleaners were given the chance to join the union and bargain collectively free of pressure from their employer, they joined in droves. In general, where workers felt safe in joining, between 70% and 80% of those attending joined during the meeting.

Collective bargaining

As this book went to press (late 2008), employers across both countries were signing a series of new collective agreements. Once this process is complete, these contracts will, indeed, change the working lives of their members. In Australia, the union has won a four-hour minimum start in buildings larger than 5,000 square metres – the key target of the campaign. (This means that it is far more likely that a cleaner can earn a living wage from the industry without having to cobble together two and three small shifts each night in different buildings and often with different employers.) Wages will go up by between 17% and 39% over the next four years – well in advance of the expected rate of infla-tion. Job security for existing cleaners when a contract shifts from one contractor to another has been vastly improved. Cleaners now have the benefit of 'mutual respect' language, which guarantees that cleaners will be treated with respect by their supervisors and supervisors will all receive training in how to treat cleaners. Holiday pay and penalty rates have been guaranteed. In New Zealand, the campaign has now been rolled into a general campaign to align the wages of cleaners in hospitals, schools and the office sector. In most areas this has happened successfully or claims are on the point of being settled. There is lit-tle doubt that owners recognise that the cost of cleaning will have to increase. The researchers have commissioned an industry analyst to cost the unions' claim – including decreases in workload in a typical building. The claim will add between 0.55% and 2.81% to building operating costs. Because of the education process that has taken place and because we engaged the whole of the large building sector, the unions' negotiators are operating in an environment where the contractors know that they can safely address the concerns of our members without risking their market share. Cleaning contracts will be let on the basis of contractors complying with the prevailing labour standards and the collective agreements being signed now set those standards. In New Zealand, the government has acted as a catalyst bringing owners, workers and employers together. Again, it has been the contractors who have been most resistant to the union having a role to play in 'their' industry. What is clear, however, is that, once Cabinet approved the agreed document, the union was given RCP rights by the contractors and the signing up of workers could proceed.

Has CleanStart been a success?

The campaign has not delivered huge numbers of new members – although density now stands at over 50% on average in Australia and in some markets between 60% and 70%. If LHMU or SFWU expected CleanStart to reverse membership decline across their unions as a whole, it will be judged a failure. But the campaign has stopped the deliberate wholesale deunionisation of the industry – not just in the targeted CBD buildings but across the whole sector: retail, schools and major buildings. The loss of these members would have been a severe blow to the LHMU in particular. Instead, union neutrality has become the norm in the industry. It has established the union as perhaps the key actor in the industry. Only the union and its members can fix the sector's labour market crisis. The aim has become to change the industry in order to organise the workers. If the bargaining is successful by providing longer jobs, increasing cleaner income and reducing turnover, the union will have secured a more easily organisable workforce. The cleaners will have a much better chance of earning a decent living and a job in which they can take pride.

The impact of CleanStart, however, is wider. The employer community has never seen an organising campaign of such sustained pressure over such a long period of time. These unions just did not go away. They knew the vulnerabilities of their targets. They knew which pressure points to push and they knew what would move the various protagonists. That all this was done in Australia in the depths of the *Workchoices* period, when the Howard government and the employers had connived in introducing the developed world's most savagely anti-union legislation, is quite remarkable. The message has not been lost on employers. If unions could pull off this kind of pressure, avoiding legal sanction, what will they be able to do under the new Rudd Labor government? Other industries have taken note. The LHMU has now launched its campaign in major residential hotels. Even before it began, owners were asking the union's organisers – 'You're not going to CleanStart us are you?'

Internally, both unions have grown in confidence. The theory worked. When overwhelming pressure was built, the industry players responded. Despite English language difficulties, fear, sometimes a poor understanding of unionism, workers were prepared to step up to take action. Australian workers, recent and long-term migrants alike, were initially uncomfortable with all that American-style noise and fervour. But they had fun at demonstrations and they were funny and they got the countries' attention. Just for once the invisible cleaners were front and centre and no one could avoid hearing their message. When bosses were truly neutral, workers would join. When the union acted powerfully – as if nothing could possibly get in its way – workers knew they were going to win. Most importantly, workers would step up to become leaders. At the LHMU National Council meeting in 2007, the local leaders of the campaign in each of the states, cleaners all of them, stood up and gave the CleanStart report – reading their presentations, shaking a lot, English often not too good – but really proud of what they had achieved.

How could all this happen?

Ten years ago, LHMU was a typical Australian union, namely, dependent on closed shop, an award system that took wages out of competition and employers that accepted the union's place in the sun. For decades it had done an honourable job of protecting the interest of workers at the bottom of the labour market. Since that old system gradually unravelled, the union has been reborn. It understands that density and organisation give it power. It sees the importance of bargaining from a position of strength rather than going to employers cap-in-hand and asking nicely. It has hired and trained a whole new generation of organisers across the country, developed lead organisers, freed its organising staff of grievances through the use of Member Service Centers in each

State. It has talked to its members about the need for change. It has tried to build its activist networks. Every state branch has had a conversation with its delegates about the need to increase fees and most states have increased fees by up to 40%. It was that move that allowed them to invest to the scale required in CleanStart.

The union understands that, in a modern economy like Australia's, it needs to be able to project its power nationally – if not globally. That means that industry campaigns must be national in scope and the state branches must find a way of working together to a common end. The union needed an enormous level of discipline. Legal attack was always our biggest fear. The union paid for the best legal advice and then every tiny little part of the union adhered to that advice rigidly. The union's links with the SEIU gave it access to some of SEIU's staff – and that was invaluable – but the real benefit it got from the SEIU relationship was the confidence that they gave to a union organising at this kind of scale for the first time. Above all, the union has developed the next generation of leaders who are passionate about the need for the LHMU to become a union that leads the way in rebuilding the power of Australian unions. Under both Jeff Lawrence – now the Secretary of the ACTU – and the current leader, Louise Tarrant, the union is prepared to risk a great deal in order to win. Employers have seen that nothing will be allowed to stand in the way of LHMU members winning.

The importance of winning

The kind of strategic approach modelled by successful organising unions is about winning improved wages and benefits through the rapidly increasing union power. The fundamental value system that underlies their work is that the benefits of unionism must not be confined to those who are already members. Rather, to defend their own interests, existing members must contribute to the organisation of their class. Failure to rise to that challenge will lead to the gradual or even rapid decline in the power of those who are already union members. CleanStart is an exemplar of such a campaign. Workers in the industry would never have risen up – even with help from their union – and organised themselves. Long-term cleaners were leaving the industry rather than fighting and even the most traditional source of new cleaners – immigrant refugees – looked for ways other than cleaning to make their entrance into the Australian labour market. That was typical of what is happening at the bottom of the labour market – where progressive unions must surely play a role in turning lousy jobs into halfway decent jobs. Even if cleaners had the drive and capacity to organise themselves, their employers lacked the power to do anything of significance about the way they were treated. They needed the analysis provided by CleanStart's research to target those responsible for the industry's labour market, namely, the building owners. Local organising in single markets would very rarely have had any impact on these immensely powerful and often global corporations.

CleanStart is unashamedly a top-down, resource-intensive campaign – because that is what it took to have any chance of winning. Initially, it did not aim to reach and educate a majority of the industry's cleaners. Instead, it focused on reaching out to and involving only an activist minority. It had a good chance of working only because the unions were able to match the power of the corporations who are the industry's decision-makers. It aimed at every stage to protect activist cleaners from retaliation by their employers. At the same time, it aimed to build a group of worker leaders who will go on to be the core of the union's worker leadership in years to come. This is critical in an open shop economy like Australia's. The industry's activists will need to play a role in maintaining the level of density already achieved and expand the campaign to retail cleaning and to smaller buildings.

Other campaigns in different industries will have different strategic approaches with a differing mix of worker and union office activity. Already, the LHMU has started its hotels campaign – similar in scope and reach. In this case, however, because the workplaces are large, great effort is being put into building organising committees in each of the hotels so that the level of organisation will largely be self-sustaining. To a far greater extent, activists are being asked to provide leadership at work right from the outset of campaigning. Even here, however, because of the size and power of the companies, the union is deploying massive resources in its determination to win and achieve a just settlement across the whole four-star hotel sector.

The deployment of such resources has come after intensive internal debate within the union. To win power in its key industries, the union has had to decide to focus its organising effort on three of those industries – childcare, cleaning and hotels – to the exclusion of all others. In a general union like LHMU, this is a tough decision as it means that all other resources are devoted to maintaining density amongst existing members through collective bargaining campaigns. That focus on three areas of growth means that there is some chance that the campaigns developed will be of sufficient scale and power to furnish a good chance of success. It does mean that workers in other relatively unorganised sectors of the union's coverage will have to wait their turn for a chance to have a voice at work. The current economic downturn will only make such a focus more important. Higher unemployment – particularly amongst the unskilled – will lead to much higher levels of fear amongst workers. That means that, before leading them in action, unions will have to build a sense of hope that action can succeed. Central to creating that sense of hope is the development of a plan for winning backed by the resources necessary to put the plan into action.

Conclusion: Does organising work?

The theory of organising works in practice only if its precepts are followed. One barely trained organiser asking workers to stand up against their boss, join the union, complain about an issue, get crushed and then appear in a case study is not a winning formula. Organising only with those ready for action, organising one workplace at a time, organising in such a way that the organised employer becomes uncompetitive and so on can only lead to defeat. In a recession, workers cannot afford defeat. To be successful, organisers must be hired, trained and given the time to win. They have to be freed of grievances. A successful union must have the capacity to organise to scale. It needs to be able to take on the whole of an industry or at least the whole of an employer. Increasingly, it needs to be able to reach out to an employer globally. Unions need to be able to make employers understand that they are not up against just their workers – they are up against whole societies.

The key aim of an organising campaign must be to force employers to be neutral. Once employers are neutral, workers can choose to join and be active in their union without fear of retaliation. If that happens then the theory of unionism works. Collective power will lead to better outcomes for workers. Employer neutrality guides the union in where it applies its organising resources. Once an employer has settled, the focus must shift to other employers not doing the 'right thing' by their workers. Organising does not mean maintaining workers in a state of 'permanent revolution'. They do not want that and their employers will not tolerate it. The process of getting neutrality can be described as partnership – although, at least in Australia, the term is a loaded one (see Crosby (2002) for a fuller discussion of neutrality and partnership).

Organisers need to be led. Lead organisers have to be prepared to hold their staff accountable for what they are doing to fulfil the strategic and tactical campaign aims. The quality of organising is important. CleanStart was better in some states than in others and that was often so because the organisers were less skilled and less well supported in the weaker states. The base of the union has to be secured. For US unions in their heartlands, this is easier. They have closed shops or fair share agreements. For the rest of the world, unions must build or rebuild activist structures and a network of neutrality agreements with employers that help the union stay on top of turnover. Unions need money and lots of it. There is no point in organising workers, exposing them to retaliation by their employer and then not having the resources to counter that threat. If a campaign starts, it must be carried through to conclusion. Above all, union leadership must have a vision of what needs to be done to rebuild worker power. They must drive every level of the organisation to organise either in already organised workplaces or in places where the union is weak. Too much is at stake for unions to be allowed to fail.

Note

More recent information on the CleanStart campaign can be gained at http://www.lhmu.org.au/campaigns/clean-start, and information on the hotels campaign at http://www.lhmu.org.au/campaigns/better-jobs-better-hotels.

10
Organising Immigrants: State Policy and Union-Organising Tactics in the Republic of Ireland

Maria-Alejandra Gonzalez-Perez, Tony Dundon and Terrence McDonough

Introduction

One of the effects and symptoms of economic globalisation has been a worldwide increase in migration (Borjas *et al.* 1996; Castles 2002; IOM 2006; Massey 1999; Rodrik *et al.* 1997; Salasar-Parreñas 2001; Stalker 2000; Taran and Geronimi 2002). Ireland, once regarded as a country of emigration, is now an economy dependent on the labour of non-Irish workers (CCI 2001; Mac Einrí 2001; Ruhs 2005). There are two divergent perceptions of non-Irish workers in Ireland. On the one hand, migrant workers are highly skilled and central to Ireland's economic boom of last decade. On the other hand, however, migrant workers are often viewed as a source of cheap labour, easily disposable and to be found primarily in the tertiary labour market. In Ireland the issue of immigrant worker rights has received considerable attention in recent years, not least in the high-profile disputes concerning the exploitation of non-Irish workers at GAMA and Irish Ferries. These disputes are important contextual events that set the scene for this chapter. Immigrant workers employed by GAMA International, a Turkish construction company, went on strike in May 2005 for over seven weeks because the company withheld workers' wages (illegally) in a Dutch bank, without their consent or knowledge. The Irish Ferries dispute brought the issue of migrant worker rights and state immigration policy to the forefront of public debate. Irish Ferries sought to lay off their entire Irish staff and replace them with lower-paid workers primarily from Eastern Europe. Significantly, this illustrated the apparent ease with which employers could replace an existing workforce with immigrant labour on lower rates of pay (Dundon *et al.* 2007). In an unparalleled display of public unity not seen in Ireland since the late 1970s, the Irish union movement organised public demonstrations and marches around Dublin in support of both the dismissed workers and the immigrant employees recruited on inferior terms and conditions of employment. Such developments in Ireland elevated the issue of foreign workers and labour standards onto a national and visibly public platform, not hitherto witnessed in Irish industrial relations.

However, union organising among migrant workers remains challenging. Many migrants are employed in lower-skilled and lower-paid industries where it is known to be more difficult to organise and recruit members (Dundon *et al.* 2007). In Ireland, migrant workers are concentrated in service occupations, production industries, construction and hotels and restaurants (DETE 2008; Turner *et al.* 2008). This is likely to affect the propensity of migrants to unionise, since joining is considered to be a function of two related factors – union availability combined with the individual's choice to join (Turner *et al.* 2008). Structural and industrial factors include size of organisation, industrial sector and occupational classification, and these largely affect union availability or presence at the workplace. For example, smaller private firms in services are less likely to recognise unions. Therefore, union availability is potentially limited for migrant workers who are employed predominantly in non-unionised sectors. Individuals' choices to join are also affected by social networks and established societal customs and norms. For example, union membership is skewed towards public sector workers in Ireland at around 42% density compared with 23% in the private sector (Turner *et al.* 2008). Thus, the established custom of unionisation is potentially alien to many migrant workers, who are mostly employed in the private sector. Furthermore, language and cultural barriers can limit access to a wider indigenous social network that may espouse union values and principles. In other words, migrant workers may be unaware of union traditions and customs (Turner *et al.* 2008). Union availability and individuals' propensity to join can also be affected by employer hostility to union organising (Dundon 2002) as well as government and state policy (Crouch 1982). For example, migrant workers may be susceptible to employer tactics of union avoidance, threats of intimidation and marginalisation given the concentration of employment in sectors such as service, construction and catering. The government's role can also affect opportunities to unionise. In Ireland, unlike the Britain or the US, there is no statutory union recognition procedure. Potentially, when faced by an anti-union employer on the fringe of the labour market, coupled with a lack of statutory protection to collectivise, the instrumental gains from unionisation poses a risky strategy for migrant workers, many of whom will be unfamiliar with Irish employment regulations and protections.

This is the context for the research reported in this chapter. Its main objectives were to subject Irish labour immigration policy to critical scrutiny, and to assess to what extent employers and unions may facilitate the integration of non-Irish workers into the labour market. The chapter is structured in six sections. Section two explains the research methodologies employed, and is followed by a review of data on the number of immigrant workers in the Irish labour market. The bulk of the evidence and analysis concerning migrant workers and state policy is considered in section four, specifically assessing the following: why foreign workers have entered the labour market, the institutional rigidities of state policy and in particular the Irish work permit system, equality and inequality in labour standards, and employer strategies in using non-Irish workers. Section five reviews union-organising activity for foreign workers. The chapter concludes by arguing that the main cause of labour exploitation and work degradation for migrant workers is based on two factors: first, it is due to the abuse of employer power, and secondly, this power is reinforced by state policy and legislation surrounding the work permit system. Arguably, for many migrant workers, the Irish labour market now conjures up not an image of opportunity, but rather a reality of social and cultural exclusion. Against this, unions have found it extremely difficult to counter the power of both employer and state in seeking to mobilise and represent migrant workers. The prospects for union organising are, to some extent, hopeful and optimistic. New initiatives and campaigning tactics are being introduced as a result of the experiences of unions internationally, particularly from organising in Australia, the US and Britain. Indeed, while union density has been in decline, the actual number of workers joining unions has increased in the Ireland (Roche 2008). However, the prognosis for union expansion and, in particular, the inclusion of migrant workers remains uncertain. One possibility is that new organising approaches have the capacity to influence the *form* of unionism in the future, with union governance structures based around a more inclusive and dynamic cadre of local activists. If the objective is to attain a workplace which is more inclusive for the non-Irish worker and still meet the demands of the

Irish economy, then current labour policy cannot be left to individual employers to respond to in opportunistic and discriminatory ways.

Methodology

Due to the sensitive nature of the study, several qualitative and ethnographic research instruments were utilised. Interviews were held with three respondent groups: key policy-makers in Ireland, national union officers, and immigrant workers. In addition, documentary material was reviewed where available, such as union policies and relevant documents from state agencies and employers' organisations. The primary research method involved an ethnographic approach which involved participant and non-participant observation and semi-structured interviews. One member of the research team was employed on the 'Diversity at Work Network project' funded by the European Social Fund and the European Union EQUAL Initiative, and was based in a number of partner institutions across Ireland (the Chambers of Commerce of Ireland, the National Consultative Committee on Racism and Interculturalism (NCCRI), and the Institute of Technology in Blanchardstown (ITB)) over a period of six months. This involved organising and participating in workshops, advising companies and immigrant workers, as well as attending conferences and events directly related to non-Irish workers, immigration policy, and a National Action Plan Against Racism. The primary ethnographic approach centred on observing interactions and issues faced by foreign workers, and how employers, unions and immigration policy responded. It also facilitated the development of relationships with the potential informants, which included immigrant workers, officials of state agencies, employer groups and unions. While the sample size may be small in comparison with national surveys, the data set contains a deeper and richer source of information surrounding migrant worker experiences as well as union forms of organising. The data is also national in scope, involving key policy advisors and activity in racism and union mobilising campaigns around Dublin together with over 20 migrant worker interviews from different parts of the country.

In total, 70 semi-structured interviews were conducted with foreign workers[1], members of ethnic minority community groups, employers, government officials, and union national officers. Some of these included focus group interviews with workers, as well as 44 one-to-one interviews with the following key informants: five union officers, five immigration policy experts in Ireland, four human resource managers in Ireland, and 30 non-Irish workers. All participants were guaranteed anonymity and were asked for their permission for audio recording and in some cases for their photographs to be taken. The coding for the data analysis for this study consisted of allocating sections of transcripts and notes into multiple categories. The process involved carefully categorising data both within previously determined themes and according to emerging issues from respondent groups. The method used was a cyclical design that constantly referred back to the transcripts, notes and documentation in order to refine the categorisation and synthesis of data in an attempt to ascertain the pertinent issues and patterns and isolate key phrases within the framework of study.

Rise of the international labour force in Ireland

With the rate and pace of economic growth over the last decade and a half, Ireland was an attractive location for foreign nationals seeking employment. Over the last 12 years, Ireland has experienced unprecedented economic expansion. From 1995 to 2000, the Irish economy grew at annual rates in excess of 8%. It has performed exceptionally strongly in the years up to 2008. Employment had expanded by close to 80% between 1992 and 2007 (CSO 2007), by which time the non-Irish labour force accounted for 10% of the working population (CSO 2007). However, recent events are expected to result in dramatic changes. The Irish economy is now officially in recession, with an estimated Exchequer deficit of €11 billion by the end of 2008, and a 2% GNP decline anticipated during 2009. Nonetheless, Ireland's current rate of immigration per capita is double that of the US. In 2007, 23,604 work permits were issued (see Figure 10.1), and this has continued to decline not because there are fewer immigrants but due to the expansion of EU member states whose citizens do not require permits. In other words, the number of non-Irish workers continued to rise, even though the number of work permits issued has declined. The impact of the current economic downturn on migratory labour flows is somewhat uncertain. While most commentators suggest many migrant workers are transient, there is an indication that many non-Irish nationals are to some extent more embedded into the Irish economy than was previously predicted (see, for example, O'Connell and McGinnity 2008).

Perhaps more interesting is the job and sector destination for many immigrants entering the labour force. As noted in Figure 10.2, before 2004 the majority of immigrant workers could be found in lower-paid

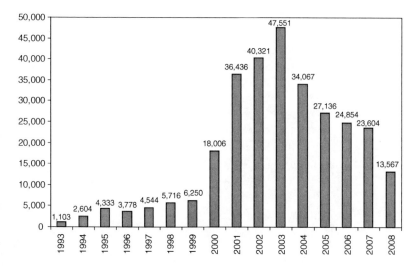

Figure 10.1 Work permits issued in Ireland 1993–2008
Source: DETE (2003, 2004, 2005, 2006, 2007, 2008, 2009).

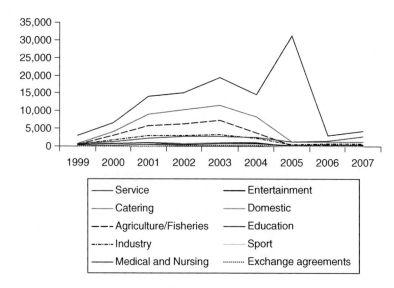

Figure 10.2 Work permits issued in Ireland (1999–2007) by sector
Source: DETE (2003, 2005, 2006, 2007, 2008).

and lower-skilled occupations in the service, catering, agriculture/
fishery sectors, whereas the numbers in more highly skilled professional occupations in the medical and nursing sectors were comparatively minimal.

Nonetheless, there have been significant changes in the sectors in
which non-EU 25 national workers are found in the Irish labour market.
As is shown in Figures 10.3 and 10.4, in 2003 Ireland had over 20 times
the number of workers in the agriculture sector under the work permit
scheme than it had in 2007. In contrast, in 2007 Ireland had almost the
same number of workers in the medical and nursing sectors employed
under the work permit scheme as it had in 2003. The increase in medical professionals is explained by migrant workers from outside the
EU who required work permits (e.g. Philippines), while reductions in
low-skilled sectors (e.g. agriculture, domestic services, catering) reflect
general employer policy of recruiting for lower-skilled occupations
from among the new accession EU member countries, especially the
Baltic states (O'Connell and McGinnity 2008). The significance here is

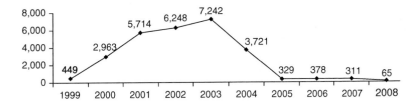

Figure 10.3   Work permits issued in the agriculture/fisheries sector in Ireland,
1999–2008

Source: DETE (2003, 2004, 2005, 2006, 2007, 2008, 2009).

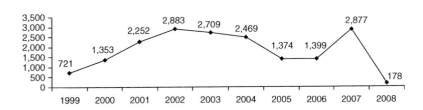

Figure 10.4   Work permits issued in the medical and nursing sector in Ireland,
1999–2008

Source: DETE (2003, 2004, 2005, 2006, 2007, 2008, 2009).

that a reduction in official work permit statistics is not an indication of declining migrant labour but a reflection of a preference for labour from among enlarged EU States.

It is important to highlight that there are important deficits in the available data (Barry 2000). For example, before the latest census data (2006) there were no reliable statistics available on the numbers of European Economic Area (EEA)[2] nationals in Ireland. They did not require specific work permits or have to report their presence to the authorities. Prior to 2002 nationality and ethnicity had not been surveyed. Against rapid labour market expansion there remains a serious deficit of reliable data at an industry or sector level for those other than non-EU nationals. One corollary is that, despite some growth in absolute union membership, density levels have declined, currently around 32% nationally (CSO 2008a). For migrant workers union density is much lower and estimated at 13% (CSO 2008a). The problem of accurate data is further compounded by illegal non-Irish workers who enter the labour market and work without permits. Further, nationals from EU-15 and, since 2004, from the new accession countries do not require permission to work in Ireland. Basically, if there is no requirement for a work permit there is no data on their participation in the labour market. Figure 10.5 shows the top 25 countries of origin for work permits issued in the period 2002–4.

Currently, it is estimated that migrant workers account for 8% of the labour force, with over three-quarters of them from Britain[3] and from Poland[4] (CSO 2007). The Irish government controls the access of non-EEA nationals through a selective immigration policy. It is a lawful requirement for every non-EEA national resident in Ireland to have a residence permit as a refugee, an asylum seeker, a non-EEA national under work permit,[5] a non-EEA national with a work visa/work authorisation[6], a non-EEA national with an Irish Green Card[7], a spouse of a work visa/work authorisation or Green Card holder, or as a student under a student visa scheme. Residence permits are usually renewed annually by the local Garda immigration office. The Irish state also controls the treatment of non-EEA nationals in the labour market through employment policy. The Work Permit Section in the DETE examines applications from employers. Employers are required to prove that the vacancy cannot be filled by an Irish national, an EEA national or another person for whom a work permit is not required. The employer should demonstrate reasonable efforts to recruit people at national and EEA levels.

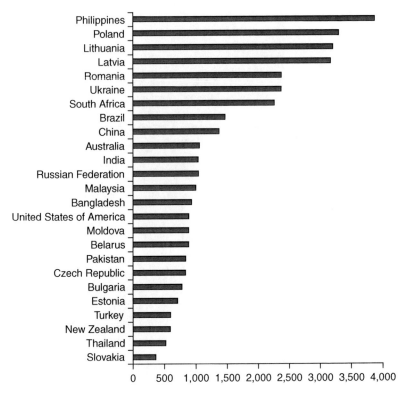

Figure 10.5   Top 25 national origin work permits issued in Ireland, 2002–4
Source: DETE (2003, 2005).

Migrant workers and state policy

The evidence from this research highlights that the Celtic Tiger image held very little reality for thousands of immigrant workers. Many were and are alienated from the social and economic boom of the last 15 years. Instead, many non-Irish national workers are subject to extensive government and employer control in both their working and personal lives (see Dundon *et al.* 2007).

A Celtic fantasy?

There are several reasons why people chose Ireland as a destination for emigration. These include expectations created by the success stories of people who had emigrated and returned home with cash to create new economic opportunities for themselves and their local communities, or who had decided to stay abroad enjoying prosperity relative to their economic counterparts at home. As one Romanian worker explained:

> *You heard stories from these places where everything is shiny and bright, where to get money is so easy, where there is job for everyone who wants it ... you see the pictures they post, you see the presents they bring when they go home at Christmas ... you see their clothes and cool electronic things ... you see how their parents managed to refurnish their home ... everyone talks about ways to send and to get money from the ones that are working abroad ... and it seems that outside things are easier than at home.* (Romanian, male, 28, kitchen porter)

For many foreign workers, the expectation of greater economic prosperity is real and significant, especially when compared with what they have left behind. One worker compared her situation in Ireland to elsewhere:

> *To work in Ireland in a B&B means that I am earning four times what I was making working in a resort in Dubai.* (Filipina waitress, 27)

However, there is a significant price to pay for many of these workers, which is part of an untold story. Immigrant workers, especially those from outside the EEA/Switzerland, are confronted with a variety of exclusion and marginalisation factors, including a lack of information and differential treatment in public services, such as hospital attention charges and social welfare support. A Latvian worker explained:

> *I didn't know how the system worked here [in Ireland], I get paid less than the Irish who do the same as me in the same cleaning company ... also I had lots of problems with my taxes for a few months, and every time I go to the tax office they seem to ignore me, they don't try to understand me ... they just don't listen ... Sometimes I think its because of my English, but most of the times I think it's because I am not Irish.* (Latvian cleaner, female, 21)

Recruitment agencies

Traditional approaches to labour migration have theorised migrants as a factor of production, motivated by social and psychological expectations of differences in wage levels between countries (Cobb-Clark 1993; Foner *et al.* 2000; Portes and Rumbaut 1996). However, this perspective runs into difficulty in that wage differentials are historically ubiquitous, and the decision to migrate may be shaped more by informal social networks that emerge between actors in the sending and receiving countries. The basis of such informal networks is often associated with a socio-psychological risk reduction effect for those involved (Fawcett 1989; Hernandez-Leon and Zuñiga 2000; Kritz *et al.* 1992; Orozco 2002; Portes and Sensenbrenner 1993; Roberts 1997; Sola-Corbacho 2002). Above all, meeting social, familial and cultural needs in an alien environment poses complicated industrial relations issues (Bronfenbrenner *et al.* 1998; Grünell and Kaar 2003; Milkman 2000; Milkman and Wong 2000; Nelson 2001; Tansey 1998; Waldinger and Der-Martirosian 2000; Waldinger and Lichter 2003).

In this regard the role of external recruitment agencies features prominently in the accounts from respondents in our sample. For example, several Filipino workers explained how they were recruited in their home country to work in a fast food outlet (with a recognised global brand name) in Ireland. The agency charged each individual a fee equivalent to €1,500 (€500 for the employment permit fee) with the guarantee of employment in the fast food company. If the permit application was refused, the agency would reimburse the individual 80% of the charged fee after a few months. We could not ascertain how much the fast food company paid for the services of the recruitment agency, but understand it was substantial. Other immigrant workers in the hotel and catering sectors explained that they paid recruitment agents an amount deducted from their salary once they started work.

From our calculations of the earnings of immigrant workers interviewed, given average accommodation and living costs, it would take 27 weeks, working 45 hours per week, to repay the recruitment expenses incurred in order to work in Ireland. Because of this network of recruitment, many immigrant workers (and their families back home) begin with undertaking a substantial debt just to be able to enter the Irish labour market. As two workers explained:

For our families, even when they miss us, to be abroad is a matter of pride... When one get the opportunity of leaving the country, our parents and other relatives lend or give us the money... it is like an investment for them. (Malaysian chef, male, 30)

Chinese parents think that to go abroad, and to learn how other people live, and to learn their language make our character stronger... they feel proud because they think I come to Ireland, and when I go back, I would be able to afford to give them better life. (Chinese worker, fast food restaurant, female, 23)

However, as important as these recruitment agencies are to the mobility of migrants, they are far from ubiquitous. For example, in another fast food restaurant, once a pool of employees had become established, informal networks replaced the role of the recruitment agent, often with the endorsement and encouragement of management. That is to say, social links between employees and their friends and family back home effectively substituted for formal (and expensive) recruitment agencies. In contrast, at the higher end of the labour market the situation was found to be quite different. Among skilled engineers, architects and especially medical and health sector employees (nurses) the use of external recruitment agencies was more extensive and embedded, with such agencies often providing assistance with permit applications on behalf of the employing organisation.

The roles of recruitment agencies, on the one hand, and the informal social networks of workers, on the other, signify emerging issues not often addressed in much of the extant research. At one extreme, formal organisations like recruitment agencies can help address a skill shortage by providing expertise for both immigrant workers and employers. At the other extreme, however, migratory labour movements are often dependent on informal information from 'pioneers', that is, workers who enter the labour market at the lower-skilled end and then feed information back to the home community for future employees. This wide range of variation has important implications for workers, state policy and union organising, which are considered next.

The work permit system

In the course of this study it was found that several factors influence the vulnerability of immigrant workers in Ireland. According to several respondents the present Irish employment scheme has led to abuse, and one example illustrates the extent of migrant worker experiences in this regard. We interviewed a female worker from Bulgaria, who had received a job description and a contract of employment under favourable conditions including accommodation. On this basis she accepted to come to work in Ireland on an employment permit as a kitchen porter. When she started work she discovered that she was not paid the agreed rate, the days off were irregular, her daily shifts changed constantly, her breaks were not paid, she had to share the room with another foreign national woman a few years younger than herself, the living conditions were very poor and located in the countryside without the possibility of socialising with people other than her co-workers. She raised the situation with her employer, who replied that if she was not happy her work permit would be cancelled. Similar cases were reported by workers of several nationalities. The net effect of the Irish work permit system is that it maintains a situation in which immigrant workers are subject to employer control, both inside and, in many situations, outside their place of employment. As one union official remarked:

> *The work permit system in Ireland establishes an unhealthy relationship because the non-EU worker is not legally allowed to change employment if they feel they have been abused or exploited ... or if they just want to change job ... the employer can control the worker with the explicit or implicit threat to deny the renewal of the work permit ... or, even more critically, they fear the loss of the permission to stay in Ireland if they are fired by the employer ... they (immigrant workers) believe that they have to make their employer happy. If not, they will have to return to their country of origin.*

The significance of this issue cannot be overstated. For example, it is the employer who applies for and subsequently owns the employee's work permit, which prohibits any labour mobility or job transfer should the individual feel dissatisfied or aggrieved. A consequence of the work permit system is that employers use this to devise their own particular supplies of labour. It is common in the catering and hotel industries to observe clusters of people of the same nationality and usually from the same region in a particular country, sharing the same language, emotional bonds and cultural ties. This phenomenon occurs due to an embedded recruitment method dependent on social networks, with migratory movements arising through the existence of links between sending and receiving communities and peoples (Gurak and Caces 1992; Krits *et al.* 1992; Milkman 2000; Orosco 2002; Portes and Sensebrenner 1993; Roberts 1997; Waldinger and Lichter 2003). For example, we found that in one fast food retail outlet around 70% of staff came not only from the same country, but from the same location within that country. Thus, clusters of workers had some connection with each other before their arrival in Ireland. They describe the relationship between themselves and their co-nationals either as 'relatives' or as a 'friend of a friend' (*paisanaje*). Basically, there is a pioneer from a certain region in a specific country who opens the road and establishes contacts with an employer, from which others follow.

This extends to issues beyond the workplace. We found, especially in the case of Filipino, Latvian, Lithuanian, Polish and Chinese workers, that they share accommodation with people from the same region; in some cases as many as four people were sharing a single person's room in order either to save money to send home, or to be able to repay recruitment agencies. Arguably, this social behaviour has contradictory impacts. Even when this behaviour seems to be adaptive because of the social and emotional support which it provides, the lack of contact with the Irish environment, culture and society can engender a vicious cycle of social and economic exclusion. This tension was noted by one state agency policy advisor:

> *In Ireland, there are no visible formed and organised ethnic communities ... The non-EU immigrant is mostly recruited abroad as an individual. In some cases they are recruited as part of a group ... generally, the worker comes to Ireland alone and doesn't have any social and family relations in Ireland ... they physically don't have anyone from whom to ask for help. The uncertain length of their period of permanency in the country, and the language and cultural differences limit their possibilities to establish and develop friendships with Irish people.*

An alteration to the current state work permit is the introduction of a 'Green Card' work scheme. Differing from the US system, which represents permanent residence for foreign nationals, the Irish one was designed only for high earners or for those who have a set of strategic occupational skills, as defined by a government-commissioned Expert Group on Future Skills Needs (EGFSN). The application for the system is made by the potential employee, and its fee (€1,000) can be paid by either the employer or the applicant. In order to apply, the potential employee should be in receipt of a full-time contract for a minimum of two years. Contrasting with the work authorisation and work permit scheme, holders are entitled to immediate family reunification and a long-term residence permit after two years.

It is critical to highlight that the Irish Green Card will replace the work permit and work authorisation schemes. This raises the issue of the future of those in Ireland under the previous work permit scheme. These changes in the Irish immigration policy dramatically affect low-paid workers, since they will no longer be able to legally remain in Ireland through a renewal of their work permit. It appears they will have no other option than to leave or to overstay their legal permission and work in the informal economy. The Irish state has apparently foreseen this as a problem, and communicated its intention to establish a 1,400-bed detention centre for foreign nationals who exceed the Green Card work and residency regulations (*Irish Times* 26 March 2008).

Inequality in labour standards

Underpinning state policy is the impact on equality and inequality in employment for migrant workers. Respondents in our sample explained that several discriminatory practices were particularly evident in their workplace. For example, many employers use the justification of a lack of proficiency in English to explain the absence of promotion to supervisory and managerial levels. Others had to work exceptionally long hours, often without overtime premium rates, which further reinforced social and cultural exclusion. Very few immigrant workers had Irish friends. Many reported a lack of free time or regular days off, insecurity and employer intimidation concerning the renewal or status of their work permit, low salaries in relation to their living expenses in Ireland, increasing economic pressures to provide money to send back home, and very little, if any, recognition of qualifications and skills attained back home. The effect is a 'low road' economy for many immigrant workers, as explained by another union official:

> *Some of them are located in low-status jobs, which it's said the Irish don't want to do anymore, such as washing dishes, picking mushrooms ... some of the immigrants are earning less than the minimum wage, they work overtime without extra pay, and for some there are weeks in which they don't have a day off... some of them have payments deducted for uniforms, accommodation... others are having the cost of the work permit deducted from their wage by employers...a number of immigrant workers came to Ireland without a detailed contract, and as a result, arrived with false expectations or a lack of knowledge about their conditions.*

According to all union respondents, key employment-related concerns of immigrant workers have been steadily increasing over the last few years. Above all, the view that most employers perceive immigrant workers as cheap labour was almost unanimous among union interviewees. Just one of the unions associated immigrant workers with a high level of education, which can be attributed to the fact that this particular union represents professionals in the health care sector. Moreover, there are identifiable barriers to immigrant workers joining unions which were consistently expressed by union officers interviewed. Scepticism about unions (especially among immigrants from former Communist states), fear of deportation, language difficulties, lack of information about employment rights, and the current work permit system were reported as particularly significant. These hurdles are magnified by a lack of social and community support for many immigrant workers.

Union organisation and representation

With the increasing spread of global labour migration, unions have faced new challenges in representing and organising migrant workers. In Ireland, migrant workers are less likely to unionise than native employees (Turner *et al.* 2008). Even though membership has grown in Ireland in absolute numbers (from 0.4329 million in 1994 to 0.5517 million in 2007), density has declined from over 43% to 31.5% over the same period (CSO 2008a; Turner *et al.* 2008). In effect, membership has not kept pace with labour market expansion, much of which includes migrants from the new EU accession states. Roche (2008) identified a number of inter related factors to explain the paradox of simultaneously increased union membership and declining density. Thus, *cyclical* influences have moderated the capacity for unions to organise among newer sectors, including those in which many migrants are employed. Then there is the impact of *structural* influences. Much expansion of employment has been among firms in difficult to organise sectors such as construction, hotels, catering and services. Thus, not only has union recruitment been unable to keep pace with employment growth, but it also has been difficult to penetrate those sectors of the economy that have grown most significantly. The net effect is both a sector and spatial barrier to union organising that has a potentially disproportionate impact on non-Irish workers (EIRO 2008d). The third factor comprises *institutional* influences. Prominent amongst these are government policy not to legislate for union recognition, mainly to buttress the concerns of non-union multinationals investing in Ireland. Institutional influences also concern the impact of the national partnership approach to industrial relations (see Allen, this volume), with an over-reliance on centralised corporatist bargaining. The net effect has been that unions no longer negotiate and engage with employers at the workplace level, diminishing the capacity for unions to mobilise at this level (EIRO 2008d).

Penninx and Roosbald (2000) posed three overarching dilemmas arising from this 'new' situation. First, unions may adopt strategies that *reject or accept* migratory flows into labour markets. Depending on the position of unions within corporatist regimes, the labour movement can seek to influence and shape state immigration policy in terms of labour market penetration. Second, unions may seek to *include or exclude* migrant workers through policy and representational structures. Finally, on accepting migrant workers into membership, unions have been faced with the issue of whether to offer *equal or special treatment* to migrant members. Special treatment would include dedicated communications in the migrants' first language or internal union governance mechanisms that allow migrant groups representational rights. According to this framework, Irish unions appear to be developing organising strategies that gravitate towards the *'accept-include-special treatment'* path for migrant workers.

However, this has by no means been easy. Despite the catalogue of concerns noted earlier, unions have found themselves in a difficult situation regarding the organisation and representation of these migrant workers. The inability of unions to *include and integrate* foreign workers is compounded by several factors: employer exploitation and intimidation, social exclusion and the lack of awareness about union roles, and, perhaps most significantly, a state policy of work permission that underpins first and foremost managerial and employer control strategies. Union membership in Ireland has remained stagnant after a period of decline, and initiatives connected with immigrant worker campaigns have failed to increase membership. Of course, membership numbers are not the only indicator of union mobilisation, and the form and character of unionisation can change as a result of campaigning and organising tactics. Arguably, as a result of the Irish Ferries dispute and large-scale public protests in Dublin, the plight of migrant workers and the role of organised labour have received renewed attention and support. It is with this point in mind that several union-organising responses can be noted to be as providing some basis for grounded optimism.

For example, a number of Irish unions are targeting migrant worker issues and using these to promote the advantages of membership. SIPTU, the largest union in Ireland, has pioneered migrant worker issues with a dedicated union officer with knowledge of Eastern European languages to work in the construction industry. Interestingly, this has been in response to the transfer of several workers defecting to the more militant Independent Workers' Union (IWU) (*Industrial Relations News* 1 September 2005). In October 2007, a Filipina worker employed as a domestic cleaner, represented by SIPTU, was awarded €7,410 by the Rights Commissioner as compensation for unpaid wages and holidays (*Industrial Relations News* 24 October 2007). In June 2007, the IWU brought to the Labour Court the case of seven Chinese female workers who worked for the Dublin-based company, Klean Fit Limited, who were abused on the grounds of retention of P45s (their employment paperwork), unpaid wages and pregnancy discrimination. At the beginning of 2008, at a meat-processing factory in county Monaghan, 20 Unite members protested because foreign nationals were paid less than Irish workers at the plant (*Industrial Relations News* 14 February 2008). It is not so much the claims and cases that are significant. Rather, it is the way the unions are using these as strategic communicative tools that offer potential as a conduit to recruitment, especially among the more difficult-to-organise sectors of the economy in which many migrant workers can be found.

National level awareness campaigns that have caught the attention of the wider business community have been pioneered by ICTU and SIPTU. One SIPTU example was to appeal to all workers to find out if their workplace was being cleaned by a reputable contract cleaning company which guaranteed that the work was being carried out by employees paid at least the statutory minimum wage and who enjoyed all other statutory conditions of employment. Other specific union campaigns have sought to make unions attractive and valuable for migrant workers by offering assistance with tax regulations and social welfare provisions. Another example is the campaign for the early ratification of the *UN Convention on the Rights of Migrants* and their families.

This has raised awareness that a migrant worker's family are often denied access rights or the right to work. Promoting the status of migrant worker qualifications and exposing a lack of education and training opportunities has been another vocal union avenue. The most noticeable campaign so far was the *Equality-Diversity Award*, first launched in November 2002 as part of the 'Anti-Racism Workplace' Week. The campaign serves to illustrate that unions, and in particular SIPTU, have adopted an advocacy mantra for migrant workers, often with resources and budgets controlled centrally rather than decentralised as might be found among union organising in Britain (see Gall 2006a). The diversity award was an initiative of the SIPTU general officers, who invited section, branch and regional committees or individual SIPTU members to nominate someone they considered to have done particularly important work countering racism and promoting racial harmony and multiculturalism. As one of the union officers argued:

There are good examples of innovation and particular attention to the needs of migrant workers such as one-day training on anti-racism and multiculturalism, cultural morning-breaks with African music and singing in the canteens of two factories. Persons were nominated whose individual work had impacted positively on the integration of immigrant workers, with actions such as contacting employers and agencies on immigrants' behalf, making sure that they were treated equally and fairly, writing a letter in their native language to each immigrant worker informing them about their rights, welcoming them to the Irish workforce and to SIPTU and offering translation for any grievance letters, assistance with issues such as housing, transport, access to medical attention, and submitting claims to the Work Permit Section and the Labour Inspectorate.

One of the most recent and potentially far-reaching in strategic terms is the result of a SIPTU Special Commission (known as the Crosby Commission after its chair, the Australian union organiser, Michael Crosby (see this volume)). Among other things, its core recommendation was to increase expenditure on organising from 6% of contributions to 25% in order to be able to effectively recruit and represent workers in the expanded labour market. Other unions have followed SIPTU. In 2008, the Mandate union, operating mainly in the retail sector, announced the inauguration of an 'organising and campaigning' model. Likewise, the Communication Workers' Union (CWU), faced with union exclusion in BT despite union recognition at BT in Britain, intends to establish an organising budget and target new companies outside its usual remit. Of particular relevance to this chapter is the CWU's production of multilingual organising materials (EIRO 2008d).

Separate union responses such as those of the CWU, Mandate or SIPTU mentioned above are also being coordinated through a new ICTU imitative to establish an 'outreach service' to target non-union workers. The key unions involved include SIPTU, CWU, Mandate, IMPACT (Irish Municipal Public and Civil Trade Union) and TEEU (Technical, Engineering and Electric Union) (*Industrial Relations News* 12 June 2007). Strategically, the objective is to target younger workers and those who are increasingly mobile and computer literate. The plan is to utilise internet technologies and social networking sites to specifically target workers who have hitherto had little exposure, time or interest in union activities. This initiative is not aimed particularly at migrants but its innovative approach is amenable to attracting workers who are difficult to reach through traditional avenues. Of course, it remains to be seen what impact these broader organising initiatives will have on union membership figures. In terms of measurable outcomes, there is only modest evidence of gains among migrant workers on a national scale, and the prognosis is far from definitive. However, it is arguable that the form of unionism is changing as a result of new union organising strategies.

First, the impact of what is defined here as 'soft' organising seems to have had a modest affect. This refers to awareness campaigns, such as anti-racism and diversity literature. In contrast, 'hard' organising relates to active recruitment drives targeted at migrant workers, protest behaviours and forms of industrial action. The 'softer' organising approach is more akin to the traditional character of Irish servicing unionism, although to some extent this is being complemented by newer organising tactics, many of which have been tested in other countries (Bronfenbrenner *et al.* 1998; Heery *et al.* 2000). It has certainly been the servicing model that has dominated most Irish unions during the Celtic Tiger years (through representing and protecting existing members). Organising migrant workers has for the most part been confined to publicity campaigns to help highlight the plight of non-Irish employees. It remains uncertain how deep or extensive the recent initiatives will penetrate into the psyche of Irish union officials. In addition, union leaders in Ireland are very much entrenched in a national, corporatist partnership model. For many in the Irish labour movement, a more assertive organising approach to tackle directly low wages and poor workplace conditions risks jeopardising relationships which have been painstakingly built-up during the partnership process. Within this context, a policy of cultural diversity and racism awareness has been the main vehicle of union campaigning with regard to migrant worker issues.

Second, while a voluntarist servicing approach remains evident in Irish labour relations, the form and character of unions appear to be altering in response to the changing industrial and political landscape. Arguably, the development of softer organising approaches has provided a platform for unions to consider harder mobilising strategies. Running alongside the cosy image of national partnership are episodes of grassroots mobilising campaigns. For example, workers at a brick factory went on strike for a few days in support of pay equality for their Czech colleagues. The higher-profile disputes may also be seen as an escalation of softer organisation methods, suggesting a shift in which unions are turning their attention from the 'sword of justice face' of unionism (Flanders 1970) towards a 'vested interest' approach specific to migrant members, as evidenced by the more militant stance of the IWU (*Industrial Relations News* 1 September 2005, 24 October 2007).

It is more probable, however, given EU expansion and the extension of legal rights for previously disenfranchised immigrant workers that unions are now able to bypass the fear and restrictions of the work permit system for EU-member migrants and tackle hostile employers head-on. Therefore the form, shape and character of union organising is now more vibrant, uneven and dynamic than a model of reliance on a few union leaders to negotiate wage settlements for the nation as a whole through partnership agreements.

In general, unions' activities and attempts to mobilise around migrant worker concerns are constrained and limited to non-traditional union concerns. Evidence of bargaining and representation over issues such as wages and working conditions is mostly confined to those migrants who are part of the official work permit system and fall under the national partnership agreement. For the most part, unions have embarked upon a strategy of services, such as free legal information and assistance in employment rights and entitlements, obtaining the required social welfare PPS (Personal Public Service) number and tax advice. Other related activities have included language training, anti-racism awareness and exposing different forms of discrimination and promoting multiculturalism. This servicing union approach has evolved through cooperation with various government agencies (e.g. the Health Service Executive and Department of Social and Family Affairs) to promote 'awareness' rather than active 'mobilisation'. Servicing, ultimately, militates against developing, nurturing and expanding grassroots activism in favour of centralised knowledge of representation. In other words, despite the emergence of strong informal networks and ties among immigrant workers themselves, unions have been unable to penetrate these networks in order to leverage recruitment among the non-Irish working population, especially in the lower-skilled occupations. Arguably, Irish trade unions remain embedded in a national corporatist regime with an image – rightly or wrongly – as a 'male, pale and stale' officialdom that is somewhat removed from the concerns of non-Irish nationals at a workplace level. That said, alternative postures towards union organising are emerging among a cross-section of unions, such as Mandate (retail), CWU (telecommunications), TEEU (engineering and manufacturing) and Unite and SIPTU (public and private sectors). To some extent this symbolises a more dynamic and engaging form of unionism with a focus on grassroots mobilisation and dedicated resources and strategic action planning.

Conclusion and discussion

Issues surrounding migrant workers and industrial relations policy look set to continue in Ireland, as well as elsewhere across the industrialised world. It remains uncertain as to whether the economic downturn will alter migratory flows in the Irish labour market and what implications this could have for union organising in the next decade. It is evident that many migrant workers are transient with the changing ebb and flow of immigration. Yet, it is also apparent that many migrant workers are embedded into occupational hierarchies and careers. To be sure, migrant workers with particular concerns and demands for union representation and collective protection will in one shape or another be a priority agenda for industrial relations policy and union organisers. Union-organising tactics have arguably begun to elevate the plight of many migrant workers onto a national (and international) stage. In Ireland, unions appear to have opted to 'include and integrate' migrant workers, as indicated by Penninx and Roosbald's (2000) framework. In addition, economic boom and the globalisation of labour and product markets have led to a demand for cross-national union activity. Unions in Ireland are seeking to learn from more advanced economies that have been addressing migrant workers' concerns and newer forms of union organising for longer, such as Australia, Britain and the US (Bronfenbrenner *et al.* 1998; Milkman 2000). Within Ireland, new multicultural currents have changed the character of the workforce, and as a consequence the *form* of representation is beginning to change, albeit in modest ways. Constrained by shrinking resources, the union response to these new developments has been variable, fragmented and often localised. This 'glocalisation' of the world economy creates a different context for the movement of labour while, at the same time, vulnerability of migrant workers has increased the need for union representation and a more aggressive organising response at the local level. It is to be expected that traditional views of migration will necessarily be found wanting, and several changes can be hypothesised in this new context.

First, migration may well continue at the top of the occupational structure as business managers, venture speculators and professionals follow capital around the globe and move to those regions specialising in jobs at the 'top' of the labour market value chain. Alarcón (2000) has found that transnational professionals occupied a privileged position because they are seen as vital to companies involved in global production processes and markets, and human capital produced else-where represents a net gain for 'information technology' companies that have the wealth and resources to choose professionals from a global pool. Ireland has recently begun to show signs of this kind of migration. In this context, Ireland has achieved success in inter-national markets through absorbing native labour into specialised and high-skilled jobs, while foreign labour served as a buffer in the lower-skilled, lower-paid service sector.

Second, the movement of labour will be increasingly globalised, with important industrial relations implications at the national and local levels. The existence of global networks of production will mean that larger percentages of the population at all locations will have experi-enced capitalist production and its associated culture. The 'compression of time and space' will make it easier to conceive of migrating, and new and emerging economic areas of the globe will become a new source of migrants. Thus, it can be hypothesised that the movement of labour will be increasingly organised by entrepreneurial groups of both a legit-imate and a criminal nature, and take place outside traditional channels and beyond the regulatory control of industrial relations institutions.

In Ireland, a neoliberal policy agenda has provided such entrepre-neurial groups (and employers) with the tools to manipulate and exploit a global labour pool at a localised level. Above all, state policy, and in particular the work permit system, does not allow non-EU nationals to change employers. Consequently, the Irish state is the gatekeeper for continued employer control over migrant workers' lives, both inside and outside their place of work. In practical terms, this means that local managers have the discretion to decide whether a non-Irish national worker can remain in Ireland or not. The power to exercise such dis-cretion often means the acceptance of managerial prerogative and the acquiescence to employment conditions dictated by local managers. It is the general perception among non-EU workers that security is depend-ent on the state's work permit system and the edict of managers, not on their performance in the job. This abuse of the work permit system among employers has affected the union movement's ability to mobil-ise and represent immigrant workers.

Even considering that the migratory process depends upon social networks and informal ties (especially at the lower-skilled end of the labour market), union organising that is targeted directly at these infor-mal networks of immigrant worker groups may be the most effective tactical strategy to mobilise and recruit these workers and change of the form and shape of union organising in the future. The data from our research and other related studies (Bronfenbrenner *et al.* 1998; Fairbrother 2000; Milkman 2000; Turner *et al.* 2008; Wills and Simms 2004) would suggest there is potential merit in considering a community unionism approach to union organising, building on softer organising tactics that may sustain inclusion and develop a broader critical mass of sympathisers and activists who may have the capacity to tackle anti-union employers and publicly campaign for changes in state policy. For example, the involvement of migrants in civic and community organisations and local church bodies could open up spaces for political participation, providing access to information to help bridge social network barriers between cultures. Exposure to new and alternative leadership experiences can enhance self-confidence, build skills and provide a platform for social and economic integration between migrants and indigenous workers across communities and workplaces. Furthermore, this could enhance the visibility of ethnic and migrant members of the community, gaining positive recognition at the local level for newcomers and already established foreign nationals. Arguably, efforts in which organisers are drawn from specific countries with a deeper understanding of the cultural nuances as well as local and sectoral concerns experienced by workers themselves could be an effective conduit for union membership through such community alliances. To achieve this, however, an organising strategy aimed at mobilising the base of the union movement will have to move much more to the fore. Such a community-based form of union organising ought to continue to pay attention to the values of equality, diversity and cultural integration, given the dichotomous low–high-skill labour market experienced by many immigrant workers in Ireland.

Notes

This chapter is a development of an earlier article, namely, Dundon *et al.* (2007) whereby the data has been updated and the analysis extended.

1. Comprising Polish, Romanian, Philippine, Latvian, Chinese, Malaysian, US, Nigerian, Pakistani, Indian, and Brazilian.
2. The EEA includes all the EU member states and Liechtenstein, Iceland and Norway.
3. According to the latest census, 112,548 British nationals live in Ireland (CSO 2007).
4. The Polish embassy estimates that roughly 120,000 Polish nationals live in Ireland (Kropiwiec and King-O'Riain 2006). Poland became an EU state in May 2004. Since then, citizens from Poland do not require legal permission to live and work in Ireland.

5. Work permits are issued to employers who employ non-EEA nationals to fill specific vacancies that they have been unable to fill from within the EEA. The employer is required to undertake an economic needs test. This in effect means that they must advertise the particular employment position for four weeks with Ireland's national employment service, FÁS, before offering the job to a non-EEA national (DETE 2005).

6. Work authorisations allow non-EEA workers in possession of skills in key areas: health and medicine, information technology, architects and engineers. Unlike work permits, work authorisations are issued to the individual and not the employer. Recipients of work authorisations are free to change employment within the economic sector of their visa. In addition, work authorisations are granted for two years and can be renewed thereafter by the immigration authorities.

7. The Irish Green Card was introduced in 2007 for highly skilled workers from outside the EU living in Ireland. They carry the prospect of permanent residence in the state after two years. It is intended mostly for occupations with an annual salary of over €60,000, and for a very restricted list of occupations with skills shortages where salaries are between €30,000 and €60,000. The discriminatory nature of these regulations is clear. It is expected that with the full implementation of the Green Card system in Ireland the existing work authorisation system will be terminated (NESDO 2006).

11
Union Organising with 'Old' and 'New' Industrial Relations Actors: Sex Workers in Australia and the United States

Gregor Gall

Introduction

With the recognition of significant decline of both labour union influence and the pervasiveness of joint union–employer regulation of the employment relationship in advanced economies, recent research in industrial relations has emphasised the importance of studying so-called 'new actors' (see, for example, *British Journal of Industrial Relations* (2006), Weil (2005a) and work on citizen advice bureaux in Britain (Abbott 2004) and worker centres in the US (Fine 2006, 2007a)). 'New industrial relations actors' are broadly defined as government and quasi-government regulatory organisations and non-governmental organisations (NGOs) which are, in turn, neither bodies of labour unions nor employers. The subtext to the recent interest in these 'new actors' is that they have emerged to try to fill some of the void left as a result of the decline of the reach of labour unionism and joint employment regulation. Another related subtext concerns whether such traditional institutions of labour market regulation are capable of being 'fit for purpose' in the 'new' environment of deregulation and globalisation, where new working patterns and forms of employment have emerged. Within these studies and commentaries, there is some debate about whether labour unions can use these intermediaries as surrogates and whether these 'new actors' signal a further step towards the continuing historical diminution of labour unionism.

However, the cases of sex workers in Australia and the US indicate that the manner of recent interest in these actors as a new discovery is somewhat ahistorical, for since the 1970s in the cases of the US and Australia (and other countries like Canada, Germany and the Netherlands), sex workers' rights groups have existed and fulfilled some of the roles that labour unions have traditionally undertaken in terms of interest representation and collective mobilisation of, and for, workers *per se*. In this early period, all relevant existing unions were particularly unwilling to campaign for or unionise sex workers as a result of the predominance within their own internal discourses of feminist and mainstream moral concerns regarding female sexual exploitation, as well as not recognising sex work as work. In addition, they baulked at the prospect of organising workers who were not regarded as 'workers' in the sense of being employed, who worked with 'grey' or 'black' economies, who were difficult to organise and of whom unions had almost no organising experience. However, cooperation between a tiny number of existing unions and the sex worker pressure groups in more recent times has resulted in the launching of unionisation projects. In the US, the Service Employees' International Union (SEIU) has played a small role, alongside the emergence of embryonic unions like the Erotic Services Providers' Union (ESPU). A similar situation pertains to Australia, where the Liquor, Hospitality and Miscellaneous Workers' Union (LHMWU) helped unionise prostitutes while the Striptease Artists of Australia (SAA) has emerged on its own to unionise exotic dancers. Nonetheless, these unionisation projects have been limited in their number, extent and purchase so that the sex worker pressure groups continue to play a significant role in interest representation for sex workers and, because of the weakness of the unionisation projects, sex worker unionism tends to operate in the same manner as the sex worker pressure groups.

Consequently, this chapter examines the following themes: first, what could be termed the potential 'union substitution' or 'union displacement' activities of these sex worker groups in organising sex workers for their interest representation prior to the more recent period in which attempts at sex worker unionisation have been made. The obvious inference here is the sense that there is a competition between different *modi operandi*; second, and indicating the complexity and variability of agency and situation, the contribution of sex worker groups to the sex worker unionisation projects, and the emergence of sex worker unionisation projects from sex worker rights groups; finally, the means by which the sex worker union projects have operated *vis-à-vis* the continuing existence and activity of their 'sister' organisations – the sex worker rights groups. The salience of looking at these 'older' 'new actors' here is that sex work, unlike most other forms of work, is heavily influenced and regulated by extra-workplace regimes (judicial, public policy, morality). In this context, and in a period of weakened labour unionism, the degree of convergence in *modi operandi* used by the sex worker union projects and sex worker rights groups is marked. In this sense, questions can be raised about the traditional ability of labour unionism – which has historically focused on rather narrow, workplace concerns – to deal with non-standard work which is regulated by the state at the formal level but unregulated in practice at the market level. The conclusion to the chapter is that the union organising of sex workers has only been possible through a combination of the *de facto* merging of activity of sex worker rights groups and sex work union projects, and a synergy between these two types of agency. The chapter begins by explaining what is meant by the characterisation of rights groups, following which the research methods used are explained. Finally, the key salient developments in both countries under study are identified and analysed.

Themes and issues

Labour unions are commonly defined as collective organisations of workers in the workplace which focus on improving the terms of the wage–effort bargain through creating collective leverage. This workplace organisation is part of a wider collective organisation comprising other workers' workplace organisations, and from this an external edifice is built which allows the aggregation of workers' resources – that is national unionism – to help and support individual workplace unionism, whether in the industrial, political or economic arena. This model of workplace representation is not necessarily wholly appropriate for all sex workers because of a number of factors, not least because they often have no fixed workplace, are often not employed and negotiate transactions with customers themselves. Yet, labour unionism is, nonetheless, evident for freelance or independent workers like actors and journalists where there is an identifiable occupation and a structured labour market, so it may be suggested that labour unionism is also not inappropriate for the entire range of sex workers. Nonetheless, two key distinctions here *vis-à-vis* conventional labour unionism are, first, the attitudes of sex workers themselves towards labour unionism for sex workers and, second, those of established labour unions, whereby there are only very small levels of positive support. Consequently, part of the perceived inappropriateness or irrelevance of labour unionism for sex workers concerns existing habits and preferences, rather than possible changed habits and preferences to labour unionism in specific and general terms. The transition from the former to the latter is most likely as a result of conscious human agency and activity (see later).

Nonetheless, in this situation the first sex worker rights groups emerged and engaged in providing a range of health and safety, educational and awareness-raising services for prostitutes. These cover safe sex, guidance on soliciting, personal safety, rights when arrested by police and tried by judiciary, how to avoid prosecution for operating a sex business and the like. Similar services or groups emerged later for other types of non-prostitute sex workers like exotic dancers. The provision of these services has been undertaken by varying amalgams of volunteer supporters of sex workers' rights, sex workers and ex-sex workers, marking out that some degree of self-agency is involved and allowing some veracity to the statements that these rights groups are providing services 'for' as well as 'by' sex workers. Service provision is the key practical aspect of interest representation but public advocacy and pressure group activity are also marked, whereby these groups undertake lobbying and representations for their constituencies to public bodies like police, local, state and federal governments and employers/operators as well as seeking to change the regimes of regulation of sex work. In this, sex worker rights groups focus upon work and related issues, primarily from outwith the worksite because of a combination of lack of physical presence as collective associations within the worksite and because the structures of the regimes of regulation of sex work exist as extra-workplace phenomena. In this sense, it would be wrong to categorise these collective associations as unions, or even quasi-unions, as they are conventionally understood (see Hecksher and Carré 2006). That does not mean that the sex worker groups cannot be categorised as workers' associations, though (notwithstanding the involvement of non-sex workers).

The sex worker rights groups are associations of lay volunteers, sometimes with employed support workers funded through public health programmes. Commonly, they are small groups of hyper-activists, often operating in an environment of no formal membership of the organisation – that is, membership application form and payment of subscription – and without democratic, participative structures such as labour unions have. More often than not they represent elite, self-selected groups constituting representation for sex workers but not always by sex workers – a particular bone of contention has been the claim of ex-sex workers to be able to represent current sex workers. Despite the virtue of having ex- (or non-) sex workers representing sex workers because of employer/operator victimisation, the separation of representatives from represented and the particular types of representatives like escorts representing prostitutes *per se* has created controversy amongst sex workers. For example, street prostitutes believe that escorts operate in a different and more secure environment and so see prostitution through a particular, unrepresentative lens.

Research methods

The approach to gathering the research data has not been based on the standard fare of interviewing sex workers and disseminating questionnaires to them in order to generate primary data because studying sex worker collective organisation presents a number of difficulties. Most sex workers are not visible for the purposes of contacting them. Street working prostitutes represent, as it were, only the tip of an iceberg. Moreover, some sex worker union activists are involved in this activity in a transient manner, where they move on to other locations of work because of victimisation for these activities, leaving no presence behind them and making them hard to track down. Access following identification is also difficult and sometimes dangerous, and sex workers often wish to retain their anonymity. These problems are accentuated by the researcher being male where most sex workers are female in an industry dominated by heterosexuality and sexism. The research was also carried out with meagre resources despite applying for grant funding – the inability to gain funding being an indication of the relative weakness of the presence of, and concurrence with, the 'sex as work' discourse in wider society.

Nonetheless, the force of these limitations was lessened and ameliorated in a number of ways. First, sex workers have themselves been extremely active in writing about their own work experiences and debating their analyses of these with each other as part of their desire for self-expression and self-understanding and, most crucially, as part of their struggle to have 'sex work' recognised as legitimate work by other sex workers and wider society. These writings have spanned the range of sex work, rather than just being about prostitution. Sex worker union activists have been particularly prolific in their writings, largely because these have formed a key medium by which to attempt to reach other sex workers with a view to collectivisation, unionisation and mobilisation. Second, and reflecting the desire to reach other sex workers and to gain legitimacy for the sex work discourse, sex worker union activists have sought to use the media to their benefit. These materials were accessed through specialist sex worker websites and the Nexis electronic data-base of newspapers and magazines. However, using these sources has its disadvantages. In the former, agendas set and areas covered emanated from the sex workers themselves, not the researcher, where the purpose has been debate and proselytising. In the latter, coverage can be spor-adic, often being a response to press releases of sex worker union activ-ists and not independent enquiry. Yet, the extent of these disadvantages was relatively limited because the specific agenda of the objective of unionisation set the parameters. More importantly, some triangulation was achieved and research questions pursued using other resources. Thus, a limited number of fieldwork interviews were conducted with sex workers and sex worker union activists in the United States in California, while structured email dialogue and correspondence were engaged in with other activists in other parts of the United States as well as with both sex workers and sex worker activists in Australia.

Australia

There are, and have been, many prostitute and sex worker rights groups in Australia which, by virtue of their nomenclature, may appear at first sight as labour unions or quasi-labour unions. These are the Private Workers' Association (PWA), Prostitutes' Collective of Victoria (PCV), Sex Industry Employment Rights Association (SIERA), Sex Workers of Tasmania (SWOT), and Workers in Sex Employment (WISE). Meanwhile, other sex worker groups have existed more as rights and advocacy groups, such as the Prostitutes' Rights Organisation for Sex Workers (PROS) and Self-Health for Queensland Workers in the Sex Industry (SQWISI). With state legislatures with the power to regulate prostitution, these groups have often operated as statewide rather than federal-wide bodies. In addition to, and alongside, the standard fare of activities (see above) for prostitutes' rights groups, a number of them have engaged in broader activities as a result of the specific environments they operate in. For example, the Private Worker Alliance, a network of independent sex workers in New South Wales, has spent many years involved in lobby-ing and HIV prevention and care, aiming for the privacy, and health and safety needs of private sex workers to be accommodated within the laws and regulations of New South Wales. But, because prostitution in this state is more brothel-bound than in many others, the PWA has also campaigned on (a) bond money, where brothel bosses charge bond money upfront (often around A$500, which is often not returned if the worker wants to leave the establishment), (b) the bullying of workers by brothel bosses, whereby, if workers try to leave the establishment and establish their own, they can experience harassment by councils, tax office and police, and (c) brothel bosses imposing fines up to A$300 for being unable to work due to illness or for being late for work.

However, some prostitutes' rights groups have moved further towards unionisation by being either its advocates or its facilitators. Thus, SQWISI called for union rights for sex workers as early as 1991 (*Courier Mail* 6 April 1991) in its evidence to the Criminal Justice Commission, and two prostitutes' rights groups (Workers in Sex Employment (WISE) and Prostitutes' Collective of Victoria (PCV)) joined the LHMWU in 1995 to recruit prostitutes to this union following the legalisation of prostitution. However, the initial momentum here has been lost as a result of meeting intra- and extra-union hostility, so that low-key recruitment was carried out through sex work support projects rather than directly. The prime hostility has taken the form of an unwillingness by different bodies within the LHMWU to provide further resources following a short period of support based upon an exacting 'make or break' rationale on gaining prostitute members. This led to the effective winding up of this unionisation project. A slightly more generous interpretation of this situation is given by Perkins and Lovejoy (2007: 158; *cf.* Sullivan 2007), who describe the dispute between the union and the prostitute union activists as resulting from a 'misunderstanding over the number of [recruited] members required by the union'. Nonetheless, but without any supporting evidence, Perkins and Lovejoy (2007: 158) went on to state that interest in sex worker unionisation is maintained and may bear fruit in the near future.

In this context of the absence at present of *bona fide* union organisations for sex workers (save the nascent SAA for exotic dancers), the Scarlet Alliance – the Australian Sex Workers' Association – has come to be identified frequently, but wrongly, as a labour union (see, for example, *ABC News Online* 25 January 2007, *Wikipedia* entry). Since its founding in 1989 as a peak organisation for sex workers and comprising sex worker rights organisations, projects, networks and groups, it is affiliated to the Australian Council of Trade Unions (ACTU) and bars sex industry business owners and operators from membership. This erroneous identification is made because of the ACTU affiliation and because the Scarlet Alliance commonly speaks of sex workers' rights in terms of labour rights but shows no signs of developing into a labour union, either on its own or in conjunction with others. The Scarlet Alliance's affiliates are the state-based sex worker and prostitute rights groups like the Crimson Coalition and United Sex Workers North Queensland. The continuation of such groups, and indeed emergence of new ones, is testament to the continued need for their services as well as the activism that sustains them. One could speculate counterfactually that their continuation might not have happened in the way it has if the sex worker unionisation projects had taken off and grown. Although the employers' and operators' organisation, the Eros Foundation, was the main force behind the establishment of the Sex Party in late 2008 (*Canberra Times* 20 November 2008), it remains to see what function this political party will provide for sex worker interests. Finally, the SAA was established as a dedicated union for dancers, given that other sex worker groups were orientated towards prostitutes. An account of its activities can be found elsewhere (Gall 2006c). In this case, those sex worker union activists who established the SAA approached a number of unions seeking help to unionise dancers under these unions' auspices before and during its existence (2001–). None of these approaches were met with enthusiasm or receptiveness.

United States

The sex workers' movement in the US began in San Francisco in the early 1970s with the founding of the advocacy and pressure group for prostitutes called COYOTE (Call Off Your Tired Old Ethics), which then operated with the subtitle of 'The Sex Workers' Rights Organization'. COYOTE subsequently developed with the founding of other COYOTE groups and affiliated prostitutes' rights groups in other US cities, as most sex worker groups in the US are city rather than state-based. However, in San Francisco by the early 1990s and thereafter, COYOTE split into the St James Infirmary (an occupational health and safety clinic run for and by sex workers), the Sex Worker Outreach Programme (SWOP – a health and rights education group), the Exotic Dancers' Alliance (EDA – an advocacy group for dancers), the Cyprian Guild (an escorts' guild support group), Sex Workers Organized for Labor, Human, and Civil Rights (SWOLHCR) and the ESPU. The separation was, in part, a parting of the ways between activists over what their priorities should be as well as a response to the development of emerging issues and subsectors of sex work.

COYOTE has comprised primarily former prostitutes and their supporters and has sought to campaign for decriminalisation and resources for prostitutes' well-being and against police harassment. One rationale for this orientation was that the criminalised status of prostitution (and attendant social morality) was viewed as the main issue facing prostitutes and from which their marginalised and stigmatised position was reinforced. Alongside this, and with prostitution remaining unlawful in the US save for Nevada's small number of regulated brothels, COYOTE activists believed that labour unionism for prostitutes was impractical because organising prostitutes would constitute an unlawful activity, as prostitution itself remained unlawful. With the rise of the 'moral majority' and the AIDS backlash, many COYOTE activists then concentrated their efforts on the creation and sustenance of the St James Infirmary and SWOP San Francisco chapter. However, with the rise of exotic dancing, the EDA emerged to provide interest representation for dancers and played an instrumental role in campaigning against stage fees and better working conditions, deploying class law actions. The highpoint of its activities was the unionisation of the Lusty Lady peepshow in San Francisco, where the dancers gained union recognition in 1996 with the help of the SEIU. Meantime, the Cyprian Guild established itself to deal with the issues facing escorts (rather than street and brothel/massage parlour prostitutes) but did not develop much beyond a mutual help group based on meetings (as opposed to public or external activity) and was unclear on whether its focus should be on escorts' rights as workers or businesses.

Frustration with the inward-looking orientation of the union members at the Lusty Lady – concerning themselves only with Lusty Lady issues – and lack of help and resources from SEIU in unionising other sex workers led a number of activists to establish SWOLCHR. It campaigned against stage fees and compulsion to prostitute in lap dancing clubs using street activity, helped file class law actions to recoup stage fees and made representations to the California Labor Commission with some SEIU assistance. The victimisation of the lead SWOLCHR activist – a working dancer – by the clubs led to the disintegration of SWOLCHR, and, with the demise of the EDA in 2004, the creation of the ESPU. It operates with a very small number of highly active (sic) sex worker activists and supporters. The ESPU's primary activities include collecting signatures to allow its proposal to get on a public ballot to facilitate a bill on decriminalising prostitution in San Francisco (following earlier but unsuccessful attempts in Las Vegas in 2002 and Berkeley in 2004 to use this same method); giving testimony to the San Francisco Entertainment Commission in 2006 on a proposed amendment to the Police Code for the regulation of live adult entertainment businesses; and submitting evidence to the Commission on the Status of Women (*PR Newswire* US 17 August 2006). The ESPU was successful in getting the proposal – known as Prop K – on the statewide ballot but was defeated by a 4:3 margin. Again, the basis for seeking to decriminalise prostitution lay in both ameliorating working conditions and then allowing unionisation to take place. In this campaign, the ESPU joined forces with other sex worker groups. In a new development for extant sex worker activity, the ESPU has worked in conjunction with the San Francisco Labor Council and Industrial Workers of the World (IWW) to proselytise for labour unionism and training sex worker activists in labour union skills.

Elsewhere in California, porn actors and actresses in the San Fernando Valley, the largest single location of pornography production in the world, tried again to unionise in 2004 following several earlier unsuccessful attempts in 1993 and 1998. However, little headway was made and the provision of an HIV-testing organisation for porn workers remains as the only lasting gain from various organising attempts by, and for, porn workers. Meantime, porn workers have engaged the services of lawyers to act on their behalf in regard to the right to 'do business' and worked with free speech coalitions *vis-à-vis* censorship and morality issues.

Outside California, the implosion of the Las Vegas Dancers' Association after the victimisation of the lead activist (Majic 2005) and the impact of the city's clubs' actions in creating a fearfulness among dancers to become involved in campaigning activities based on opposition to the *status quo* has meant that there is now no labour unionism to speak of in Las Vega (see Gall 2006c). However, the Sin City Alternative Professionals Alliance (SCAPA), an independent chapter of SWOP (US), has been able to act as a resource, advice and advocacy centre. SCAPA is an affiliate of the US-wide Desiree Alliance, a coalition of sex workers and health and educational professionals formed in 2005, which advocates for sex workers' human, labour and civil rights and has set itself the task of 'be[ing] part of efforts to reinvigorate the sex workers' rights movement in the US. Therefore, all of our actions...focus...on building leadership and constructive activism in the sex worker population' (Desiree Alliance website). Meantime, the *Spread* magazine – 'a magazine by sex workers for sex workers', according to is website, and established in 2005 – seemed to fill in for the long-defunct *Danzine* sex workers' magazine. Concomitantly, sex workers have founded internet chat rooms and blog sites like *boundnotgagged* (linked to the Desiree Alliance) for other sex workers to discuss their work issues.

Summary

Examples exist in both Australia and the US of sex worker rights groups and extant labour unions acting in a complementary manner in proximity to, and at a distance from, each other by virtue of either working together to organise and unionise sex workers or providing representation to state bodies. In regard to the latter, the political activities of the sex worker rights groups are a reminder that labour unionism (national unions or peak federations) also deploys extra-workplace political lobbying to pursue interest representation in general terms and where the relative disorganisation of unionised workers (by time and space) compels unions to look for other levers of influence. There is little evidence that sex worker groups have constituted forces for 'union substitution' or 'union displacement' in either historical or contemporary terms, in the sense that labour unionism has shown little interest in organising sex workers and has rebuffed many approaches for such activities from sex workers. Indeed, where unionisation projects have taken place, these have just as often involved sex worker activists approaching existing unions rather than setting up their own, and these activists have been the catalyst to the *de facto* unionisation of sex workers on the ground. Also of note is that, when unionisation projects have been set up, many of these have engaged in activities which are similar to or replicate those of sex worker rights groups. This indicates much about the nature of the regulatory regime of sex work and the weakness of sex worker unions.

Conclusion

The projects to establish the unionisation of sex workers in both Australia and the US have been on a very small scale and of very limited success, indicating both the inhospitable operating environment and the determination of activists. Having emerged from sex worker rights groups, the underlying dynamic of the rationale for unionisation has now fallen back into those continuing sex worker rights groups because of the inability of the unionisation projects to lay down self-sustaining roots. While this close, symbiotic relationship may yet yield further attempts at unionisation, there is also a multifaceted tension between the two. Sex worker rights groups can provide a supportive environment for activists who wish to embark on unionisation projects, but they can also provide a self-limiting one. This self-limitation can take the form of substitution or displacement, even though the formal purposes of each are different within the remit of interest representation. This could be expressed as: because there are no sex worker unions, there are sex worker rights groups and because there are sex worker rights groups, there are no sex worker unions.

Unlike many other 'new' industrial relations actors, there is an authenticity to the sex worker rights groups inasmuch as, while they cannot claim numerical representative status, they are far more of, and, by the workers concerned rather than professional advocates servicing a client base as in the case of many other 'new' actors. In the case of sex workers, it is clear that the process of creating the organisational representation structures of interest group formation amongst workers as workers can take place without unions and without necessarily being centred on, and in, the workplace. Here, the discourses of sex as work and sex work as an occupation have been critical. And, if the distinction between unions and the 'new' industrial relations actors is that the former organise in workplaces and along occupational lines, relying on collective bargaining as the principal method for improving terms and conditions of work, and the latter operate outside of workplaces, in communities, and deploy tactics other than collective bargaining as a means of trying to defend or raise labour standards, then the sex worker groups do something quite distinct. Because of the nature of sex worker–operator–client relationships, the sex workers' groups can help sex workers modify their own behaviour and actions so as to provide for relatively more control over their work and their worksites, even if this is a collectively provided service for individual deployment. Overall, the study of sex workers in this chapter provides further evidence that so-called 'new' industrial relations actors can provide worksite representation for workers, even atypical workers. Whether the perceived inappropriateness or irrelevance of labour unionism for sex workers concerns an existing situation rather than future or all situations remains to be seen.

12
Reconstructing Construction Unionism: Beyond Top-Down and Bottom-Up

Dale Belman and Allen Smith

Introduction

The decline of the US organised labour movement is an oft-told tale. Total membership declined from 21 million in 1979 to 15.7 million in 2007, with density dropping from 24.1% to 12.1% (Hirsch and MacPherson 2008b). Even these gloomy numbers hide a harsher reality. In the same years, private sector membership fell from 15.1 million to 8.1 million, with density plunging from 21.2% to 7.5%. Only an increase in public sector members saved unions from greater decline. In 1973, the 3.1 million public sector members comprised only 17% of all members. In 2007, they numbered 7.5 million, now 48% of the total. Only one private sector industry has experienced significant union growth – construction. Paralleling other unionised sectors, construction union membership dropped from 1.6 million in 1973 to 1.45 million (1979) to 1.14 million (1989) to 0.9 million in 1992. However, membership rose to 1.276 million in 2001, an increase from 1992 of 0.37 million or 41%. In addition, with a 2007 membership of 1.193 million, the construction unions have largely maintained hold of that growth through two economic downturns.[1] By contrast, despite all the attention rightly paid to the innovative tactics used by SEIU's Justice for Janitors campaign, the number of unionised janitors declined from 0.39 million in 1993 to 0.37 million in 2001 and 0.31 million in 2007. This growth in construction union membership paralleled an increased ability to protect wages. In 1977, union construction wages were 41% higher than non-union wages in the sector, the figure declining to 33% in 1993. However, the ratio in 2006 was still 33%, the highest union wage-premium of any sector. Actual construction union wages show the same pattern. Yet, wages alone are an increasingly inaccurate measure as total union pay due to rising benefit costs. These combined wage and benefit increases have ranged from 3.8% to 4.5% annually since 1998, higher than the rate of inflation (Construction Labor Research Council, various). Another source is prevailing wage determinations in markets where union collective bargaining agreements are the *de facto* determination.

This stabilisation and slow improvement in construction is largely unknown. It reflects years of efforts to rebuild membership, recover market share in existing areas and move into new ones. The better-known tactics – salting, stripping, COMET and comprehensive campaigns – have utilised adversarial approaches that undercut the 'open shop' and its institutions. Less well known are the experiments with cooperative strategies – strategic partnerships, joint labour–management efforts and new forms of labour agreements. Finally, a number of construction unions have restructured themselves to adapt to changes in construction markets, particularly by changing their geographic dimension – and administrative structure of locals – in hope of supporting bargaining and growth and gaining efficiencies in organisational administration. It is apparent this experimentation has not resulted in a single successful path for reorganising construction. Rather, these different approaches are complementary and are effective when used in concert. While it is not certain that construction unions will continue to improve their position, they have created a foundation of knowledge, tactics and reputation that they can build on in reasserting their role in the sector. Moreover, given current projections for energy, petrochemical, and public works construction, and consequent demand for trades, union membership may enter a new period of significant growth.

Our discussion of these issues reflects the authors' long-standing relations with construction unions. Allen Smith has worked for the International Association of Sheet Metal Workers and the Building and Construction Trades Department of the AFL-CIO and now works as an independent consultant to construction unions (locals, district councils and internationals). Dale Belman has worked closely with construction unions and unionised employers in Michigan and the Midwest.

The construction sector

Unions in construction face fundamentally different issues in reorganising workers and increasing market representation from those elsewhere.

The occupational structuring of construction is highly differentiated, with workers more defined by their occupation than by their employer. Skills are specific to separate trades, and once workers have acquired substantial skills within a trade they usually do not move to another. Most firms are also occupationally structured, providing a specific type of services such as electrical, heating or plumbing. Even general contractors seldom employ more than the basic trades and may obtain these trades by subcontracting to specialists. Construction is unique among the organised industries in being dominated by small operators; there are a small number of large firms, but these do not employ the majority of workers. One reason is the specialisation of trade and work such that employers tend to specialise in particular types of trade within certain types of work, and in particular geographical regions. Because construction projects are inherently temporary, and work varies considerably between employers, the workforce has to be mobile between projects and often between employers.

Historically, inter-project and inter-employer mobility of the construction labour force provided a strong bond between workers, unions and employers. Unions acted as labour market intermediaries, providing the information and certification needed by employers to be able to hire workers with confidence (as well as to workers who are mobile and peripatetic). Joint labour–management committees supervised the craft training programmes that provided skilled workers to the industry and resolved the public goods problem inherent in single firm training schemes. Finally, joint labour–management organisations provided a range of benefits and services, such as health care and pensions, to a mobile workforce (see below). These strong ties and the craft nature of production provided the unions with a close relation to employers (which does not exist in many other sectors), with many employers formerly being, or continuing as, craftworkers who have created their own companies. But these strong ties also created an interdependence that, in contrast to other sectors, precludes many employers from walking away from a unionised labour force. And, of course, construction unions historically as craft unions, thus, exercised a degree of craft professionalism in terms of regulating entry and standards to the craft which has usually been absent from many other unions and sectors.

But mobility has also made union–employer relations less stable than in other industries. Employers who can find sufficient non-union labour can easily become 'open shop' employers despite long relationships with unions. Another characteristic is the depth of cyclicality of work and employment. Construction is sensitive to demand conditions and interest rates. When demand is weak, construction employment declines rapidly, and when demand is strong there is more work than the existing workforce can complete in the desired time. Finally, migrant workers comprise an increasing proportion of the workforce, and opposition to unions comes from both construction employers and construction clients.

Such characteristics underlie a unique industrial relations system that arose in construction after 1945. Weil (2005b) suggested its seven key characteristics are: (i) hiring arrangements where unions held control over the pool of available workers for job assignment through hiring halls or related arrangements; (ii) provision of entry skills and standards (apprenticeship) and ongoing skill enhancement via labour–management programmes administered at the relevant trade and geographical level; (iii) wage, benefit, and working condition agreements spanning a designated geographical area, typically at a local (metropolitan or submetropolitan) area; (iv) formalised labour–management dispute resolution mechanisms to resolve workplace conflicts *vis-à-vis* conduct of work, safety and health problems and ongoing administration of contracts; (v) formalised labour–management dispute resolution mechanisms to resolve conflicts arising between trades and contractors regarding assignment of work (i.e. resolving jurisdictional disputes); (vi) joint labour–management financing and administration of apprenticeship and journeymen training through multi-employer organisations; and (vii) joint labour–management financing and administration of health and pension benefits through multi-employer funds. While this system proved effective in maintaining union influence until the 1970s, changes in construction markets, labour law, and owners' attitudes served to undermine the position of organised labour.

Important union underpinnings have been mutual support between construction unions and limitations on employer ability to operate 'open shop'. Until the 1970s, union members could honour pickets and refuse to work on projects employing non-union workers in other trades. In effect, union control of labour in critical trades limited 'open shop' opportunities in other trades where they had a presence. Also labour law restricted signatory employers' ability to operate 'open shop' subsidiaries. Two decisions by the US Supreme Court fundamentally changed this, making mixed sites possible by the presence of a neutral gate and allowing construction employers to establish 'open shop' subsidiaries. Such subsidiaries could draw on the knowledge and experience of the contractor's professional staff, reducing the hurdle to operate effectively. But legal changes alone did not cause rapid union decline in the 1970s and 1980s. The locus of construction shifted from the well-organised downtowns into suburbs and more rural areas and, because much of it was residential, light commercial and low-rise, construction became simpler. This offered opportunities for 'open shop' contractors to use less skilled non-union labour. Larger owners also supported the development of 'open shop' through the Business Round Table. Large clients developed the capacity of 'open shop' by having new 'open shop' contractors work on projects and then bring in union contractors to make repairs. Over time, the 'open shop' developed the capacity to handle the work on its own. The move to 'open shop' was accelerated by the recessions of the 1970s and 1980s, for in slack times many union members 'stick their card in their shoe' and work for 'openshop' contractors. However, as work on the union side recovered more slowly than that in the 'open shop', and the second recession dragged on, many workers remained with 'open shop' contractors, providing them greater capacity than they otherwise would have been able to achieve on their own (Allen 1988).

Finally, the labour relations system itself limited the union ability to respond to change. Both construction workers and employers are, in Perlman's (1928) terms, job conscious – they view work opportunities as inherently limited. This view, which is consonant with the highly cyclic dynamics of work and employment within construction, leads them to hold work and employment opportunities very tightly. Union members are often unwilling to take in new members or expand apprenticeship programmes because of concerns about unemployment during cyclic downturns. Similarly, employers do not favour unions organising new employers if the new employers will enter markets staked out by current signatory employers. This protection of employment opportunities has limited unions' ability to expand in times of secular employment growth. The orientation toward protection of employment opportunities for current members leads the union sector to handle periods of high labour demand through extended working hours and, if needed, with temporary union memberships. These approaches protect current members' income and employment opportunities, but at the cost of limiting the growth of union capacity and creating a partially trained labour force for the 'open shop'.

New strategies for building membership and recovering market share

The seriousness of the decline was recognised and the response came in many different forms, which can be divided into three categories: adversarial, cooperative, and restructuring. They are discussed individually before examining how they are used together to increase membership and promote market share recovery.

Adversarial strategies

Adversarial strategies are the highest-profile approach to increasing union presence and they have played a central role in the stabilisation and growth of construction unions. 'Union organising' workers has not played a key role prior to the 1990s. The transitory nature of projects and the workforce and variability of employment at any given employer made getting employers to sign collective agreements and creating employer-side bargaining organisations far more important than direct organisation of workers. The control of skilled labour required employers to come to the union to obtain the workers they required. Workers were bound to the unions by training and benefit programmes, employers by their need for workers. This difference between construction unions and other unions is embodied in labour law; in no other industry are unions permitted to sign pre-hire agreements with employers, agreements that set forth the terms and conditions of employment before workers are hired and without a vote for collective representation. The historical craft strategy did not continue to work well in an environment in which 'open shop' contractors had access to sufficient numbers of skilled and semi-skilled workers. 'Open shop' work structure differed considerably from that used in the unionised construction (Northrup and Foster 1975). Rather than using small crews of highly trained self-directing workers, the 'open shop' used relatively few highly skilled workers as foremen and many lesser-skilled workers. Employers were able to obtain sufficient numbers of skilled workers by employing former union members and doing some training, and recruiting workers with few or any skills from among manual workers and then migrants. The altered work structure freed many employers from having to deal with the unions to obtain skilled labour, leaving unions with little leverage to compel these employers to sign collective agreements.

In response to this and the resultant membership decline, union leaders began to organise 'open shop' workers, particularly skilled ones, either under their current employers or by bringing them over to unionised employers. Construction Organising Membership Education Training (COMET) is the best known of the bottom-up organising methods used here from the late 1980s, and combined organising and membership education. Local members had to be educated to build support for taking in new members. Previously, local members saw any move to let in new workers as creating a longer wait for obtaining employment for themselves. Construction unions had a variety of ways to limit membership, from accepting only small numbers of new apprentices, to requiring large initiation fees, to having multiple classes of members which effectively restricted jobs to long-time members. The unions had little power to change these local policies, so each local had to be convinced, a slow process that remains incomplete.

COMET organising was not about signing up new employers, although that did happen. Its main tools were salting and stripping. Salting concerned allowing union members to work for non-union contractors with a view to learning about contractor and workforce with the aim of taking concerted action on behalf of the salt and workers interested in union representation. Of course, non-union contractors were usually very unhappy with this, frequently taking action against the salt that would violate labour laws, leaving the company ensnared in unfair labour practices. Stripping concerned individual recruitment. A union organiser, sometimes by salting and sometimes by site visits, identified non-union workers who would like to join the union. The organiser then worked to take the worker in, usually during periods of full employment so the recruit could go straight to work. Again, this could lead to organising a company if it were done by taking significant numbers of workers in and preventing contractors from completing contracted jobs. Again, this was not the usual result. Stripping off the most capable employees allowed the union to meet job calls and weakened the non-union operator. It is likely most new members joined in this way, not by signing the company and assuredly not by an NLRB election. The use of unfair labour practice charges as part of salting and stripping has been limited by decisions by the NLRB which have limited salts' rights to be considered as employees and the amount of back pay they can receive.

Unions emphasised stripping journeymen rather than apprentices or lesser-skilled 'open shop' workers. Stripping off skilled workers is advantageous to the unionised employer, hurting 'open shop' employers more than stripping less skilled workers. Unions were also confronted with difficult issues of where to place less skilled workers in their apprenticeship programmes. Some unions have tried to evaluate stripped workers and place them in appropriate classes to provide a full set of the skills expected of journeymen, but this approach has proven difficult to implement. There is often considerable tension between organisers and apprenticeship trainers, as the former want to take in large numbers of 'open shop' workers while the latter believe the organisers often recruit workers who do not have the requisite skills and abilities to qualify for the apprenticeship programme. Some local unions oppose organising for reasons including that it interferes with running the annual apprenticeship contest. The construction unions also developed expertise with comprehensive campaigns against specific 'open shop' contractors and 'open shop' organisations.

Comprehensive campaigns are a new step for construction unions. For many years, 'open shops' have waged effective political and legal campaigns against prevailing wage laws and other institutions that support the construction unions. Although this was a regular topic of complaint by union leaders, little was done to place them into the position of playing defence. Yet many are vulnerable because of violations of employment law with respect to benefit payments, use of independent contractors, and workers' compensation fraud, to name a few issues. Increased efforts to bring these matters to light and prosecute them diverts 'open shops' from attacking unions, ties up resources, levels the playing field and opens up a possibility of some implicit agreement to maintain the *status quo* with respect to labour law.

Cooperative strategies with construction employers and owners

Cooperative strategies have always been a part of the union toolkit, with the distinction between employee, manager and owner being narrower than in most other industries. Because of small firm size, construction managers are accessible to employees and there are multiple points of contact between managers and union members. Movement from employee to manager or owner, and back, is common. Many new firms are begun by craft workers and older firms often bring managers up from the trades. Union members regularly fill many of the lower-level managerial positions, such as foreman and supervisor, and members may be called upon to serve as estimators and in other professional jobs. Some unions, such as the International Brotherhood of Electrical Workers, provide training to members who want to start new firms. Small firm size has also necessitated the development of cooperative institutions linking firms to other firms and unions. Unions bargain with employer associations, but also interact with these associations in the joint administration of training programmes and benefit funds. Few construction firms are sufficiently large to provide training, pensions or health insurance on their own, and worker mobility between firms limits the value of firm-specific services. Instead, such services are provided through Taft-Hartley joint labour–management trusts and are funded with fixed charges per hour worked. These trusts are overseen by representatives of employers and unions and require ongoing contact and cooperation between the parties. Cooperative efforts between labour and management are then embedded in the structure of the employment relationship. This has provided a basis on which new cooperative institutions to promote unionised contractors have been developed.

Formal labour–management cooperation as a method of regaining market share

One of the earlier forms of cooperative programme intended to regain market share for unionised construction was that of industry promotion funds. These funds allowed signatory contractors to submit proposals for subsidies to help win projects. The proposals were selected by a joint labour–management board. The funds, which are a limited form of cooperative programme, have had some success in preserving work for union construction and stabilising employment. More ambitious are ongoing labour–management efforts to promote unionised construction. Tri-con, in Peoria, Illinois, is one of the most successful of these efforts. Early in its development as a labour–management effort to regain market share, Tri-Con established that clients were uninterested in whether work was done unionised or 'open shop'. Rather, they were concerned with the perceived value of the project. The members of Tri-Con created a construction organisation and trademark, Better-Bilt, which provided access to a full range of construction services including architects, financing, construction law, and, of course, construction. Although organised around a labour–management cooperative relationship, marketing and an evolving reputation have made Better-Bilt a recognised brand for high-quality reasonably priced construction. Part of its success has been establishing internal systems for maintaining quality and limiting conflict between parties in the organisation. Using the Better-Bilt name, Tri-Con has been successful in regaining market share in its region. The efforts of the Quad City Labour–Management Cooperation Committee in Iowa and Illinois came out of the rapid decline in the construction unions and contractors in the early and mid-1980s. Over time, the unions and contractors have learned to handle internal differences and focus on providing the client with a better value proposition than the 'open shop'. The committee has funded a full-time executive to promote union construction and to serve as a first-line mediator of project disputes. The labour–management committee has also adopted a standard umbrella agreement that assures the construction owner against labour shortages or other factors that may disrupt the project. Again, these efforts have been used to rebuild the presence of union construction in the Quad City Area.

There has been considerable movement in the joint-apprenticeship organisations in many trades to modernise training, to take advantage of new learning technologies and to upgrade the workforce even after completion of apprenticeships. For example, the United Association of Plumbers and Pipefitters (UA) and the Mechanical Contracts Association (MCA) have created a series of new training centres with video links so that, when appropriate, skills can be taught from the national training centre. The UA and MCA are also seeking ways of merging the apprenticeship training with college education so as to provide members with the opportunity to earn degrees in construction management and other related studies. The Iron Workers' union has built on its capacity in training members to obtain voluntary recognition from the largest ironwork firm in the High Plains and southwest. The critical shortage of craft workers has been paralleled by a critical shortage of supervisors. The Iron Workers also agreed to train existing members as supervisors to run this firm's rod tying crews in return for recognition. The members going through this programme will be trained in Spanish as well as in supervisory skills. The union will gain at least 2,000 members.

Improving value proposition for owners

Owners, the individuals and firms that pay for buildings, have formerly only had arm's-length relations with the construction industry. When there was work to be done, projects were put out to bid and owners, with the aid of their construction departments, would evaluate them. This limited the degree to which unions and unionised employers could influence owners' decisions. Over the last 20 years, conscious effort has been made to become involved in owner decisions about projects earlier in the process. Some examples are regional efforts to work with owners to standardise drug and safety training and establish multi-owner/multi-employer skill testing. Programmes provide savings as employees do not have to recertify for each new job. Finding common drug testing standards has proven more elusive, as many owners want their own programmes, but the economies of joint programmes are attractive and may bring owners around. Another example of this has been public multi-owner/multi-employer skills testing. Prior to their development, workers demonstrated mastery of appropriate skills at each employment site where this was required, which was time and cost-consuming. The Boilermakers have implemented public testing in some areas of the country where members demonstrate their skills in a public site where employer and owner representatives can attend. Passing these tests qualifies the employee to work on attending owners' projects for a set period, often three years. As these are done on weekends, there is minimal cost to employers or owners.

Project labour agreements

The increasing use of Project Labour Agreements (PLA) by unions and joint labour–management committees reflects another cooperative approach to establishing better relations with owners. A PLA is a pre-hire, collective bargaining agreement, which governs the terms and conditions of employment on a project. PLAs are normally used on large projects of long duration. The advantages for contractors and clients are that they are assured a timely supply of labour, no-strike/no-lockout provisions assure jurisdictional and contract issues will not interfere with the project, and, to varying degrees, the PLA will reconcile sometimes disparate provisions of local collective bargaining agreements across trades. With a PLA, a project manager need be concerned primarily with one unified agreement rather than as many as 15 local ones. For unions, PLAs are a guarantee that collectively bargained terms and conditions will be enforced, for all contractors agree to abide by the PLA as well as any provisions of local agreements that are specifically referred to in the PLA or not otherwise limited by the PLA. As a practical matter this means that all contractors agree to use union referral mechanisms (e.g. hiring halls), pay union rates, contribute to jointly administered (i.e. union sector) benefit programmes and, in general, operate as unionised contractors while on a project whether they are usually unionised contractors or not.

PLAs are particularly attractive to owners on time-sensitive projects, in periods in which there is a shortage of labour, or when there is concern about the effect of increases in the price of labour on costs. Although PLAs historically have been between owners and unions, they are often used by labour–management committees as part of a package to attract owners to build 'union'. An advantage of having the PLA jointly developed by a labour–management committee is that the owner will likely be familiarised with its advantages. PLAs with public bodies have proven particularly important to construction unions. Thus, while sometimes used on relatively small projects, such as school reconstruction, their use on very large public projects such as the Boston Throughway and, prospectively, the $30 billion Alaska Gas Pipeline project assures that these projects are built under collectively bargained conditions and that signatory contractors will not be disadvantaged in the bidding process by adhering to these standards.

Strategic engagement with owner associations

The construction unions have also undertaken strategic initiatives with owners. In part because of a critical shortage of skilled craft labour, energy companies have been engaged in joint meetings with unions and employers on issues of mutual concern for more than a decade. More recently, the construction unions have engaged the Construction Users Round Table (CURT) in discussions. CURT, an organisation of large industrial owners, is a spin-off of the Business Round Table. Problems with the ability of 'open shop' to provide a sufficiently skilled workforce pushed CURT to meet with construction unions to find means of working together. This relationship has been fraught with problems, for CURT uses 'double breasting' and has been reluctant to make commitments to use unionised contractors in return for expansion of union craft apprenticeship programmes or other changes. Despite such limitations, this is a new relationship and contrasts strongly with the solidly anti-union approach of the Business Round Table.

Limitations of cooperative strategies

Although cooperation with employers and owners has been an important dimension of constructions unions' recovery, it has also placed limits on this. Weil (2005b) found established unionised employers may be unwilling to move into unfamiliar markets and equally unwilling to see the new employers organised, as these contractors may create future competition. Such employer views complement tendencies among union members against new markets and organising and can add powerfully to institutional inertia. If the unions accept such limits, it inherently limits their growth and allows the 'open shop' to claim emerging opportunities. There are, however, examples of locals moving ahead with organising new markets and employers despite resistance from existing signatory employers (Weil 2005b). Although this can create conflict between employers, union leadership and members, new organisation, with or without the support of signatory employers, is critical to the rebuilding of construction unions.

Restructuring the trades

The growth of the union construction industry is due to more than success in dealing with outside groups more effectively. It is also the outcome of an ongoing transformation of the unions and their membership. Although construction is sometimes viewed as the industry time forgot (*Boston Globe* 12 August 2007), there has been considerable change in its structure of employment and units of capital, inter-capital relations, technology and markets since the 1950s. Technological change has reduced the skill needed for some types of work, while allowing new products and methods to emerge which require new skills. The changes in the industry and its labour force have compelled rethinking of who is recruited into the unions, how they are recruited and trained, and how the unions are structured. This is an ongoing process but one that has progressed further than is recognised by those outside the construction sector.

Changing member attitudes

There has been ongoing discussion within some unions about members' attitudes toward the job, employer and customer. At issue is engaging workers in improving efficiency and performance in construction and addressing some cultural norms that impede higher levels of performance. Some of this, paralleling the UAW's efforts with its paid education leave programme, is about educating members about the position of their employers and industry. Some is about redefining the relationship between craft worker, owner and owner representative. The IBEW has developed a code of excellence for its members that addresses issues of timeliness, productivity and behaviour and is starting to screen applicants to apprenticeship programmes for work motivation and attitude. Others have developed programmes for improving administration of locals, setting clearer goals for members, and signing up 'open shop' contractors on the basis of a union value proposition. Programmes work on issues of inclusiveness and diversity, a critical issue for unions, as construction brings in migrant workers. These efforts may be viewed as mirroring those concerning the changing structure of work in manufacturing 40 years ago. The efforts then led, over time, to new work structures, such as the GM production system, with its lean managerial structure and the devolution of responsibility and control of production (Block and Berg, forthcoming). Although the union work structure provides more autonomy and control over work than existed in manufacturing, current discussions are almost entirely focused on employee change rather than analysing the employment relationship, determining how this causes inefficiencies and conflict, and then developing methods of improving performance.

Of course, changing member attitudes can result in new union leadership. Indeed, without strong support from the business manager of a local union, organising efforts there will not succeed. These disputes invariably bubble upwards, as top leaders of each union evaluate how hard locals can be pushed toward more organiser-friendly policies. These tensions, in part, created contested elections for the leaderships of two of the largest unions, the IBEW and UA. In the former, the challenger and a key figure pushing organising lost to the incumbent by 5:1 while, in the latter, the organising director lost by 2:1 to the incumbent. As both candidates had argued for more aggressive organising strategies, fallout from their defeats likely weakened organising efforts in both unions for a period.

Enlarging administrative units to better reflect labour markets

Construction has always been a footloose industry consisting of regional and national as well as local markets. The extent of local markets has increased with the rise in individual mobility. While once construction workers might not work more than 50 miles from their home, today workers will regularly drive 70 or 100 miles to worksites every day. Thus, previously distinct construction labour markets, formerly separate, are now often one. These redefined markets have posed challenges for union administrative structures developed when markets were far more local. Contractors will approach different locals, meaning that relationships can be varied and complex, potentially pitting local against local. The existence of many small locals within a single labour market is also disadvantageous as pension and health funds are organised by locals and small funds cannot take advantage of economies of scale in their operation.

There has been a steady move towards creating union and employer institutions that are more congruent with emerging labour markets, while the form varies by union. The most dramatic of these is the consolidation of the Brotherhood of Carpenters structure into regions. It has created geographically large regions on a statewide basis, for example, and placed operational control of union activities in the hands of regional directors and staff. Further, in order to reduce local political influence over staff, business agents are employed by regions, being appointed rather than elected. This regional structure allows contractors to be bid work throughout the region and carry their workforce with them. It also allows the allocation of resources, such as staff, to areas where they are needed. Although the locals remain, and continue to elect their officers, much of the bargaining and other functions are now located in the region. Among other construction unions, only the painters have taken such bold steps toward restructuring, but most have moved in this direction. There has been considerable consolidation of locals so that locals better correspond to labour markets, typically through the merger of smaller ones into larger ones. But such consolidations are less common in larger metropolitan areas where large locals maintain sufficient financial and political power to resist efforts of the international toward merger.

Adapting occupations to meet the challenge of residential construction

Unions have also been adapting their occupational categories to changes in the demand for skills. Residential construction has been the fastest-growing segment of the industry for the last decade. While housing accounted for 45% of construction in 1995, by 2006 it accounted for 55% in the *US Census* of 2007. Although construction unions had some role in the residential housing industry in the past, particularly in larger cities where unions were strong, their role in the current housing market has been limited. This reflects, in large part, their focus on the better-paid and more skilled industries within construction such as heavy highway, heavy commercial and industrial construction. Skills and compensation have been structured for these markets. Most of the unions that potentially have a role in residential construction have been moving toward creating occupations and training programmes intended to make it possible for them to operate in this market. For example, the International Brotherhood of Electrical Workers (IBEW) and the National Electrical Contractors Association (NECA) have developed a three-year residential wireman apprenticeship. This apprenticeship does not provide the full range of skills as the inside wireman apprenticeship, but also does not take five years. Graduates of the programme are prepared to work in residential and light commercial construction under residential collective bargaining agreements.

In some areas, the United Association of Plumbers (UAP) has taken a different approach in having a residential training programme rather than an apprenticeship. Those who go into this programme are trained, relatively rapidly, for residential and light commercial work, and work under a different agreement from members who are working in heavy commercial and industrial work. Although their pay is lower than other members', they carry full health and pension benefits, making their work considerably more attractive than working under 'open shop'. The UAP promoted this programme in Michigan by offering extended warranties on new construction done by signatory contractors. The residential workforce can upgrade over time into the better-paid parts of the industry, but residential work provides a port of entry for workers into the union. The Sheet Metal workers in Toronto have taken yet another approach in developing a piecework system for residential and light commercial. This substantially reduces the cost of union labour while allowing members to maintain their income.

Both the United Brotherhood of Carpenters (UBC) and the Labourers have approached the residential market with a new occupation, the homebuilder. This occupation includes virtually all of the skills needed for residential construction. A single crew can pour foundations, do framing, dry walling and roofing, and finish carpentry, heating, electric and plumbing. This approach has been particularly successful in western Pennsylvania, where UBC members currently command 40% of the residential market. This wall-to-wall approach creates jurisdictional issues with other trades, but, given the lack of union engagement in residential, this has not become an issue between the UBC and the other unions. Although it has not created new occupations, the Roofers have *de facto* recognised residential roofing as a distinct trade in their organising residential roofers in Las Vegas and other areas.

Although union efforts to establish themselves in residential will be slowed by the sharp downturn in new home construction, this offers more than an increase in membership. First, it establishes labour standards in a construction industry which had been poorly remunerated. Second, residential has been an important point of entry for new construction firms. As they develop knowledge and expertise, these firms can move into light commercial and the survivors may over time move into more skilled and demanding parts of construction. By forgoing involvement here, unions have ceded this source of new firms to the 'open shop' and suffered consequences as light commercial construction has been increasingly dominated by the 'open shop'. Re-engagement may benefit unions both by increasing the number of new union firms and by reducing the opportunities available to the 'open shop'.

Organising migrant workers without regard to legal status

Construction is a port of entry for documented and undocumented immigrant workers. This is reflected in the rapid increase in Hispanic workers in construction. Because many migrant workers in construction are undocumented, they are vulnerable to exploitation such as low wages, non-payment of wages, not receiving benefits and not having protection provided by social insurance such as workers' compensation and unemployment insurance. Undocumented workers are particularly common in residential construction, but substantial numbers are present elsewhere. Migrant workers, especially undocumented workers, pose difficulties for the construction unions. Some trades, such as roofing, painting and dry walling, have been adversely affected by the large inflow of undocumented migrants. And rapid decline of some unionised trades in the South and Southwest can be attributed to competition from 'open shop' firms using undocumented workers.

There is agreement amongst unions that current migrant workers need to be provided a path to citizenship, but there are also considerable differences on what to do before passage of comprehensive immigration reform. Carpenter, labourer, and roofing unions, for example, have implemented programmes to organise without regard to immigration status. The Roofers have gone as far as providing personal identifiers to members other than social security numbers so that the undocumented can participate in health and welfare programmes. Similarly, these organisations have not limited entrance to their apprenticeship programmes to those with documentation. In contrast, other unions, often those which are less affected by undocumented workers, have implicitly excluded undocumented workers because of difficulties in entering them in programmes that require extensive documentation. Even those unions which actively recruit migrant workers face issues in retaining these workers in their ranks. Employers may be reluctant to take on undocumented workers, particularly as states and localities pass laws penalising those employing undocumented workers. Even if one employer is willing to hire undocumented workers, other unionised employers may not and this restricts workers' ability to maintain employment. 'Open shop' employers have proven willing to have workers deported rather than recognise unions supported by undocumented workers.

Conclusion

We have separately examined a variety of distinct strategies and efforts, and many times they have been pursued individually. However, these efforts are complementary and work best when combined into a single effort. Thus, stripping the most able workers away from 'open shop' contractors will complement efforts to offer contractors a skilled workforce only if the local union is able to assess these new members' skills and place them at the appropriate level in the training programme, or bring them directly to journeyman status. Internal barriers must also be over-come. Similarly, increasing the unionised workforce, either through an expansion of the apprentice programme and/or stripping qualified 'open shop' workers, is unlikely to increase union market share if signatory contractors are unwilling to bid on work beyond their normal projects. Creating a job targeting programme can help. Moreover, restructuring locals into regional bodies may create necessary organising resources. However, structural changes alone will not create winning conditions if the members and unionised contractors feel too excluded from the new forms of decision-making.

Construction has developed a series of approaches which, when used together, may provide the foundation for reunionisation and building union leverage. However, success is not assured. Many factors could slow or prevent unions here. First, strategies are complex, requiring more than skill to implement – they need adequate human resourcing. Second, these strategies go against some long-held approaches of union leaders and members, such as taking in large numbers of new members without increased amounts of work. That the new members may be Hispanics entering a still largely white unionised workforce may add to the resistance. One restructuring common among other unions but largely absent from those in construction has been union mergers. While unions like SEIU and UNITE-HERE have added members and scale in this way, construction unions have made no such efforts. Indeed, the 'localist' construction culture that has allowed the development of a broad range of tactical innovations may prevent such an approach. The construction unions are profoundly AFL-style unions in an increasingly CIO-economic world. This issue remains unaddressed in this chapter as it remains largely unaddressed among construction unions.

Notes

1. Membership numbers are for private construction workers, excluding about 0.15 million unionised construction workers directly employed by government.
2. COMET1 and COMET2 differed in focus. The former was more focused on educating members to accept bringing in new members; the latter was more tactical, with an emphasis on salting and stripping.
3. This structure parallels those of the joint boards used in the needle trades since early in the last century.

13
Contrasts and Contradictions in Union Organising: The Irish Mushroom Industry

Francisco Arqueros-Fernández

Introduction

This chapter describes the recent efforts of SIPTU, the largest union in Eire with 225,000 members, to eradicate underpayment and mistreatment of migrant agricultural workers in the Irish mushroom industry through an 'organising' approach between 2006 and 2007. SIPTU used a top-down, bureaucratic approach to improve mushroom workers' standards and organise these workers. SIPTU tried to implement an 'organising' model of labour unionism by using an apparatus trained to 'service' existing union members while concomitantly negotiating at a high level with employers and the state in the context of national social partnership (see Allen, this volume). Accordingly, SIPTU's campaign in the mushroom sector managed to increase the rate of employer compliance with legal labour standards by lobbying state agencies rather than by deploying workforce pressure at workplace level. This achievement, however, fell short of the mark that SIPTU set itself when it launched its campaign to 'clean up' the mushroom industry. This chapter argues that a participative, militant grassroots dynamic within unions is a necessary condition to implement a proper 'organising' model.

The chapter presents the outcome of extensive fieldwork carried out in County Monaghan between 2005 and 2007 which was supplemented by secondary sources thereafter. Initially, the research focus was to describe and explain the two major structural changes that the mushroom industry underwent in the last quarter-century. But, at the beginning of 2006, the underpayment and mistreatment of migrant workers in mushroom farms came into the focus of the mass media.

The Migrant Rights Centre Ireland (MRCI) set up around that time the Mushroom Workers Support Group (MWSG). These events refocused the priority of the research, leading to a study of SIPTU's organising campaign in the mushroom industry. The research method was ethnography, based on participant observation where the researcher worked first on a mushroom farm and then as a participant observer in the MWSG. Firstly, the chapter describes the context in which SIPTU's recruiting and organising campaign took place, followed by an overview of the Irish mushroom industry and a description of SIPTU's organising campaign. Finally, the chapter discusses the inherent contradictions in the union-organising project that SIPTU tried to apply, comparing and contrasting this with the work that MRCI is doing with mushroom workers.

Unions and migrant workers in Ireland

A sizeable body of literature on unions covers responses, with more failures than successes, to the decline that the labour movement has experienced in the developed countries since the 1980s (see, for example, Moody 1997a, 2007; Munck 2002; Clawson 2003). This decline has two main, connected features: decreases in union density, and in membership militancy and democratic participation. Migrant and low-paid workers in general constitute the main groups of workers outside the labour movement. Unions in Ireland are trying to organise migrant workers because of ideological reasons so that they present a rights-based approach 'grounded in a belief in inalienable rights for all people and opposition to discrimination and exploitation' (Krings 2007: 49). According to Krings (2007), these ideas are also based on self-interest because employers can use migrants to undermine the wages and working conditions of Irish workers. However, evidence presented by Krings (2007: 46–7) indicated that there was only limited evidence that migrant workers have actually contributed to lower wages and working conditions of Irish workers (save for the Irish Ferries dispute in 2005, which ended with the displacement of Irish workers by migrants on cheaper wages). Nevertheless, Krings (2007: 51) suggested that the 'self-interest' was likely to focus on 'any section of the workforce that remains outside of the remit of unions [because they] automatically undermine their bargaining position'. Since union density in Ireland has declined sharply since the mid-1980s (Allen, this volume), unions' bargaining power has sharply decreased. Therefore, it seems to make sense to organise non-unionised workplaces, including those with a high proportion of migrant workers. What is interesting is that Krings placed the need to organise migrant workers in the context of the renegotiation of social partnership in 2006. Those negotiations became the main means for unions to try to enforce employment standards. The ICTU refused, according to Krings (2007: 51), to engage in those negotiations until they got some assurances because:

> [a]mong unions the expectation is that with this stronger enforcement architecture, the rights of both indigenous and migrant workers are protected and that the latter are not longer a cheaper option of the former ... [but this] cannot be enacted by legislative change alone. This is particularly true as often migrant workers are not aware of their rights and may sometimes be satisfied with less than they are entitled to. Thus, the task for unions is to convince migrant workers to actively involve themselves by joining a ... union.

Therefore, national partnership agreements alone cannot guarantee the implementation of labour standards. Rather, workers must get actively involved by joining a union. The problem here is that unions are trying to turn towards an organising strategy while also trying to avoid any confrontation at the workplace, that being the key objective of social partnership. Union officials, in practice, do not believe in the feasibility of strike action or collective (as opposed to bureaucratic) bargaining on the part of migrant workers, particularly those on work permits. So, they prefer to rely on the legal mechanisms to resolve industrial conflicts. In practice, as we will see later, they prefer 'to organise workers' rather than 'get workers organised'. As a union official said:

> ... due to the work permit scheme, if immigrant workers strike, they have the underlying threat of dismissal, the consequences of which might include the loss of their permit to stay in Ireland or deportation. Immigrant workers must be made aware that they have other ways to fight for their rights, and they must have confidence that there is enough support in the Irish legal system to prevent unfair treatment. Irish policy and legislation should be adequate to immigrant workers. (Gonzalez-Perez et al. 2008)

This strategy of relying on 'the Irish legal system', rather than on workplace militancy, is the product of the fear they attribute to migrant workers and their reluctance to challenge their employers. Union officials interviewed by Krings (2007) also cited obstacles to organising such as the lack of communication between migrant workers and unions due to language, and the presence of migrant workers in sectors where unions are weak. Many also said that Eastern European workers do not like unions because of negative past experiences with state-controlled unions (Krings 2007, researcher's fieldwork notes). A SIPTU union official involved in its recruitment mushroom farm campaign, in a moment of despair, referred to the individualism of Eastern Europeans as the most important obstacle to organising these workers: '[They] don't help each other out, unlike the Irish when they were abroad. I don't believe [organising] is going to work' (fieldwork notes).

Such arguments can be better shown to reflect union officials speaking of their lack of resources and the bureaucratic framework within which they fight out industrial disputes rather than any ideological opposition to organising new workers *per se* or an ideological affinity to a mutual gains agenda. The bureaucratic structure of unions can present a major obstacle to new organising and membership participation. The SIPTU President for the Electronics and Engineering Branch and a member of the Dublin Regional Executive Committee (Derwin 2005) argued that around 20 years of partnership agreements have turned union officials into 'amateur lawyers and advocates at the Labour Court', transferring collective bargaining 'from the workplace to the heights of Government Buildings'. As a result, 'for many, full general meetings are a nostalgic memory. Some branch AGMs have long been getting attendances below 5%' (Derwin 2005; see also Allen, this volume). Yet at the same time, and since 2001 when SIPTU decided to set up an organising unit, which later included bilingual organisers, in order to reverse falling density rates, migrant workers and particular industries were targeted, with around 30,000 having joined SIPTU. But the union used a top-down approach. Recruitment did not involve members' activism. It was the job of a 'professional core of organisers'. For many union officials, weighed down with individual casework, this merely added to their work (Allen, this volume). This type of approach, therefore, was not suitable for recruiting new members as well as turning them into active members who were 'empowered' workers. Moreover, Krings (2007) reported that SIPTU's campaign to recruit migrant workers in the mushroom industry had helped to improve working conditions and workers' incomes but yielded few new recruits.

So, whilst there has been a turn to organising, it has arguably been constrained and coloured by the context of the union and regulatory environment into which it has been inserted. An organising approach is currently at odds with SIPTU's long-term practices and structures; this does not mean, however, that the organising turn is not both a positive and a necessary move.

Irish mushroom industry: Development, crisis and migrant workers

The mushroom industry in Ireland has been characterised, even before the arrival of migrants, by poor wages and working conditions for a predominantly female workforce. The modern period of this industry started in the 1980s with the setting up of satellite networks based on non-written contracts between growers and marketing groups, which also supplied growers with compost (their main input). Contract farmers were required to make an initial investment of IR£20,000 for a three-house farm. The labour force in this contracting system consisted of the grower and his wife, although part-time pickers – women from the neighbourhood – would help with the harvesting. The satellite networks expanded until the mid-1990s, when the number of farms reached around 500 and the average farm size comprised 5–6 houses. But prices started to fall in the 1990s because of overproduction. In order to keep margins up, growers increased yields by expanding growing surface, and by increasing compost productivity. In 2006, there was an average of around 20 full-time female pickers per farm, and one or two male general operators. Since harvesting is a manual operation that currently absorbs 25% of farm gate prices, reducing labour costs became the key issue in the industry. Growers used piece rates to increase harvesters' productivity, leading to degrees of exploitation characteristic of early capitalism. Picking rates went from an average of 15 pounds per hour (lbs/h) in 1981 (*Northern Standard* 6 August 1981) to around 45 lbs/h in 2006. The most significant increase in workers' exploitation (by working harder and decreasing piece wages) took place when migrant workers became dominant. Growers reduced piece rates from €0.2 per pound of mushrooms picked to €0.15/lb between 2000 and 2003 for migrant workers. In some farms, piece rates went as low as €0.11/lb.

Non-EU migrant workers on work permits started to arrive in the horticultural sector in 1999. The Irish economic boom in the late 1990s created an acute labour shortage in the industry exactly at the same time that this labour-intensive industry was expanding production. By 2001, it represented 40% of the horticultural workforce at primary production level (4,080 workers). In the industry, migrant workers constituted 70% of all workers (1,940 workers) (An Bord Glas 2002). By 2006, around 95% of mushroom workers were not Irish. After May 2004, most mushroom workers became EU members after new accessions and did not need work permits any more. Some mushrooms growers started to report higher staff turnover of their formerly 'committed' and 'hard-working' Lithuanian and Latvian workers. Therefore, they demanded that DETE allow them to bring Thai and Chinese pickers on work permits. The lobbying by SIPTU and MRCI early in 2006, however, stopped a replacement of workers in mushroom farms.

SIPTU's recruiting campaign

Between 2001 and 2004, some scattered news stories (see, for example, *Irish Times* 22 February 2005, 12 July 2005) about abuses of foreign workers appeared in the media. A group of mushroom workers from one farm contacted MRCI in April 2004 and described working days of 16–17 hours, average hourly wages of between €2.2 and €2.5, exposure to chemicals, and tyrannical work regimes. In February 2005, a socialist member of parliament, Joe Higgins, highlighted in the Dail the case of the GAMA construction workers who were working 80 hours per week for wages between €2 and €3 per hour for unskilled workers when the registered employment agreement rate for the lowest-paid operative in construction was at the time €12.96 an hour (*Irish Times* 9 February 2005). Their strike between March and May 2005 brought to the forefront the underpayment of migrant workers in Ireland. The case of Irish Ferries in late 2005, on the other hand, spiralled into a 100,000-strong ICTU-called demonstration in Dublin – the largest since 1979 (*Irish Times* 10 December 2005) as well as in other cities, showing the level of public concern about the threat of a 'race to the bottom' in the Irish labour market. All this took place at the same time as government, unions and employers were preparing the renegotiation of the national social partnership pact. Against this background, in early 2006 a grower fired all his 17 mushroom pickers after a walkout over changes to working conditions. The workers had suffered working weeks of 80–100 hours for around €250 per week (*Irish Times* 19 January 2006). The straw that broke the camel's back was that all workers would have to finish picking at the same time, implying that faster pickers would help the slower ones and, therefore, take part of the (piece) wages of the latter. Without having had any previous union contact, the workers walked out and went to the local SIPTU office. They asked SIPTU to mediate for them. When a SIPTU official made a phone call to the farm, the official was informed that the workers had already been replaced and that SIPTU should find alternative jobs for them.

This gave SIPTU more evidence about the lack of law enforcement and worsening of incomes and working conditions for migrant workers. At the end of March 2006, SIPTU launched a campaign to 'clean up' the mushroom industry around the issues of sweatshop conditions, workers' dismissal and the 'race to the bottom'. The union announced a recruitment-cum-organising campaign, and started negotiations with employers and DETE in order to get some guarantees that the government would effectively enforce existing labour standards through the Labour Inspectorate. Just before this, the MRCI had started on its own initiative, the MWSG, by gathering information about the working conditions and building a network. The MRCI supplied SIPTU with information and, thus, exerted a significant influence on the first stages of SIPTU's campaign. Initially, MWSG approached workers by organising open meetings. Then with EU funding, it hired a Latvian former mushroom worker to act as a community worker. This worker built on the small network of contacts the group already had. Members' meetings took place once a month from late 2006, with attendances of between 14 and 20. The members discussed their work experiences and two community workers proposed lines of action based on these discussions. In early 2007, members relaunched the group as Agricultural Workers Association (AWA).

SIPTU set up a basic structure to carry out its campaign but without a special branch for agricultural workers, or a specific EUO. Local branches were to deal with any recruits. One of the rural branches, for instance, consisted of one branch official (officially called a branch organiser) and two part-time secretaries performing data entry work. The organiser's work consisted of casework. SIPTU's organising campaign was, thus, going to charge these already overworked union officials with recruiting and organising as well as developing activists, and without any knowledge of the sector or spoken languages. However, SIPTU (2006) presented this in a disingenuous light:

> *SIPTU has put together a special group of full-time organisers from all over the country to co-ordinate the [u]nion's efforts to improve pay and working conditions in the mushroom picking industry ... Members of the group comprise union organisers from [nine areas].*

Moreover, the initial recruiting work was to fall on the Lithuanian organiser working in the organising unit, but most of her time consisted of servicing the growing number of Eastern European workforce SIPTU members who were fluent in Russian (Lithuanians, Latvians, Russians, and Ukrainians) throughout the whole of Eire. How she was to allocate time to go out and recruit mushroom workers was not clear. Nonetheless, some recruiting took place during 2006. Around 10 workers out of an around 100-strong workforce in County Kildare joined, and in three farms in three different counties some workers approached SIPTU and joined. A local SIPTU organiser, on her own initiative, tried to overcome the campaign's shortcomings and its under-resourcing by working with the MWSG bilingual community worker. This unofficial arrangement meant SIPTU would take the legal cases and MWSG would help to mediate the contacts with these workers. Some of these workers also became MWSG members. Simultaneously, MRCI was contacting workers in several counties and taking up their cases but also trying to get them to join MWSG.

Yet by late 2006, seven months after launching the campaign, no further attempts to recruit and organise had been undertaken. SIPTU officers put up some posters in Eastern European shops in a number of towns with mushroom farms appealing to mushroom workers to join. There were some phone calls from migrant workers to SIPTU's organising unit, but mainly to ask for jobs in mushroom farms (fieldwork notes). Except for a small number of workers approaching SIPTU, union officers carried on with their normal duties. The SIPTU organising team did not have a recruitment plan for the whole 2006 and almost no time was set aside for migrant worker recruitment. SIPTU did not intend to employ a full-time bilingual organiser focused on the mushroom sector (fieldwork notes).

SIPTU's campaigning energies, instead, went mainly to negotiating and lobbying at the top with employers' representatives and state agencies. Due to adverse publicity for growers that this campaign generated, and the pressure from DETE and the Labour Inspectorate, a handful of the largest growers decided to set up a body to negotiate an Employment Regulation Order (ERO) – an agreement on payment and working conditions for an employment sector made by a Joint Labour Committee and registered with the Labour Court – for the mushroom industry, leaving the ERO for agricultural workers. The deal was that the new ERO would end overtime rates in exchange for union recognition. For some SIPTU officials, this was the only way to get union recognition. For some large and efficient employers, the new ERO would reduce labour costs and avoid 'bad press' that was damaging the sector's public image. Small growers, however, were completely opposed to union recognition because they were not willing to pay even the minimum wage for agricultural workers (fieldwork notes). For large growers, the new ERO offered the possibility of gaining market share by pushing small and inefficient growers out of business. In early 2007, a draft ERO was agreed between SIPTU and the Mushroom Growers Committee, headed by Monaghan Mushroom and Dewfresh Mushrooms. The Growers Committee now had to convince mushroom growers to open their farms to a union recruitment campaign. The agreement included the provision that SIPTU members in mushroom farms had to vote for the ERO.

The recruitment campaign in two northern counties took place in early 2007 (which the researcher observed through field visits and interviews). In one, the Lithuanian organiser carried out the initial visits to mushroom farms together with the local branch organiser. She explained in Russian that the new ERO included no overtime pay, but that they would get the minimum wage, 20 days' holidays and a Sunday work bonus if they joined and voted for the agreement. This was better than their current terms. The organiser offered workers the forms, asked people to fill them in, and got nearly everyone to join. In the other county, the local SIPTU organiser visited farms with an interpreter but only a tiny number filled in application forms – 10 in 5 visits compared with 40 forms in 3 visits for the other organiser. The difference was attributable to the ability to speak Russian and engage on that basis, while the success of the Russian-speaking organiser questions to some extent the supposed obstacles to migrant organising, namely, individualism and suspicion of unions. According to SIPTU, several hundred completed forms were collected during the recruitment campaign agreed with the Growers' Committee between March and April 2007. This meant that these union fees, some union officials recognised, would be enough to pay at least one full-time organiser. Yet, there were no plans for hiring an organiser.

SIPTU's recruitment, on the other hand, faced opposition from many growers, who did not allow access to their farms. In a press release in July, SIPTU (2007a) announced it was abandoning the plan for an ERO for the whole industry because of 'the failure of the Employers' Group to live up to previous commitments'. SIPTU, however, still claimed that 'to have [workers] represented and organised by the union' was the only way to 'ensure the proper maintenance of employment standards'. Therefore, SIPTU decided to use the Agreement reached for an ERO as the basis for Registered Employment Agreements (REA) with the individual employers that were willing to sign up. The rest of the farms would still be covered by the ERO for agricultural workers. The first and only REA until the time of writing (late 2008) was signed in late 2007 between SIPTU and Drimbawn Mushroom Ltd, a division of Monaghan Mushrooms Ltd (SIPTU 2007b, EIRO 2008c).

In the meantime, however, the membership applications collected in the recruitment campaign were not followed up. SIPTU strategy in practice consisted in waiting to reach agreements with employers first and organise later. Only after the first REA was signed did SIPTU's organising unit put in place a plan to train shop stewards and to organise union branches where the union had reached agreements with employers. It could be argued again that SIPTU followed this strategy because of lack of resources. But it also can be argued that organising was subordinated to 'partnership' with employers, although the union always presented organising as the chief strategy to 'clean up' the mushroom industry. This fact highlights the contradiction generated when a union tries to apply an organising model through a structure developed in the context of partnership and casework.

SIPTU was more successful in improving working conditions by putting pressure on the DETE and its Labour Inspectorate, without organising workers *per se*. After it launched its recruitment campaign in one of the northern counties in March 2006, some growers there started to improve wages and working conditions. For example, one grower started to pay overtime after getting a tip-off from his producer organisation that SIPTU was inspecting the farms. The grower gathered all the workers together, warning them not to talk to anyone about their jobs because SIPTU could close the farm and everyone would lose their jobs. In fact, SIPTU had met with DETE representatives and gained assurances that the Department of Agriculture and Food (DAF) was not going to give capital investment grants to growers who did not comply with fair labour standards. Again, this was not quite the case, for DAF declined to MRCI to release the names of the individual growers getting these grants, although DETE promised to start inspecting the farms. Around October 2007, the inspectorate carried out 55 visits – around 50% of all farms – but found very little evidence of irregularities. More important, because of its impact upon growers, was an Employment Appeals Tribunal award of €342,600 to the workers who walked out over conditions (see above). At the same time, MRCI was putting pressure on growers and government bodies, and its mediation on behalf of workers recovered €250,000 in back wages for approximately 100 workers on 20 different farms across Ireland in 2007 (*Mushroom Newsletter* January–March 2008).

Levels of non-compliance, however, remained high according to sources from MRCI (fieldwork notes). But labour inspectors could not find evidence of unlawful breaches unless workers collected these themselves and at their own risk. Even when this did happen, growers only paid a maximum of six months' wages in arrears when found at fault. Generally speaking, the labour inspectorate and courts do not want to put farms at the risk of closure. For example, between 2006 and 2007, labour inspectors performed 3,944 inspections, finding 296 cases of breaches, but only one prosecution was initiated (*Irish Times* 15 February 2008). The alternative for workers is to join a union to fight for their entitlements. Union officials, by contrast, attributed a low level of union consciousness to migrant workers, and preferred to focus their energies on top-level negotiations, as we have seen.

Workers' consciousness

Workers' consciousness is highly uneven, being not just an expression of workers' direct work experience. Migrant workers tend to have worked in their home countries, having absorbed different political traditions, and are subject to extra-work influences. A mushroom picker's diary from a farm is illustrative:

> 30 Oct 2003: I would like to join an Irish trade union and start fighting for my rights. Working day for 14 hours, like in Russia before the socialist revolution. I wanted to call home but we finished our job at 21.30. No time for calling!

> 14 Dec 2003: [Our] very poor translator told us that [the boss] wasn't happy with our job. According to her, we were slow. Next day [the boss] was fighting with the Latvian workers. We asked about a break at 6 o'clock in the evening. [My friend] was crying... was threatened not to get 3rd work permit. Now pickers have 3 breaks instead of 4; we have our meals all together. The employer is our master.

> 25 Dec 2003: We had very hard days before Christmas!... To stand at the conveyer belt for 14 hours, then we had to re-pack the whole pallet of mushrooms. Somebody made a mistake about the dates! Nobody said 'thank you for your job'. Our employer considered us to be at his complete disposal for his money!

> 2 Jan 2004: New Years Eve, good day! We went to bed at 5.30am but we had to go to job by 8am! Nobody considers us as human beings! This week no day off! We were told no day off, you had one day on Christmas!

Here, there is no sign of rejection of unions because of previous work experience in a former 'communist' country. Rather, this mushroom worker linked her oppression to power relations between workers and boss. It led her to think of becoming a union member as the only way out, in spite of her early socialisation in Ukraine in the 1970s and 1980s. Similarly, for other migrant workers from former 'communist' countries, there seemed to be little inherent resistance to unions.

At MWSG meetings, the most active members believed that unions had to prove that they could solve problems before workers would join them. Others wanted to know more about unions. Two MSWSG members from one farm joined SIPTU, but most of the other workers did not, while three other MWSG members joined the Independent Workers' Union but could not convince their fellow farm workers to join with them because these Ukrainians workers were willing 'to do anything for the boss in order to get their work permits renewed'. No mention was made of union dislike and only fear of the employer was cited. Furthermore, the success of the Lithuanian SIPTU organiser could partly be attributed to the recruitment taking place on the farm and with the farmer's agreement. Here, the chances of getting their entitlements seemed high and made joining the obvious step to take.

Previous experiences in unions or political organisations in former 'communist' countries did not predispose the most forthcoming members of MWSG against unions, although they were not convinced that Irish unions were effective enough. Some of them were actually proud of their young communist organisation membership in their youth, recalling with pride at MWSG socials the responsibilities they held and the speeches they made during that time. One MWSG member had studied Marx's *Capital* as a part of his academic training in Belarus. After leaving his job in Minsk, he worked for two years on a mushroom farm. One night after a meeting, he recounted that he first thought that workers in the 'west' had rights and these were respected but that his time on the mushroom farm reminded him of the type of capitalism that Marx had described in Britain in the mid-nineteenth century – which he thought was something of the past. Another mushroom worker, who challenged her employer on her own, stated that if her employer could make any money at all, it was because workers picked the mushrooms. Employers, in her opinion, made profits on the backs of workers.

These ethnographic samples are not representative of all mushroom workers. The migrant workers observed were quite aware of their oppression at the workplace and they constituted the most militant section of all mushroom workers. Most of them were former mushroom workers who had taken a case against their employer (some of them while in this employment). They challenged the farm regime and that experience radicalised them politically. The MWSG meetings contributed to this, as was their role. Any account of working conditions was presented in terms of workers versus bosses – two social groups with opposed interests. This response emerged organically but not spontaneously. It matched their immediate experiences and the MWSG was instrumental in igniting it. The founder of the MWSG defined its goals: (i) to bring migrant workers together; (ii) to offer a space where they can share their experiences; (iii) to work on the main issues that affect the lives of these immigrant workers; and (iv) to allow them to decide how far they want to go in challenging their current situation at work or in society. One part of MWSG meetings involved the need to look for allies, particularly amongst unions, in order to empower workers. From the beginning, the MWSG founder community contacted worker unions, local Citizen Information Centres, county partnerships, and any kind of organisation that could support the process of empowerment of agricultural workers.

Yet, it would be a mistake to believe that the work of MRCI with mushroom workers took place smoothly or easily. Although it dealt with over 100 cases in mushroom farms and gained workers €250,000 compensation in 2007, the number of workers active in it never rose above 20 and members were not active in running the group or publishing the *Mushroom Newsletter*, edited by MRCI. All the work fell on the two full-time MRCI community workers. Nevertheless, in August 2007 the MWSG became the Agricultural Workers Association, legally independent, with the goal of giving members full control of the organisation.

Fear, rather than lack of information, was one of main obstacles to organising. One of the MWSG members, who had worked in the Kilnaleck farm, recalled how she and her co-workers had worked 36 hours non-stop, and it was normal practice to start work at 4 a.m. and finish in the evening or close to midnight. She recounted:

> *We were very tired but we had to continue ... We didn't know anything about the law when we were working in the farm ... We signed contracts with the work agency before we started in the farm. They said that we were going to get the minimum wage, and everything was legal, hours too. But we needed the money. We had to work. What could we do [about it]? We could do nothing. (fieldwork notes)*

These workers saw no alternative for a long time. But in January 2006, 17 of them walked out and no pickers stayed behind, for the tipping point was a change in work practices on top of the existing conditions. Three days after the walkout, SIPTU arranged a meeting with labour inspectors with media gathered around. The workers told, through an interpreter, their story and then broke up into smaller groups. They greeted positively suggestions of collective forms of action, indicating a change in consciousness and that they had overcome any fragmentation, individualism and suspicion of unions. Yet, no one pursued this further and no one led this group into further collective action. The mood passed and SIPTU just took up their cases. Perhaps it was complicated to organise a group based on only 17 workers from a single farm. Yet, some of these workers joined later the MWSG, becoming active within it. Some other MWSG members came from group cases taken up by MRCI between 2004 and 2006.

Fear of losing jobs, the need to guarantee incomes in spite of mistreatment and underpayment, and an unfamiliar linguistic, social and cultural environment were serious obstacles to organising. Yet, the Kilnaleck workers, in a really oppressive work environment and without any outside support, decided to walk out and go to the nearest union office. SIPTU officials complained of obstacles to organising and migrants' workers lack of collective consciousness. But, when the Kilnaleck walkout took place, this group of workers did not become organised into a union. The features discussed above all made workers potentially more receptive to collectivism and combination via unions, but this did not prefigure the kind of unionism they would engage in or be receptive to, namely, servicing or organising modes. Similarly, these features did not necessarily determine the chances of collectivism of whatever form being successful. However, the form of unionism and collectivism that was on offer to the migrant workers was not one that required their active involvement, for caseworkers, labour inspectors, labour commissioners or labour courts mediated their agency. In fact, while MRCI was able to incorporate some of the Kilnaleck workers into the MWSG, SIPTU was not able to get them union-organised. Therefore, it is necessary to examine the approach and consciousness of the unions as institutions.

SIPTU as an 'obstacle'

The MRCI tried to work as closely as possible with SIPTU, but SIPTU did not try to work in partnership with it. MRCI set up the MWSG in order to create a space where workers could articulate their demands. By contrast, SIPTU did not create any such spaces where workers could come together and share their experiences and ideas. SIPTU did not allocate resources such as a bilingual full-time organiser. Yet, MRCI with fewer resources was able to make use of the services of an interpreter in all the meetings of MWSG, and got EU funding in 2006 to hire a full-time bilingual community worker for one year. SIPTU employed most of its efforts and resources in negotiating with employers and the state over the implementation of labour standards, the opening of farms to unions and so on in the context of the renegotiation of social partnership in 2006. SIPTU did well according to partnership standards at these negotiations, but not at organising. It was good at what it was doing, but this was not union organising. Its bureaucratic structure, overdeveloped during the era of national partnership, was not suitable for organising workers in low-paid jobs from scratch. Agriculture has never been an easy sector to organise. And, according to a SIPTU official, the cost of organising these workers outweighed the benefits, particularly as resources were scarce. Migrant workers were much easier to recruit, and in higher numbers, in larger companies in other sectors of the economy, particularly where the union already had branches. The question that arises is why SIPTU decided to organise in the mushroom industry. A conference in Lurgan in June 2006 on unions and migrant workers shed some light on this.

Lurgan conference: A signifier of different methods and ideas

SIPTU and Unite, the two largest general unions in Ireland, are seeking to implement an organising 'model', as is mandate, the retail sector union (*Irish Times* 21 April 2008). At a conference in Lurgan in 2006, organisers from SIPTU and Unite spoke of their organising methods. The first from Unite was a fluent Portuguese speaker who organised in the food industry. Her view was that unions were losing power and needed to recruit new layers of workers such as women, migrant workers and the low-paid in the increasingly growing non-unionised economic sectors. She stressed that organisers had to leave their offices, going out to workplaces to identify leaders and the best recruiters, and establish links with community networks. She emphasised the necessity to establish personal relations inside and outside the workplace. The approach this organiser was putting forward came from unions like the SEIU in the US and the vision of social movement unionism (see Moody 1997a, 2007). The one important feature that the Unite organiser left out was the need to democratise unions. By contrast, the SIPTU organiser said very little about organising, focusing instead on the lack of legal mechanisms to enforce labour standards. The number of labour inspectors, in his opinion, was insufficient and SIPTU's main demand in renewing the social partnership agreement concerned increasing their number. The economy, it was argued, needed migrants but exploitation had to be avoided. The organiser finished by saying that 16,000 migrants had joined SIPTU, and that this union had three non-Irish organisers, two Polish and one Lithuanian.

Here, we find a considerable contrast in methods and approaches. While Unite might practice external and top-down organising, it does – at least – practice a form of organising. And, in Ireland, Unite has been critical of social partnership, rejecting the latest national wage agreement in November 2008 (*Irish Times* 18 November 2008). But the difference is also arguably ideologically rooted. The two unions align themselves differently in relation to the main tendencies within the logic of collective bargaining. Unions negotiate with employers and do so within the framework of the reproduction of capital in which the interests of wage-labour and capital can be seen as interlinked and complementary (Lebowitz 2003). Therefore, since unions primarily engage in collective bargaining over the price of labour-power, they do not challenge this cycle. A basic contradiction between labour and capital, however, also develops from the same logic of collective bargaining. Capital manifests its inner logic in the production and realisation of surplus value through the competition of many capitals. In this way, capital reproduces and produces a fragmented working class (Lebowitz 2003: 81–7). The labour movement, on the other hand, in order to successfully carry out its bargaining goals, needs the combination of as many segments of workers as possible. By trying to establish a monopoly over the commodity labour in order to strengthen its bargaining power, unions also tend to push wages out of competition, which also means a rejection of the capitalist economic principle of productivity and competition. Collective bargaining, therefore, challenges the labour market institution. And there cannot be capitalism without a labour market (Weeks 1981).

While SIPTU mainly aligns with the first tendency, it is still caught in the double logic of collective bargaining. As Krings (2007) argued, there were both ideological reasons and self-interest involved in SIPTU's drive to organise migrant workers at a national scale. Because of 'self-interest' to maintain its bargaining power and position as the largest union, it seeks to struggle against the decreasing union density that national social partnerships have helped cause. This means it needs to organise those 'outside' the traditional remit of unions. SIPTU presented its campaign in the mushroom industry as aimed at getting migrant workers organised. It argued this was the only way to get minimum labour standards implemented. Yet, it did not allocate the necessary resources to organising to do this. SIPTU officials engaged in the campaign did not believe that organising was going to work. In the mushroom campaign, successful recruitment only took place when it was agreed with employers. Organising was subordinated to partnership, and participation and grassroots activism to the quantity of recruits.

As SIPTU's campaign took place when the unions, employers and state were engaged in negotiations over the 'Towards 2016' partnership agreement, there was a general feeling that employers were going to use migration and outsourcing to lower wages and labour standards. SIPTU successfully connected with workers' concerns with its use of the phrase, 'the race to the bottom'. It can be deduced from this, allied to the account above, that SIPTU laid more store by meeting the employer challenge in the corporatist forum than in the industry or its workplaces. This was all the more so when SIPTU's organising approach was heavily coloured by its bureaucratic tendencies and top-down approaches developed for the period of social partnership deals. The requirement of active participation of union members was de-emphasised. In spite of this, SIPTU's campaign contributed to highlighting migrant worker mistreatment, prompting state agencies to inspect mushroom farms. After this, working conditions and wages were improved. Now, it is much easier for workers to stand up and criticise employers, and SIPTU is recognised in the farms of the largest mushroom employer. Fortuitously, small farms, the worst offenders, are disappearing due to a crisis of overproduction.

This chapter has limited itself to SIPTU's organising campaign in the mushroom industry. Future research on SIPTU's organising should attempt to draw comparisons with other, and more successful, campaigns in sectors that the union has targeted in order to understand what results are peculiar to the campaign in the mushroom sector. Nonetheless, it seems evident that a coherent organising approach must involve the active participation of workers and members. Workers need unionisation in order to turn spontaneity into organisation. But this requires reversing current bureaucratic approaches and ideological perspectives in relation to social partnership. How that might come about is a different question.

Note

The research undertaken was possible thanks to a three-year scholarship from the Irish Research Council for the Humanities and the Social Sciences. Thanks are due to Gregor Gall for extensive help in revising this chapter.

14

Union Renewal and Young People: Some Positive Indications from British Supermarkets

Iona Byford

Introduction

The focus of this chapter concerns union renewal and young people. If unions are to be revitalised, one of the key groups of potential members that need to be encouraged to join, and more crucially to become active participants in union matters at their places of work, are young people (those workers aged between 16 and 24). The findings from the research for this chapter indicate that, despite gloomy predictions for the future of union membership in general and amongst young people in particular, young people will still join unions where the union culture is well embedded at the workplace and where shop stewards provide a strong influence in encouraging membership, union education and active participation. This is more likely to occur where an organising agenda for union revitalisation is being followed as compared with a partnership strategy.

In terms of union renewal in Britain, the prospects look gloomy with a continuing decline in union density from 28.3% in 2006 to 28% in 2007 (BERR 2008). Absolute union membership remains relatively stable at between 6.5 million and 7.0 million but is not growing. In lieu of this position, union renewal efforts are more critical than ever. Given that the majority of union members in Britain are over 40 years old, if the movement is to have a vibrant future it needs to recruit young workers. One of the relatively easier and cheaper contexts within which union renewal could take place is amongst non-members (sometimes referred to as 'free riders', of whom there are 3.3 million) in already unionised workplaces where there is recognition (Metcalf 2005). Some young workers in supermarkets are amongst this category of non-members. These young people may be easier to recruit in these workplaces because there should be union representatives who know who the non-members are, and where a continuing persuasion to join may elicit results.

The research for this chapter also investigated the different employment relations environments created within the workplace by the union, in this case the Union of Shop, Distributive and Allied Workers (USDAW), through following the contrasting renewal strategies of either partnership or organising. In general, the organising stewards created a workplace environment where membership was 'the norm' and where the problems at work were largely attributed to the employer. Under the partnership approach, the problems at work were less likely to be attributed to the employer and a more consensus-oriented approach was utilised. The emphasis on recruitment within organising would seem to lend itself to membership growth more easily than the lesser impetus behind the consensus approach of partnership. According to USDAW (2006), 20% of all young workers work in retail, reflecting the recent expansion of employment in a growing sector and, therefore, a potential growth area for recruitment amongst young people.

This chapter is organised in four sections: the first section examines the extant literature concerning union renewal and more specifically the role and impact of young people within that process, and the second is concerned with the research methods deployed. The third section details the findings of the research and the last discusses the results and draws some conclusions.

Partnership and organising

As Heery (2002) has argued, partnership and organising can coexist in the *realpolitik* of labour unionism. Labour–management cooperation strategies under different guises have historical precedents but not necessarily any degree of longevity, indicating that current partnership practices are not necessarily new in terms of accommodation with the employer (Gospel 2004). According to Stuart and Martinez Lucio (2005: 1), 'Partnership represents an attempt to shift the culture of employment relations away from zero-sum and adversarial relationships' whereby partnership with the employer is 'a defining feature of the new industrial relations settlement for the millennium'. Currently, it is actively supported and promoted through funding and policy by the 'new' Labour government and some employers in both public and private spheres as well as the TUC as a way to conduct 'better' employment relations at the workplace (Undy 1999). What labour–management partnership manifestly entails is imprecise, as are its implications, for these can change with circumstance, and are usually dependent on the union, employer and sector involved (Badigannavar and Kelly 2004). Overall, from a union perspective partnership offers some prospects for renewal in that it allows a presence at the workplace which may other-wise not be tolerated and it offers scope for action in that it is a vehicle to support and operationalise a broadening of the scope of union par-ticipation in management decision-making (Haynes and Allen 2000). The six principles of partnership according to the TUC (2001) that should be adhered to when signing a partnership agreement are: (i) the quality of working life; (ii) employment security; (iii) transparency of actions from management; (iv) recognition of the legitimacy of differ-ent management and union interests; (v) a shared commitment to the success of the organisation; and (vi) the idea of mutual gains. There are both advocates (Ackers and Payne 1998; Brown 2000; Brown and Oxenbridge 2002) and detractors (Danford *et al.* 2005; Gall 2008; Kelly 1996; Taylor and Ramsay 1998) concerning the effectiveness of partner-ship with the employer, both in terms of the regulation of the employ-ment relationship and also as a union renewal strategy. Examples of organisations following the formal employer and union partnership approach are Tesco, Blue Circle Cement, parts of the NHS and the civil service (Badigannavar and Kelly 2004). It is worth noting that these agreements have no legal status and can, therefore, be reneged upon by either party at any time.

Martinez Lucio and Stuart (2005) and Danford *et al.* (2005) consid-ered that the current debates around partnership as a renewal strategy in the terms in which it has been constructed, that is, one of binaries advocating moderation (partnership) as opposed to militancy (organis-ing) or based solely around the TUC principles. They found this to be problematic and advocated a broadening of the issues into looking at how partnership is constituted within the political economy and soci-ology of workplace relations. Martinez Lucio and Stuart (2005: 800) indicated that union policy regarding partnership in reality 'emerges from the way in which trade unionists perceive the actions, intentions and trajectories of management and employers'. They conceptualised three different types of partnership: nurturing, transitional and coer-cive. They argued that the tendency in Britain, due to the lack of wider institutional support, was for partnership agreements to be of either a transitional or a coercive nature, and that, in order to work effectively, both parties to partnership agreements need to build a relationship built on trust. By using a study of MSF (Manufacturing, Science and Finance union) partnership strategies in a variety of workplaces and by investigating both political and workplace-based activities, Martinez Lucio and Stuart (2005) identified a number of generalisable issues that are problematic for unions when undertaking partnership as a renewal strategy. The independence of the union was a concern in a partnership setting, with the 'cost' being high on the union side in terms of the purpose and scope of its activities. Partnership as a union renewal strategy may have a place in terms of generating new members, through the employer's consent to union presence, but it remains problematic for union independence and union effectiveness. There are also problems with the amount of influence workers can have on the wider renewal project within partnership environments due to the constraints inherent in their nature, for example, the limits around negotiating processes in terms of the role of shop stewards and the content of their bargaining agendas.

The organising model has been defined as involving a process of organising workers so that they are empowered to define and pursue their own interests through the medium of collective organisation (Heery *et al.* 2000). This is achieved through a union-building approach to membership growth in which the union fosters activism, leadership and organisation amongst workers, which should provide the nucleus around which recruitment can occur. Organising comes as a suitable strategy in response to the intensification of work, lack of job security, growing inequality and a move away from Keynesian economic policies and the idea of a welfare state from 'cradle to grave'. According to Kelly (1996), the appropriate response to this strategy is to adopt a more militant approach and organise aggressively in order to extend union benefits to unorganised workers and, crucially, to enable unionised workers to become more participative in their unions at work. Organising as a renewal strategy predominantly emerged as a response to union decline and a 'race to the bottom' for employment conditions under neoliberalism (see Bronfenbrenner 2003).

In Britain, the key response of the union movement, as represented by the TUC, was to establish the Organising Academy in 1998 as a lead body to disseminate 'organising' amongst affiliates. Yet recruiting activists from within the workplace can still be more difficult than it used to be, for previously the people most likely to become active were 'organically connected to vibrant working class communities in industrial towns and cities' and, therefore, came with an embedded sense and knowledge of collective consciousness (Wills 2005: 140). The modern workforce is likely to be drawn from a wider group of people whose roots are not in the same community as their workplace; hence the case for indirect recruitment, away from the workplace, as means to connect with these worker (Wills 2002a). Moreover, the context for organising is still difficult, in that unions need to recruit something in the order of 0.5 million per year just to maintain current density levels (Heery *et al.* 2000). So organising as an approach to revitalise trade unions has made some inroads into the 'easier' areas and contexts for renewal but is only achieving modest aims overall, and in some contexts there do not appear to be any other ways forward in terms of either increased government support or changes to recognition law to make it easier to expand union membership (Gall 2007, 2009b; Metcalf 2005; Yates 2002).

Young people and unions

Since the 1980s, density amongst young people has declined from 45% in 1989 to 20% in 1998 and only 10% in 2004 (Pascual and Waddington 2000). In 2007, density for 16–24-year-olds was 9.2% (BERR 2008). Density amongst younger workers is considerably lower than that for older workers (Haynes *et al.* 2005), with two key factors seemingly explaining the relative difference and the low density for young people. Thus, turnover amongst young workers is high and the sectors within which they work are less inclined to be well unionised or unionised at all (see below). Young people, according to Beck (1992), Giddens (1990), Phelps Brown (1990) and Alvin and Sverke (2000), have a more individualised notion of their relationship with their own work, employers, politics and society in general as opposed to a collectivist attitude more typical of older workers. However, Haynes *et al.* (2005) and Gomez *et al.* (2002) rejected this, for their findings indicated that young people had a favourable attitude towards unions – it was just that they often worked in places where unions were not present and they showed a tendency to move from job to job when they were unhappy at their workplaces. It should also be noted that young people are not a homogenous group and, thus, should not necessarily be considered as having automatically shared interests or experience of employment (Kahmann 2002). Consequently, union campaigns to target young people specifically can run the risk of missing their target. The single most important predictor of whether a young person will join a union is union recognition in his or her place of work (Payne 1989). There is evidence also that young people actually want unions to pursue traditional issues on their behalf, namely, better terms and conditions rather than the other specific policies only aimed at young people (Kahmann 2002). Evidence also indicates that young union members are more likely to have had union-active parents and that, for young people in particular, peers and colleagues are more important influences than family (Kahmann 2002). Another hurdle for unions trying to encourage membership amongst young people is that financial cost of membership is an issue when weighed against perceived benefits which may or may not materialise at the workplace (Alvin and Sverke 2000).

There is debate about the exact ages (16–19 or 16–24) that qualify workers as young, and therefore as young union members (Pascual and Waddington 2000). According to the TUC (2004), some 4.5 million young people are in the labour market, equating to 17% of the working population. Forty per cent of young people work in distribution, hotels and restaurants. The proportion of young people employed in these various sectors varies with their age even within the definition of young people. For example, 64% of 16-year-olds work in distribution, hotels and restaurants, but by the time they are 25 years old that figure drops to 19%. In the public sector, the figures go from 5% at 16 to 26% by the time they are 25 years old, with similar changes reflected in the figures for the banking, finance and insurance sector (TUC 2004). Nationally, only one worker in ten is a union member among young people, and if they are part-time the density figure drops to 5%.

Kahmann (2002) argued that young people must be allowed to have a real impact on unions through participative structures that contain 'new autonomies' and less paternalistic behaviour. Young union activists are fairly scarce and, as Payne (1989: 126) pointed out, there is also a difference in that young men, either full- or part-time, are more likely to be active than all young women, regardless of the type of employment contract. Frege (2000) indicated that a move towards unions transforming themselves into more of a social movement model may attract young people, but this is unlikely to be achieved in the near future. The DTI Consultation report (2007) on workplace representatives also suggested that young people may be attracted to unions and participating in union activities through an emphasis on policies concerning equality and the environment. In this respect, there is a greater prospect of such change. In terms of other research findings, Blanden and Machin (2003) and Gomez et al. (2002) argued that for young people the social capital they bring to the workplace in the form of the views of other family members and their peer group is influential in how they relate to unions. This affects the subsequent likelihood of union joining and participation. Thus, Hartley (1992: 178) suggested: 'the group climate is significant for young people as they are socialised into the workplace'.

But, just as importantly, the relationship between young people and any political institutions, unions included, has suffered from an alienation which 'may point to the dissolution of certain sociocultural milieus as well as the exhaustion of a traditional political discourse' (Kahmann 2002: 33). Indeed, as Fernie (2005: 16) observed: 'It takes a certain type of individual to get excited by the terms "regional council" and "composite motion" and these sorts of leisure activity certainly cannot compete with a night in with the play station.' Pascual and Waddington (2000: 24) have categorised the reasons already cited by a range of other authors for the decline in membership amongst young people: attitudinal (comprising notions of individualism and union instrumentality); union-specific (refers to union structures and processes and issues of trust for young people in union officials); and structural (consisting of location of employment for young people, lack of union recognition in those workplaces and more educated young people from higher education needing a different form of union representation from manual workers). They also provided four factors inclining young people not to join unions: lack of knowledge of what unions are and what they do; many young people working in small, independently owned enterprises; young people may have a poor and negative image of unions predominantly acquired from watching television, where unions are seen as conflict generators; and young people, more than other, older workers, having more insecure, temporary, casualised jobs with greater inter-job and inter-employer mobility. Visser (2002: 416) also suggested that if young people do not join the union in their first few years of working life then they are unlikely to do so thereafter.

In responding to these issues, unions have pursued a variety of policies, from trying to change their image by promoting themselves through education programmes in schools and universities and also at music festivals to having specific agendas to attract young people in terms of addressing issues specific to them such as the minimum wage rate, and by reforming their structure so that there is less emphasis on the hierarchical procedures and dull meeting formats and more of a structure that encourages both membership and participation, for example, youth sections, forums and committees (Pascual and Waddington 2000). In Canada, the UFCW union has been successful in encouraging young people to become active in their union through a long-term grassroots-focused campaign, in terms of education and involvement, supported by union structures both financially and ideologically (Liu and O'Halloran 2006). And Kahmann (2002: 34) concluded: 'There are no signs that a lost generation may be succeeded by an upsurge in membership without any substantial organisational and political changes' such as those exemplified by the UFCW. Currently, the organising of young people takes place within the overall setting of a wider employment relations structure in the retail sector, which has experienced a degree of change within the last 20 years.

Employment relations in retail

Up until 1988, multi-employer bargaining had been the norm in supermarkets with the exception of Sainsbury's and Marks and Spencer. In 1988, Tesco decided to negotiate individually with USDAW, which precipitated the decentralisation of bargaining across the retail sector (Jackson *et al.* 1991). For ten years, Tesco and USDAW negotiated around 'the Retail Agreement', but dissatisfaction on both sides eventually led to the signing of a partnership agreement in 1998 (Haynes and Allen 2000). The partnership agreement specifically omits negotiation of pay with the union. The agreement has been subject to some changes in recent years but remains predominantly as it was originally drawn up. Sainsbury and USDAW signed an improved national agreement called 'Getting it Right' in 2002, which also allows only minimal union influence in pay negotiations. USDAW is the predominant union representing workers in the supermarket sector and currently has 389,000 members. It sits on the right of the political spectrum and has strong links to the Labour Party. Recruitment for USDAW is an important and constant priority as there is a high turnover of staff in retail (Upchurch and Donnelly 1992). It has a pragmatic approach to gaining new members and pursues both an organising and a partnership approach dependent on the employer concerned. USDAW has had its own Organising Academy based on the TUC model since 2002, and by November 2008 hoped to have trained 110 new organisers.

A further context in which the USDAW case studies operate is that of the regional dimension. In 2007, in the private sector union density was 21.5% in north-west England, 12.5% in south-east England and 14.5% in south-west England, where the research was undertaken (BERR 2008). In terms of the sector, union density in the regions was 15.4%, 8.5% and 11.6% respectively (BERR 2008). In terms of union density amongst young people (16–24-year-olds), the figures were 13.7%, 7.0% and 8.4% respectively (BERR 2008).

Research questions and methods

The most salient research questions arising from the extant literatures are: why do some young people decide to join unions at all; what are the strongest influences on that decision; do they then participate to the same degree as their older colleagues in union activities; and what is the impact of the different union renewal strategies at the workplace on young people and their interaction with unions? The research sites to examine these questions were located in the private service sector. Union density in the private sector overall is low at around 16% (BERR 2008) and these research sites, thus, provide a good indicator of how young people and unions within unionised workplaces relate to each other and what prospects there are for revitalisation of the union movement from the perspective of young grassroots members and 'never' members. A key methodological research task was to elicit responses from the young workers themselves, thereby providing a worker perspective on the issues concerned as opposed to a view articulated by union officials. The research sites were in two local branches of two different high street supermarkets. Both supermarkets were unionised and represented by USDAW and both employed a high percentage of young people. USDAW used a partnership strategy with one employer and an organising strategy with the other. The respondents were asked to complete a questionnaire at their place of work which explored their attitudes to unions, whether they were members or not. Young people also contributed to focus groups and added comments on their questionnaires. Some 122 young people took part in the research and 80% were classed as unskilled workers.

Research findings

The findings showed that overall density was 47% among young people, 78% of whom had permanent jobs, either full- or part-time. In the partnership setting, 29% of young workers were union members, compared with 65% in the organising setting. The most important reason given for joining was the same as for older people, namely, for protection at work. This supports previous findings that young people will join unions in a supportive environment and that their reasons for joining – protection at work and the improvement of pay and conditions – are similar to those of the rest of the workforce (Gomez *et al.* 2002; Haynes *et al.* 2005). One of the most important considerations for young part-time workers in deciding whether to join the union was cost. In the organising setting, where the hourly rate of pay was lower than in the partnership environment, 42% of non-members cited cost as a reason for not joining. In the partnership setting it was 20%. In terms of member participation, 44% of respondents participated in union affairs at their workplaces to a greater or lesser extent. This ranged from 46% reading the union newsletter to 9% voting in union elections and 12% who regularly visited the USDAW website. At the Tesco store, 42% of the workers were between the ages of 16 and 26, while at Sainsbury the percentage of workers in this age category was 48%. The types of contract that young workers (see Table 14.1) have will now be examined alongside length of service, for both of these factors could be influential on the likelihood of young workers to join and participate.

Thus, nearly 80% had permanent jobs with one-fifth having temporary contracts. The level of temporary contracts amongst young workers was a much higher percentage than for other age groups in the two workplaces. The percentage of young, full-time, permanent employees at nearly 40% is also surprisingly high, indicating that for many young people this is their main employment and not undertaken alongside other activities. The majority of young workers, perhaps unsurprisingly, had less than two years' service. Ninety-four per cent of these young workers had no dependent children, but 6% had a variety of caring responsibilities, including children. In terms of union revitalisation, a crucial measurement was how many of these young workers became members and whether there were any differences between the two strategies used *vis-à-vis* increased activity and participation. Both workplaces have the common baseline of being unionised and recognised.

Alongside the average density being 47% for young workers (which is much higher than the national economy average), 45% also had never

Table 14.1   Contract type and length of service for young workers

Which of the following best describes your current employment contract and how many years have you been with your current employer?

Full-time, permanent	39%
Part-time, permanent	39%
Temporary, full-/part-time	22%
< 2 years' service	63%
2–5 years' service	31%
5–10 years' service	6%

Source: Author's research.

been members. This was a higher percentage than in any other age group. The most significant difference in terms of young people joining unions in this research, as shown in Table 14.2, is the difference between membership rates under partnership (29%) and under organising (65%). This would seem to indicate that the strategy employed at the workplace is critical in determining whether young people join unions or not. The membership of workers over the age of 50 is also of interest and reflects a previously strong workplace union culture and an enduring relationship with a union over a working lifetime. This again emphasises the importance of joining a union when young as membership is likely to continue.

Why young people chose to join the union at their workplaces will now be examined (see Table 14.3). The most important reason for joining the union was for protection at work, as it is with other age groups. Thirty-five per cent joined because it was encouraged by the employer, this being three times higher than for any other age group. Twenty-three per cent (compared with 18% for all workers) joined as a result of encouragement by shop stewards or colleagues, and, taken in tandem with the lower percentage of joining because of belief in unions, this suggests their positive knowledge and positive experience of unions were low. This was reflected in a comment from one of the shop stewards who often conducted inductions. She reported:

> *I mean the first thing I do is ask 'who knows what unions do?' and nine times out of ten you'll probably get, out of twelve people, three or four that actually look like they know what you're talking about. All the rest is completely blank faces. And I literally run through briefly what we do, what we're here for.*

This finding (employer inducement and lack of awareness) also supports arguments from those arguing that more partnership between

Table 14.2 Union membership by age

Status	Tesco/Partnership (%)	Sainsbury/Organising (%)
All ages	50	67
All ages, never been member	40	24
16–26 years of age	29	65
16–26, never been member	64	28
>50	71	72

Source: Author's research.

Table 14.3 Joining a union – young people

Why did you join the union?	16–26-year-olds (%)	Average for all other age groups (%)	Partnership 16–26 years old (%)	Organising 16–26 years old (%)
For protection at work	59	72	54	60
Encouraged by the employer	35	10	50	20
Best way of improving pay and conditions	29	45	13	33
Believe in union principles	22	38	9	27
Encouraged to join by the shop steward	23	18	9	35
For fringe benefits like cheap insurance	2	5	4	0
Encouraged to join by colleagues	12	5	9	15

Note: Multiple responses possible.
Source: Author's research.

employers and unions at the workplace will encourage the joining and subsequent participation of more young people in roles as union representatives (see, for example DTI 2007: 22). The evidence was that, although the partnership environment was supportive of union joining, the organising environment elicited more members and, therefore, the likelihood of developing activists was increased due to a larger pool of young people being exposed to active union processes at work. In terms of other personalised influences, 25% of young respondents had other family members who were also union members and 6% had a shop steward in their close family.

In terms of union participation at the workplace, only 4% of young people fully participated as opposed to 19% of 26–50-year-olds and 25% of the over-fifties (and see Table 14.4). Participation was self-defined in terms of the degree to which they engaged with the union and its activities at the workplace. Fifty-six per cent of young people did not participate at all in union activities, as opposed to 34% of 26–50-year-olds and 26% of the over-fifties. However, the impact of the type of renewal strategy pursued by the union arguably had an impact on participation rates. If all the participation categories of response are taken together for partnership and organising, then it can be shown that under the partnership arrangement only 23% of young members

Table 14.4 Union participation of young people

How much do you participate at your workplace?	All members (%)	Young members (%)	Young members (partnership) (%)	Young members (organising) (%)
Not participate at all	34	56	77	51
Sometimes on a random basis	21	22	14	28
Only when there are important issues at work	21	13	9	10
When asked to by the shop steward	5	4	0	8
Fully participate	19	4	0	3

Source: Author's research.

took part but under the organising agenda that figure was 49%. Thus, organising offered a more promising strategy for engaging young people in union activities at the workplace. This is because they can see that participating in union activities can make a positive difference to their workplaces.

Those who choose not to join USDAW will now be assessed (see Table 14.5). As has been previously intimated, this group may provide important indicators for developing future renewal strategies, for analysis of their responses may contribute to finding out why so many young workers choose not to join even in unionised workplaces.

Not being asked to join a union is often given as the most popular reason for not joining (TUC 1989). For example, Kerr (1992: 43) cited that this was the case for 39% of non-members while Cregan and Johnson (1990: 90) found that this was the case for 40% of non-members. In the two supermarkets, 32% overall were not current members (although a small percentage had previously been members). The percentage of non-members was higher at 46% amongst young people and higher still under the partnership agenda. The comparison is that in the organising setting 28% of young people had never been union members and under partnership the figure was 64%. The largest single reason for not joining was cited as being because they did not see themselves as 'union' people. This needs unpacking as to the reasons why they feel this way, particularly as the idea of feeling negative towards unions as a result of being 'Thatcher's children' has been largely dismissed (Gomez *et al.* 2002; Haynes *et al.* 2005). It may be attributed to the fact that they did not see themselves as being able to 'fit' in with the identity that many

Table 14.5   Non-members/young workers renewal strategy

If not a union member, why is this?	Young workers (%)	Young workers (partnership) (%)	Young workers (organising) (%)	All non-members (%)
Do not see myself as a union person	49	54	45	44
Prefer to negotiate my terms and conditions individually	26	17	37	29
Unions are ineffective at the workplace	10	14	5	19
Costs too much	31	20	42	31
Gain the collectively negotiated benefits anyway	9	6	5	19
Employer may see me as being a troublemaker	5	3	0	9

Source: Author's research.

young people felt characterised union membership, that is, being male and working in manufacturing.

For the young workers, many of whom are part-timers, cost is an important factor in their consideration, particularly for those working in the organising environment. This is because the wage differential with the minimum wage in the organising environment for young people is lower than in the partnership environment. For those under 18 years of age, the pay rates were £4.14 (organising) and £4.62 (partnership), and for those over 18 but under 26 years of age it was £5.55 (organising) and £6.02 (partnership). There was also evidence that many young people felt that they could negotiate a better deal with the employer for themselves as compared with through the union. This may reflect an attitude of individualisation in terms of the employment contract amongst young people, as opposed to a more collectivist view held by many older workers, who have predominantly experienced their early employment in a different political and economic context. This view held by young people was at least partially formed because they saw the union as being weak in terms of negotiating the most important parts of their employment contract, and in many cases they were unsure of the processes and structures used to come to an agreement with the employer. A quote from a young respondent illustrates some of these issues as follows: 'the trade union is partially owned by Tesco's; they aren't independent and offer no protection or valid help'. The findings here have significance in their own right for Visser (2002) found that union joining and subsequent activity are more likely to happen and persist if they are undertaken in the early stages of an employee's working life. There was also evidence amongst this sample of young workers that there were a number of 'free riders', which may indicate that as long as they were in unionised workplaces they would continue with these attitudes (although the percentage was higher when averaged out across all age groups).

Discussion and conclusions

In the two research sites, the organising strategy was shown to be more effective than the partnership strategy in terms of encouraging young people to both join and participate in union affairs in the workplace. The strongest influence in the organising environment was the shop steward. In the partnership environment, the strongest influence on union joining was the employer. The fact that membership was encouraged by the employer was significantly more influential in encouraging young people, particularly in the partnership setting (50%), to join than other, older workers (10%). Young people were found to be no different from their older workplace colleagues in their motivations for joining, with the most popular reason cited as 'protection at work'. This finding also confirms other research which found that young people do not always have separate issues at the workplace but actually share many of the wider concerns of the workforce and, therefore, special recruitment campaigns organised centrally by the parent union aimed at potential young members may miss their intended targets. The cost of belonging to a union was a significant reason cited by young people for non-membership (Alvin and Sverke 2000) alongside not seeing themselves as being a 'union person'.

The research for this chapter found that the type of renewal strategy impacts on the likelihood of young people joining the union in their workplace. In general, organising elicits a more positive response to both union joining and subsequent activity than partnership, representing a more positive model for renewal (see Bronfenbrenner 2003). Young people would seem to willingly participate in union activities at the workplace if encouraged and if they are 'allowed' to. This is provided they feel that their contribution can make a difference (see Kahmann 2002). Passivity of participation in the partnership setting confirms other findings (Danford *et al.* 2005). The organising strategy has had limited gains but looks as if it is the best policy at present (see Gall 2007). Supermarkets could be an important site for illustrating how young people and their relationship with unions currently stand, in that the percentage of young people's employment that is dependent up on the retail sector is higher than it is for other sectors of the economy, and where coupled with an existing union presence – a crucial determinant in union joining (Payne 1989).

In terms of looking forward to the future of the union movement, the lack of young activists – as identified in this research – is a cause for concern. It takes years to move from being a union member to becoming an activist, particularly in workplaces where the local shop stewards have long tenure and are generally perceived by the membership to be doing a 'good job' and to be 'experts' in what they do. This research indicated that, although young people were joining the union particularly in the organising environment, moving them forward to becoming active participants is at present a few steps further away. In order for this to happen, education of members, including young members, in the role and the purpose of the union at their workplace and as a movement for wider social change needs to be undertaken. It needs to become an urgent priority, especially in already unionised workplaces, for unions to feel more assured of an optimistic future and for young people to feel that they can play a part in that potential resurgence.

References

Abbott, B. (2004) 'Worker representation through the Citizens' Advice Bureaux', in Healy, G., Heery, E., Taylor, P. and Brown, W. (eds) *The Future of Worker Representation*, Routledge, London, pp. 245–63.

Ackers, P. and Payne, J. (1998) 'British trade unions and social partnership: Rhetoric, reality and strategy', *International Journal of Human Resource Management*, 9/3: 529–50.

Acuff, S. (2006) 'The AFL-CIO union movement: Strategy and vision to build worker power' (blog.aflcio.org/2006/09/01).

AFL-CIO (2005) *Executive Council Report 2005*, Twenty-Fifth Constitutional Convention, AFL-CIO, Washington DC.

Alarcón, R. (2000) 'Skilled immigrants and cerebreros: Foreign-born engineers and scientists in the high-technology industry of Silicon Valley', in Foner, N., Rumbaut, R. and Gold, S. (eds) *Immigration Research for a New Century: multidisciplinary perspectives*, New York: Russell Sage Foundation, pp. 301–21.

Allen, K. (2000) *The Celtic Tiger: the myth of social partnership*, Manchester: Manchester University Press.

Allen, S. (1988) 'Declining unionization in construction: The facts and the reasons', *Industrial and Labor Relations Review*, 41/3: 343–59.

Alvin, M. and Sverke, M. (2000) 'Do new generations imply the end of solidarity? Swedish unionism in the era of individualisation', *Economic and Industrial Democracy*, 21/4: 71–95.

American Rights at Work (2008) 'Why can't 60 million Americans get what they want?' April 10 (www.americanrightsatwork.org).

Amicus@Honda Newsletter (2005) 'Breakthrough in weekday overtime dispute', Issue 8.

AMIEU (WA) (2003) 'Statement on Live Shipping' (www.wa.amieu.asn.au).

An Bord Glas (2002) *Horticultural Labour Force Review*, unpublished report, Dublin.

Archer, M. (2003) *Structure, Agency and the Internal Conversation*, Cambridge: Cambridge University Press.

Baccaro, L., Hamann, K. and Turner, L. (2003) 'The politics of labour movement revitalization: The need for a revitalized perspective', *European Journal of Industrial Relations*, 9/1: 119–33.

Bacon, N. and Blyton, P. (2000) 'Industrial relations and the diffusion of teamworking', *International Journal of Operations and Production Management*, 20/8: 911–31.

Bacon, N. and Blyton, P. (2004) 'Trade union responses to workplace restructuring: Exploring union orientations and actions', *Work, Employment and Society*, 18/4: 749–73.

Bacon, N., Blyton, P. and Morris, J. (1996) 'Among the ashes: Trade union strategies in the UK and German steel industries', *British Journal of Industrial Relations*, 34/1: 25–50.

Badigannavar, V. and Kelly, J. (2004) 'Labour-management partnership in the UK public sector', in Kelly, J. and Willman, P. (eds) *Union Organisation and Activity: the future of trade unions in Britain*, London: Routledge, pp. 110–26.

Bagguley, P. (1997) 'Beyond political sociology? Developments in the sociology of social movements', *Sociological Review*, 45/1: 147–61.

Barry, U. (2000) *Building the Picture: the role of data in achieving equality*, Dublin: Equality Authority.

Beck, U. (1992) *Risk Society: towards a new modernity*, London: Sage.

Beck, U. (1994) 'The reinvention of politics: Towards a theory of reflexive modernization', in Beck, U., Giddens, A. and Lash, S. (eds) *Reflexive Modernization: politics, tradition and aesthetics in the modern social order*, Cambridge: Polity Press, pp. 1–55.

Becker, C., Brudney, J., Cohen, C. and Flynn, J. (2006) 'Neutrality agreements take center stage at the National Labor Relations Board', *Labor Law Journal*, 57/2: 117–28.

Beguin, J. (2005) 'Industrial relations in the European steel industry', *EIROnline*, Dublin.

Behrens, M., Fichter, M. and Frege, C. (2003) 'Unions in Germany: Regaining the initiative?', *European Journal of Industrial Relations*, 9/1: 25–42.

Benz, D. (2002) 'Organizing to survive, bargaining to organize', *Working USA: The Journal of Labor and Society*, 6/1: 95–107.

Bernstein, I. (1960) *The Lean Years: a history of the American worker 1920–1933*, Baltimore, MD: Penguin Books.

BERR (2008) *Trade Union Membership 2007*, Department for Business, Enterprise and Regulatory Reform, London.

Beynon, H. and Wainwright, H. (1979) *The Workers' Report on Vickers*, London: Pluto Press.

Billewicz, J., Zapart, M. and Strycz, W. (2007) 'Unpublished group interview with the representatives of the Lower Silesia region of NSZZ Solidarność', 3 July.

Blanden, J. and Machin, S. (2003) 'Cross-generation correlations of union status for young people in Britain', *British Journal of Industrial Relations*, 41/3: 391–415.

Block, R. and Berg, P. (2009, forthcoming) 'Joint responsibility unionism: A multi-plant model of collective bargaining under employment security', *Industrial and Labor Relations Review*.

Blyton, P. and Turnbull, P. (2004) *The Dynamics of Employee Relations*, 3rd edn, Basingstoke: Macmillan.

Bohle, D. and Greskovits, B. (2007) 'Neoliberalism, embedded neoliberalism, and neocorporatism: Paths towards transnational capitalism in Central-Eastern Europe', *West European Politics*, 30/3: 443–66.

Borjas, G., Freeman, R. and Lawrence, K. (1996) 'Searching for the effects of immigration on the labour market', *NBER Working Papers*, No. 5454.

Bosch, G. and Charest, J. (2008) 'Vocational training and the labour market in liberal and coordinated economies', *Industrial Relations Journal*, 39/5: 428–47.

Bosch, G. and Weinkopf, C. (2008) 'Low-wage work in Germany: An overview', in Bosch, G. and Weinkopf, C. (eds) *Low-Wage Work in Germany*, New York: Russell Sage Foundation, pp. 19–112.

Bourdieu, P. (1990) *The Logic of Practice*, Stanford, CA: Stanford University Press.

Bouwman, T., Van de Camp, A. and Tom, T. (1994) *Net Werk: over werken in de automatisering* [Just work: On working in ICT], STZ advies & onderzoek, Amsterdam.

British Journal of Industrial Relations (2006) Special Edition on New Actors in Industrial Relations, 44/4: 601–756.

Brenner, M. (2008) 'SEIU reformers challenge union's direction at Puerto Rico convention', *Labor Notes*, 352: pp. 3, 10.

Bronfenbrenner, K. (2003) 'The American labour movement and the resurgence in union organizing', in Fairbrother, P. and Yates, C. (eds) *Trade Unions in Renewal: a comparative study*, London: Routledge, pp. 32–50.

Bronfenbrenner, K. (2007a) 'Race, gender, and the rebirth of trade unionism', *New Labor Forum*, 16/3–4: 142–8.

Bronfenbrenner, K. (ed.) (2007b) *Global Unions: challenging transnational capital through cross-border campaigns*, Ithaca, NY: ILR Press.

Bronfenbrenner, K. and Hickey, R. (2004) 'Changing to organize: A national assessment of union strategies', in Milkman, R. and Voss, K. (eds) *Rebuilding Labor: organizing and organizers in the new union movement*, Ithaca, NY: Cornell University Press, pp. 17–61.

Bronfenbrenner, K. and Juravich, T. (1998) 'It takes more than house calls: Organizing to win with a comprehensive union-building strategy', in Bronfenbrenner, K., Friedman, S., Hurd, R., Oswald, R. and Seeber, R. (eds) *Organising to Win: new research on union strategies*, Ithaca, NY: ILR Press, pp. 19–36.

Bronfenbrenner, K., Friedman, S., Hurt, R. W. and Oswald, R. A. (eds) (1998) *Organizing to Win: new research on union strategies*, Ithaca, NY: Cornell University Press.

Brown, W. (2000) 'Putting partnership into practice in Britain', *British Journal of Industrial Relations*, 38/2: 299–316.

Brown, W. and Oxenbridge, S. (2002) 'The two faces of partnership? An assessment of partnership and co-operative employer/trade union relationships', *Employee Relations*, 24/3: 262–76.

Brudney, J. (2005) 'Neutrality agreements and card check recognition: Prospects for changing paradigms', *Iowa Law Review*, 90: 819–86.

Brudney, J. (2007) 'Neutrality agreements and card check recognition: Prospect for changing labor relations paradigms', *Advance: The Journal of the ACS Issue Group*, 1: 11–31.

Burawoy, M. and Verdery, K. (1999) 'Introduction', in Burawoy, M. and Verdery, K. (eds) *Uncertain Transition: ethnographies of change in the post-socialist world*, Lanham, MD: Rowman & Littlefield Publishers, pp. 1–17.

Burchielli, R. and Bartram, R. (2007) 'What makes organising work? A model of the stages and facilitators of organising', Working Chapter, La Trobe University School of Business, Bundoora.

Buttigieg, D., Deery, S. and Iverson, R. (2007) 'Union mobilization: a consideration of the factors affecting the willingness of union members to take industrial action', *British Journal of Industrial Relations*, 46/2: 248–67.

Carter, B. (2006) 'Trade union organizing and renewal: a response to de Turberville', *Work, Employment and Society*, 20/2: 415–26.

Carter, B. and Cooper, R. (2002) 'The organizing model and the management of change: A comparative study of unions in Australia and Britain', *Relations Industrielles*, 57/4: 712–91.

Castles, S. (2002) 'Migration and community formation under conditions of globalization', *International Migration Review*, 36/4: 1143–68.

CCI (2001) *Economic Immigration: Survey*, MORI MRC/Chambers of Commerce of Ireland, Dublin.

Charlwood, A. (2002) 'Why do non-union employees want to unionise? Evidence from Britain', *British Journal of Industrial Relations*, 40/3: 463–91.

Charlwood, A. (2004) 'Influences on trade union organizing effectiveness in Britain', *British Journal of Industrial Relations*, 42/1: 69–93.

Churches, S. (1992) 'Aboriginal heritage in the wild west – Robert Bropho and the Swan Brewery site', *Aboriginal Law Bulletin*, 56/2: 9–10.

Clawson, D. (2003) *The Next Upsurge: labor and the new social movements*, Ithaca, NY: ILR Press.

CNA/NNOC (2008) 'About us' (www.calnurses.org).

Cobb-Clark, D. (1993) 'Immigrant selectivity and wages: The evidence for women', *American Economic Review*, 83/4: 986–93.

Cobble, D. (2001) 'Lost ways of unionism: historical perspectives on reinventing the labor movement' in Turner, L., Katz, H. and Hurd, R. (eds) *Rekindling the Movement: labor's quest for relevance in the 21st century*, Ithaca, NY: Cornell University Press, pp. 82–96.

Cockfield, S. and Lazaris, M. (2007) 'Building community support for union campaigns', in Buttigieg, D., Cockfield, S., Cooney, R., Jerrard, M. and Rainnie, A. (eds) *Trade Unions in the Community – Values, Issues, Shared Interests and Alliances*, Melbourne: Heidelberg Press, pp. 210–14.

Cockfield, S., Rainnie, A., Buttigieg, D. and Jerrard, M. (2009) 'Community unionism and union renewal: Building linkages between unions and community in Victoria, Australia', *Labor Studies Journal*, 34/4 (page numbers forthcoming).

Cohen, S. (2006) *Ramparts of Resistance: why workers lost their power, and how to get it back*, London: Pluto Press.

Cohen, S. (2008) 'The 1968–1974 labour upsurge in Britain and America: A critical history, and a look at what might have been', *Labor History*, 49/4: 395–416.

Cooper, R. (2001) 'Getting organised? A white collar union responds to membership crisis', *Journal of Industrial Relations*, 43/4: 422–37.

Cregan, C. and Johnson, S. (1990) 'An industrial approach to the free rider problem: Young people and trade union membership', *British Journal of Industrial Relations*, 28/2: 84–104.

Crosby, M. (2002) 'Next steps in union renewal', in Forbes-Mewett, H. and Griffin, G. (eds) *Unions 2002: future strategies for the union movement*, Monograph No. 15, National Key Centre in Industrial Relations, Monash University, Melbourne, pp. 127–46.

Crouch, C. (1982) *Trade Unions: the logic of collective action*, London: Fontana.

Croucher, R. and Cotton, E. (2009) *Global Unions, Global Business: global union federations and international business*, London: Middlesex University Press.

CSO (2007) *Principal Statistics*, Central Statistics Office of Ireland, Dublin.

CSO (2008a) *Quarterly National Household Survey: union membership Q2 2007*, CSO, Dublin.

CSO (2008b) *Quarterly National Household Survey Q2 2008*, CSO, Dublin.

D'Art, D. and Turner, T. (2003) 'Union recognition in Ireland: One step forward or two steps back?', *Industrial Relations Journal*, 34/3: 226–40.

Dail Debates (1971) Volume 253, Column 1943, 19 May.

Dail Debates (1990) Volume 397, Column 377, 15 March.

Danford, A., Richardson, M. and Upchurch, M. (2003) *New Unions, New Workplaces: a study of union resilience in the restructured workplace*, London: Routledge.

Danford, A., Richardson, M., Stewart, P., Tailby, S. and Upchurch, M. (2005) *Partnership and the High Performance Workplace*, Basingstoke: Palgrave.

de Turberville, S. (2004) 'Does the "organizing model" represent a credible union renewal strategy?', *Work, Employment and Society*, 18/4: 775–94.

de Turberville, S. (2007) 'Union organizing: A response to Carter', *Work, Employment and Society*, 21/3: 565–76.

Derwin, D. (2005) 'Solidarity not social partnership – why SIPTU should say no to another partnership deal' (irishsocialist.net/publications_against_social_partnership_siptu_member_des_derwin.html).

DETE (2003) *International Workers Statistics*, Department of Enterprise, Trade and Employment, Dublin.

DETE (2004) 'Tánaiste introduces new arrangements for spouses of skilled non-EEA nationals', press release, Department of Enterprise, Trade and Employment, Dublin.

DETE (2005) 'Statement by Minister Micheál Martin to Seanad Éireann in relation to Rights of Migrant Workers', press release, Department of Enterprise, Trade and Employment, Dublin.

DETE (2006) *Statistics and Company Listings for 2005*, Department of Enterprise, Trade and Employment, Dublin.

DETE (2007) *Statistics and Company Listings for 2006*, Department of Enterprise, Trade and Employment, Dublin.

DETE (2008) *International Workers*, Department of Enterprise, Trade and Employment, Dublin.

Dribbusch, H. (2003) *Gewerkschaftliche Mitgliedergewinnung im Dienstleistungssektor: ein Drei-laender-vergleich im Einzelhandel* [Union Organizing in the Service Sector: a three-country comparison in retail], Berlin: edition sigma.

Dribbusch, H., Bispinck, R., Van Klaveren, M. and Tijdens, K. (2007) *Exploring Collective Bargaining Coverage in Eight EU Member States*, Woliweb project, University of Amsterdam, Amsterdam.

DTI (2007) *Workplace Representatives: a review of their facilities and facility time*, London: DTI.

Dufour, C. and Hege, A. (2002) *L'Europe Syndicale au Quotidien: la representation des salaries dans les entreprises en France, Allemagne, Grande-Bretagne et Italie* [Everyday Unionism in Europe: the representation of workers in France, Germany, Great Britain and Italy], Brussels: Peter Lang.

Dundon, T. (2002) 'Employer hostility to union organising in the UK', *Industrial Relations Journal*, 33/3: 234–45.

Dundon, T., Gonzalez-Perez, M. and McDonough, T. (2007) 'Bitten by the Celtic Tiger: Immigrant workers and industrial relations in the new "glocalised" Ireland', *Economic and Industrial Democracy*, 28/4: 501–22.

Early, S. (2003) 'AFL-CIO's organizing summit looks at "best practices" – but leaves much unexamined', *Labor Notes*, 287: 7, 10.

Eaton, A. and Kriesky, J. (2001) 'Union organizing under neutrality and card check agreements', *Industrial and Labor Relations Review*, 55/1: 43–59.

EIRO (2003) 'Germany: Union membership continues to fall', Eironline, Dublin.

EIRO (2005a) 'Germany: Unions take new initiatives to tackle membership decline', Eironline, Dublin.

EIRO (2005b) 'Ireland: Union density declines to around a third', Eironline, Dublin.

EIRO (2006) 'Germany: Union membership decline slows down', Eironline, Dublin.

EIRO (2007a) 'Germany: Decline in union membership levels in 2006 less acute than in previous years', Eironline, Dublin.

EIRO (2007b) 'Ireland: Trade unions launch new membership recruitment drive', Eironline, Dublin.

EIRO (2008a) 'Germany: Trade union membership decline arrested in 2007', Eironline, Dublin.

EIRO (2008b) 'Ireland: Union develops new organising strategy for non-unionised companies', Eironline, Dublin.

EIRO (2008c) 'Ireland: Agreement seen as milestone for mushroom industry', *EIROnline*, Dublin.

EIRO (2008d) 'Ireland: Union strategies to recruit new groups of workers', *EIROnline*, Dublin.

European Commission (2001) *Social Protection in Europe*, Office of Official Publications of the European Communities, Luxembourg.

European Commission (2002) *Employment in Europe 2002*, European Commission DG for Employment and Social Affairs, Brussels.

European Commission (2005) *Employment in Europe*, Office of Official Publications of the European Communities, Luxembourg.

European Commission (2006) *Employment in Europe 2006*, European Commission DG for Employment and Social Affairs, Brussels.

European Commission (2007) *Statistical Annex of European Economy*, Office of Official Publications of European Commission, Luxembourg.

Eurostat (2005) *Europe in Figures: Eurostat Yearbook 2005*, Office of Official Publications of the European Communities, Luxembourg.

Fairbrother, P. (2000) *Trade Unions at the Crossroads*, London: Mansell.

Fairbrother, P. and Stewart, P. (2003) 'The dilemmas of social partnership and union organisation: Questions for British trade unions', in Fairbrother, P. and Yates, C. (eds) *Trade Unions in Renewal: a comparative study*, New York: Continuum Press, pp. 158–79.

Fawcett, J. (1989) 'Networks, linkages, and migration systems', *International Migration Review*, 23/3: 671–80.

Federal Mediation and Conciliation Service (2000, 2004) *Annual Report*, Washington DC: FMCS.

Fernie, S. (2005) 'The future of British unions – introduction and conclusions', in Fernie, S. and Metcalf, D. (eds) *Trade Unions: resurgence or demise?* London: Routledge, pp. 1–18.

Ferrarotti, F. (2002) *On the Science of Uncertainty: the biographical method in social research*, New York, Oxford: Lexington Books.

Findlay, P. and McKinlay, A. (2003) 'Organising in electronics: Recruitment, recognition and representation – shadow shop stewards in Scotland's "Silicon Glen" ', in Gall, G. (ed.) *Union Organising: campaigning for trade union recognition*, London: Routledge, pp. 114–32.

Fine, J. (2006) *Worker Centers: organizing communities at the edge of the dream,* Ithaca, NY: ILR Press.

Fine, J. (2007a) 'A marriage made in heaven? Mismatches and misunderstandings between worker centres and unions', *British Journal of Industrial Relations,* 45/2: 335–60.

Fine, J. (2007b) 'Why labor needs a plan b: Alternatives to conventional trade unionism', *New Labor Forum,* 16/2: 35–44.

Fink, L. (2003) *The Maya of Morganton: work and community in the Nuevo New South,* Chapel Hill, NC: University of North Carolina Press.

Fiorito, J. (2004) 'Union renewal and the organising model in the United Kingdom', *Labor Studies Journal,* 29/2: 21–53.

Fiorito, J. and Jarley, P. (2008) 'Why don't they organize?' Presented at the Labor and Employment Relations Association, New Orleans 2008.

Fiorito, J., Jarley, P. and Delaney J. (1995) 'National union effectiveness in organizing: Measures and influences', *Industrial and Labour Relations Review,* 48/4: 613–35.

Flanders, A. (1970) *Management and Unions: the theory and reform of industrial relations,* London: Faber.

Fletcher, B. and Gapasin, F. (2008) *Solidarity Divided: the crisis in organized labor and a new path toward social justice,* Berkeley, CA: University of California.

Fletcher, B. and Hurd, R. (1998) 'Beyond the organizing model: The transformation process in local unions', in Bronfenbrenner, K., Freidman, S., Hurd, R., Oswald, R. and Seeber, R. (eds) *Organizing to Win: new research on union strategies,* Ithaca, NY: Cornell University, pp. 37–53.

FMCS (2000, 2004) *Annual Report,* Federal Mediation and Conciliation Service, Washington DC.

FNV (1987) *FNV 2000 – voorstellen tot vernieuwing van de FNV* [FNV 2000 – Proposals for Renewing the FNV], Amsterdam: FNV.

FNV (2007) *The Dynamic Triangle – Sole Traders and the FNV,* Amsterdam: Labour Department FNV.

Foerster, A. (2001) 'Confronting the dilemmas of organizing: Obstacles and innovations at the AFL-CIO Organizing Institute', in Turner, L., Katz, H. and Hurd, R. (eds) *Rekindling the Movement: labor's quest for relevance in the 21st century,* Ithaca, NY: ILR Press, pp. 155–81.

Foner, N., Rumbaut, R. and Steven, J. (eds) (2000) *Immigration Research for a New Century: multidisciplinary perspective,* New York: Russell Sage Foundation.

Forrester, N. (2005) 'Learning for revival: British trade unions and workplace learning', *Studies in Continuing Education,* 27/3: 257–70.

Freeman, R. and Rogers, J. (2002) 'Open source unionism: Beyond exclusive collective bargaining', *Working USA: The Journal of Labor and Society,* 5/4: 8–40.

Freeman, R., Hartog, J. and Teulings, C. (1996) *Pulling the Plug: an analysis of the role of mandatory extension in the Dutch system of labour relations,* The Hague: OSA.

Frege, C. (2000) 'Das organisierungsmodell in den USA und seine bedeutung fur Deutsche gewerkschaften' ['The organising model in the USA and its meaning for German trade unions'], *Gewerkschaftliche Monatshefte,* 3: 140–9.

Frege, C. and Kelly, J. (2003) 'Union revitalisation strategies in comparative perspective', *European Journal of Industrial Relations,* 9/1: 7–24.

Frege, C. and Kelly, J. (eds) (2004) *Varieties of Unionism: strategies for union revitalisation in a globalizing economy,* Oxford: Oxford University Press.

Frege, C., Heery, E. and Turner, L. (2004) 'The new solidarity? Trade union coalition-building in five countries', in Frege, C. and Kelly, J. (eds) *Varieties of Unionism: strategies for union revitalization in a globalizing economy*, Oxford: Oxford University Press, pp. 137–58.

Gabriel, J. (2006) 'Organizing the jungle: Industrial restructuring and immigrant unionization in the American meatpacking industry', *Working USA: The Journal of Labor and Society*, 9/3: 337–59.

Gall, G. (ed.) (2003) *Union Organising: campaigning for trade union recognition*, London: Routledge.

Gall, G. (2004) 'Trade union recognition in Britain, 1995–2002: Turning a corner?', *Industrial Relations Journal*, 35/3: 249–70.

Gall, G. (2005) 'Union organising in the "new economy" in Britain', *Employee Relations*, 27/2: 208–25.

Gall, G. (2006a) 'Introduction: The fruits of labour', in G. Gall (ed.) *Union Recognition: organising and bargaining outcomes*, London: Routledge, pp. 1–25.

Gall, G. (ed.) (2006b) *Union Recognition: organizing and bargaining outcomes*, London: Routledge.

Gall, G. (2006c) *Sex Worker Union Organizing: an international study*, Basingstoke: Palgrave.

Gall, G. (2007) 'Trade union recognition in Britain: A crisis of union capacity?', *Economic and Industrial Democracy*, 28/1: 78–109.

Gall, G. (2008) *Labour Unionism in the Financial Services Sector: struggling for rights and representation*, Aldershot: Ashgate.

Gall, G. (ed.) (2009a) *Union Revitalisation in Advanced Economies – Assessing the Contribution of 'Union Organising'*, Basingstoke: Palgrave.

Gall, G. (2009b) 'What is to be done with "union organising"?', in Gall, G. (ed.) *Union Revitalisation in Advanced Economies – Assessing the Contribution of 'Union Organising'*, Basingstoke: Palgrave, pp. 1–16.

Gajewska, K. and Niesyto, J. (2009) 'Organising campaigns as "revitaliser" for trade unions? The example of the Lidl campaign', *Industrial Relations Journal*, 40/2: 156–71.

Gardawski, J. (1997) *Przyzwolenie ograniczone: robotnicy wobec rynku i demokracji* [Limited Consent: workers in the face of the market and democracy], Warsaw: Wydawnictwo Naukowe PWN.

Gardawski, J. (2001) *Związki zawodowe na rozdrożu* [Trade Unions at the Crossroads], Warsaw: Instytut Spraw Publicznych.

Gaus, M. (2008a) 'Workers win test of "card check" ruling', *Labor Notes* website, February 4 (www.labornotes.org).

Gaus, M. (2008b) 'Hotel workers rising campaign pays off in L.A.', *Labor Notes*, 352, July: 5.

Giddens, A. (1990) *The Consequences of Modernity*, Cambridge: Polity Press.

Glaser, B. (1978) *Theoretical Sensitivity: advances in the methodology of grounded theory*, Mill Valley, CA: Sociology Press.

Glaser, B. and Strauss, A. (1967) *The Discovery of Grounded Theory: strategies for qualitative research*, Chicago, IL: Aldine Publishing Company.

Goedhard, N. and Tijdens, K. (1993) *Beroepsbinding en vakbondsorientatie in de schoonmaak* [Occupational Bonds and Union Orientation in Cleaning], Amsterdam: Industriebond FNV.

Goldfield, M. (1987) *The Decline of Organized Labor in the United States*, Chicago, IL: University of Chicago Press.

Goldthorpe, J., Lockwood, D., Bechhofer, F. and Platt. J. (1968) *The Affluent Worker: industrial attitudes and behaviour*, Cambridge: Cambridge University Press.

Gomez, R., Gunderson, M. and Meltz, N. (2002) 'Comparing youth and adult desire for unionisation in Canada', *British Journal of Industrial Relations*, 40/3: 519–42.

Gonzalez-Perez, M., Dundon, T. and McDonough, T. (2008) 'Organising immigrants: State policy and union organising tactics in the Republic of Ireland', paper presented to International Labour Process Conference, Dublin.

Gospel, H. (2004) 'Markets, firms and unions: A historical-institutionalist perspective on the future of unions in Britain', in Fernie, S. and Metcalf, D. (eds) *Trade Unions: resurgence or demise?*, London: Routledge, pp. 19–45.

Graham, S. (2006) 'Organising out of decline – The rebuilding of the UK and Ireland shop stewards movement', Union Ideas Network (uin.org.uk/content/view/236/125/).

Greene, A., Black, J. and Ackers, P. (2000) 'The union makes us strong? A study of the dynamics of workplace union leadership at two UK manufacturing plants', *British Journal of Industrial Relations*, 38/1: 75–93.

Grünell, M. and Kaar, R. (2003) 'Migration and industrial relations', *EIROnline*, Dublin.

Guest, D. and Peccei, R. (1998) *The Partnership Company: benchmarks for the future*, London: IPA.

Gunnigle, P., Collins, D. and Morley, M. (2005) 'Hosting the multinational: Exploring the dynamics of industrial relations in US multinational subsidiaries', in Boucher, G. and Collins, G. (eds) *Working in Ireland*, Dublin: Liffey Press, pp. 125–44.

Gunnigle, P., Turner, T. and D'Art, D. (2002) 'Counterpoising collectivism: Performance related pay and industrial relations in greenfield sites', *Economic and Social Review*, 36: 565–80.

Gurak, D. and Caces, F. (1992) 'Migration networks and the shaping of migration systems', in Kritz, M., Lim, L. and Zlotnit, H. (eds) *International Migration Systems: a global approach*, Oxford: Clarendon Press, pp. 150–76.

Harcourt, M. and Lam, H. (2007) 'Union certification: A critical analysis and proposed alternatives', *Working USA: The Journal of Labor and Society*, 10/3: 327–45.

Hardiman, N. (1988) *Pay, Politics and Economic Performance in the Republic of Ireland*, Oxford: Clarendon Press.

Harteveld, L. (2006) 'Draagvlak vakbeweging' ['Support for trade union movement'], *Zeggenschap*, 17/4: 20–1.

Hartley, J. (1992) 'Joining a trade union', in Hartley, J. and Stephenson, G. (eds) *Employment Relations: the psychology of influence and control at work*, Oxford: Blackwell, pp. 163–83.

Haynes, P. and Allen, M. (2000) 'Partnership as union strategy: A preliminary evaluation', *Employee Relations*, 23/2: 164–87.

Haynes, P., Vowles, J. and Boxall, P. (2005) 'Explaining the younger-older worker union density gap: Evidence from New Zealand', *British Journal of Industrial Relations*, 43/1: 93–116.

Hecksher, C. and Carré, F. (2006) 'Strength in networks: Employment rights organisations and the problem of coordination', *British Journal of Industrial Relations*, 44/4: 605–28.

Heery, E. (2002) 'Partnership versus organizing: Alternative futures for British trade unionism', *Industrial Relations Journal*, 33/1: 20–35.

Heery, E. (2003) 'Gewerkschaftliche Strategien gegen die Mitgliederschwund' ['Union organizing in comparative perspective'], *WSI-Mitteilungen*, 56/9: 522–7.

Heery, E. and Simms, M. (2008) 'Constraints on union organizing in the United Kingdom', *Industrial Relations Journal*, 39/1: 24–42.

Heery, E., Delbridge, R., Simms, M., Salmon, J. and Simpson, D. (2003) 'Organising for renewal: A case study of the UK's Organising Academy', in Cornfield, D. and McCammon, H. (eds) *Labour Revitalization: global perspectives and new initiatives*, Oxford: Elsevier, pp. 79–110.

Heery, E., Simms, M., Simpson, D., Delbridge, R. and Salmon, J. (2000) 'Organising unionism comes to the UK', *Employee Relations*, 22/1: 38–57.

Hermanussen, R. (2008) 'Hotels: Industry restructuring and room attendants' jobs', in Salverda, W., van Klaveren, M. and Van der Meer, M. (eds) *Low-Wage Work in the Netherlands*, New York: Russell Sage Foundation, pp. 177–205.

Hernandez-Leon, R. and Zuñiga, V. (2000) 'Market carpet by the mile: The emergence of a Mexican immigrant community in an industrial region of the US historic South', *Social Science Quarterly*, 81/1: 49–66.

Hertog, J. and Mari, C. (1999) *Management of Change and Human Resources: transfer of learning in the European steel industry: final report*, Eurofer and Social Affairs Committee, Brussels.

Heyes, J. (2007) 'Training, social dialogue and collective bargaining in western Europe', *Economic and Industrial Democracy*, 28/2: 239–58.

Hirsch, B. and MacPherson, D. (2008a) *Union Membership and Coverage Database* (www.unionstats.com).

Hirsch, B. and MacPherson, D. (2008b) *Union Membership and Earnings Data Book*, Washington, DC: Bureau of National Affairs.

Hobsbawm, E. (1992) 'Introduction: Inventing traditions', in Hobsbawm, E. and Ranger, T. (eds) *The Invention of Tradition*, Cambridge: Cambridge University Press, pp. 1–14.

Holgate, J. and Simms, M. (2008) 'Is there an organising "model"? An empirical critique', paper presented at BUIRA conference, Bristol.

Hooiveld, J., Sprenger, W. and Van Rij, C. (2002) 'Twintig jaar na FNV 2000 (1)' ['Twenty years after FNV 2000 (1)'] *Zeggenschap*, 13/3: 34–40.

Huldi, C. (2002) 'Family obligations and the transition to working life: The influence of parenthood and family obligations on the transition to employment of university graduates', *Education and Training*, 44/4/5: 208–16.

Hurd, R. (1998) 'Contesting the dinosaur image: The labour movement's search for a future', *Labour Studies Journal*, 22/4: 5–31.

Hurd, R. (2004) 'The failure of organizing, the new unity partnership, and the future of the labor movement', *Working USA: The Journal of Labor and Society*, 8/3: 5–25.

Hurd, R. (2007) 'US Labor 2006: Strategic developments across the divide', *Journal of Labor Research*, 23/2: 313–25.

Hurd, R. (2008) 'Neutrality agreements: Innovative, controversial, and labor's hope for the future', *New Labor Forum*, 17/1: 35–45.

Hyman, R. (1999) 'Imagined solidarities: Can trade unions resist globalization?', in Leisink, P. (ed.) *Globalization and Labour Relations*, Cheltenham: Edward Elgar, pp. 94–115.

Hyman, R. (2001) *Understanding European Trade Unionism: between market, class and society*, London: Sage.

Hyman, R. (2007) 'How can trade unions act strategically?', *Transfer*, 13/1: 193–210.

International Labour Organisation (1992) *Recent Developments in the Iron and Steel Industry in Sectoral Activities Programme Report 1*, ILO, Geneva.

IOM (2006) *Migration facts and figures*, International Organization for Migration, Geneva.

Jackson, M., Leopold, J. and Tuck, K. (1991) 'Decentralisation of collective bargaining: the case of the retail food industry', *Human Resource Management Journal*, 2/2: 29–45.

Jarley, P. (2005) 'Unions as social capital: Renewal through a return to the logic of mutual aid?', *Labor Studies Journal*, 29/4: 1–26.

Jenkins, C. (1995) *The Politics of Social Protest*, Minneapolis, MN: University of Minnesota Press.

Jenkins, J. (1983) 'Resource mobilization theory and the study of social movements', *Annual Review of Sociology*, 9: 927–53.

Jerrard, M. (2000) '"Dinosaurs are not dead": The AMIEU (Qld) and industrial relations change', *Journal of Industrial Relations*, 42/1: 5–28.

Jerrard, M. (2007) 'Building alliances to protect jobs: The AMIEU's response to live animal export', in Buttigieg, D., Cockfield, S., Cooney, R., Jerrard, M. and Rainnie, A. (eds) *Trade Unions in the Community – Values, Issues, Shared Interests and Alliances*, Melbourne: Heidelberg Press, pp. 185–200.

Johnston, P. (2002) 'Citizenship movement unionism: For the defense of local communities in the global age', in Nissen, B. (ed.) *Unions in a Globalized Environment: changing borders, organizational boundaries, and social roles*, Armonk, NY: M.E. Sharpe.

Jordan, L. and Bruno, B. (2006) 'Does the organising means determine the bargaining ends', in Gall, G. (ed.) *Union Recognition: organising and bargaining outcomes*, London: Routledge, pp. 181–97.

Kahmann, M. (2002) *Trade Unions and Young People: challenges of the changing age composition of unions*, European Trade Union Institute, Brussels.

Kelly, J. (1996) 'Union militancy and social partnership', in Ackers, P., Smith, C. and Smith, P. (eds) *The New Workplace and Trade Unionism: critical perspectives on work and organisation*, London: Routledge, pp. 77–109.

Kelly, J. (1998) *Rethinking Industrial Relations: mobilization, collectivism and long waves*, London: Routledge.

Kerr, A. (1992) 'Why do public sector workers join unions? An attitude survey of workers in the health service and local government', *Employee Relations*, 14/2: 39–54.

Kersley, B., Alpin, C., Forth, J., Bryson, A., Bewley, H., Dix, G. and Oxenbridge, S. (2006) *Inside the Workplace: findings from the 2004 Workplace Employment Relations Survey*, London: Routledge.

Kirton, G. (2005) 'The influences on women joining and participating in unions', *Industrial Relations Journal*, 36/5: 386–401.

Kloosterboer, D. (2007) *Innovative Trade Union Strategies*, Amsterdam: FNV.

Kochan, T. and Osterman, P. (1994) *The Mutual Gains Enterprise: forging a winning partnership among labour, management and government*, Boston, MA: Harvard University Press.

Kozek, W. (2003) 'Destruktorzy: tendencyjny obraz związków zawodowych w tygodnikach politycznych w Polsce' [Destructors: the biased picture of trade unions in political magazines in Poland], in Kozek, W. (ed.) *Instytucjonalizacja stosunków pracy w Polsce* [Institutionalisation of Labour Relations in Poland], Warsaw: Wydawnictwo Naukowe Scholar, pp. 161–85.

Krings, T. (2007) ' "Equal rights for all workers": Irish trade unions and the challenge of labour migration', *Irish Journal of Sociology*, 6/1: 43–61.

Kritz, M., Lim, L and Zlotnit, H. (1992) (eds) *International Migration Systems: a global approach*, Oxford: Clarendon Press.

Kropiwiec, K. and King-O'Riain, R. (2006) *Polish Migrant Workers in Ireland: Polscy Migranci Pracujacy w Irlandil*, Community Profiles Series, NCCRI, Dublin.

Kurczewski, J. (2006) 'The social functions of Solidarity', *Polish Sociological Review*, 153/1: 111–27.

Lebowitz, M. (2003) *Beyond Capital*, 2nd edn, Basingstoke: Palgrave.

Lewin, D. (1986) 'Public employee unionism and labor relations in the 1980s: An analysis of transformation', in Lipset, S. (ed.) *Unions in Transition: entering the second century*, San Francisco, CA: ICS Press, pp. 251–64.

Lipsig-Mumme, C. (2003) 'Forms of solidarity: Trade unions and community unionism', ACTU Organising Centre (www.actu.asn.au/organising/news/1053579943_13456.html).

Liu, A. and O'Halloran, C. (2006) 'Mobilising young people: A case study of UFCW Canada youth programmes and initiatives', in Kumar, P. and Schenk, C. (eds) *Paths to Union Renewal: Canadian experiences*, Toronto: Broadview Press, pp. 191–200.

Lopez, S. (2004) *Reorganizing the Rust Belt: an inside study of the American labor movement*, Berkeley, CA: University of California Press.

Lustig, J. (2002) 'New leadership and its discontents', *Journal of Social Policy*, 33: 1–5 (www.csus.edu/org/cfa/Lustig1.htm).

Lyddon, D. and Darlington, R. (2001) *Glorious Summer: class struggle in Britain, 1972*, London: Bookmarks.

Mac Einrí, P. (2001) 'Immigration into Ireland: Trends, policy responses, outlook', Irish Centre for Migration Studies (NUIC) (migration.ucc.ie/irelandfirstreport.htm).

Majic, S. (2005) 'Live! Nude! ... organized workers? Examining the organizational efforts of sex workers in Las Vegas, Nevada', chapter presented to the Institute for Women's Policy Research's Eighth International Women's Policy Research Conference, Washington DC.

Martin, A. (2008) 'The institutional logic of union organizing and the effectiveness of social movement repertoires', *American Journal of Sociology* 113/4: 1067–1102.

Martinez Lucio, M. and Stuart, M. (2005) ' "Partnership" and new industrial relations in a risk society: An age of shot gun weddings and marriages of convenience?', *Work, Employment and Society*, 19/4: 797–817.

Mason, B. and Bain, P. (1993) 'The determinants of trade union membership in Britain: A survey of the literature', *Industrial and Labour Relations Review*, 46/2: 332–51.

Massey, D. (1999) 'International migration at the dawn of the twenty-first century: The role of the state', *Population and Development Review*, 25/2: 303–22.

Maurice, M., Sellier, F. and Silvestre, J. (1986) *The Social Foundations of Industrial Power: a comparison of France and Germany*, London: MIT Press.

McCarthy, N. (2009) 'Union organising in a recognised environment – a case study of mobilisation', in Gall, G. (ed.) *Union Revitalisation in Advanced Economies – Assessing the Contribution of 'Union Organising'*, Basingstoke: Palgrave, pp. 107–30.

Meardi, G. (1996) 'Trade union consciousness, east and west: A comparison of Fiat factories in Poland and Italy', *European Journal of Industrial Relations*, 2/3: 275–302.

Meardi, G. (2000) *Trade Union Activists, East and West: comparison in multinational companies*, Aldershot: Gower.

Meardi, G. (2007) 'More voice after more exit? Unstable industrial relations in Central and Eastern Europe', *Industrial Relations Journal*, 38/6: 503–23.

Meerman, M. and Huppes, G. (1993) *Werk aan de winkel* [Work to Be Done], Leyden: Wetenschapswinkel.

Metcalf, D. (2005) 'Trade Unions: Resurgence or perdition? An economic analysis', in Fernie, S. and Metcalf, D. (eds) *Trade Unions: resurgence or demise?* London: Routledge, pp. 83–117.

Meyer, D. and Cooke, W. (1993) 'US labour relations in transition: Emerging strategies and company performance', *British Journal of Industrial Relations*, 31/4: 531–52.

Milkman, R. (ed.) (2000) *Organizing Immigrants: the challenge for unions in contemporary California*, Ithaca, NY: Cornell University Press.

Milkman, R. and Voss, K. (eds) (2004) *Rebuilding Labor: organizing and organizers in the New Union Movement*, Ithaca, NY: Cornell University Press.

Milkman, R. and Wong, K. (2000) *Voces desde la lucha, la organización de trabajadores inmigrantes en Los Angeles*, Center for Labor Research and Education, Los Angeles.

Ministerie van Sociale Zaken en Werkgelegenheid (SZW) (2006) *Voorjaarsrapportage CAO-afspraken 2006* [Spring Report on Collective Agreements 2006], SZW, The Hague.

Mishel, L. and Walters, M. (2003) 'How unions help all workers', *Briefing Paper*, Economic Policy Institute, Washington, DC.

Moody, K. (1988) *An Injury to All: the decline of American unionism*, London: Verso.

Moody, K. (1997a) *Workers in a Lean World*, New York: Verso.

Moody, K. (1997b) 'Towards an international social-movement unionism', *New Left Review*, 225: 52–72.

Moody, K. (2007) *US Labor in Trouble and Transition: the failure of reform from above, the promise of revival from below*, London: Verso.

Mrozowicki, A. and van Hootegem, G. (2008) 'Unionism and workers' strategies in capitalist transformation: The Polish case reconsidered', *European Journal of Industrial Relations*, 14/2: 197–216.

Müller, T., Platzer, H-W. and Rüb, S. (2003) 'Globalisierung und gewerkschaftliche Internationalisierung – Zur Politik der Global Union Federations', *WSI Mitteilungen*, 11: 666–72.

Munck, R. (2002) *Globalisation and Labour: the new 'Great Transformation'*, London: Zed Books.

Munro, L. (2001) 'Caring about blood, flesh, and pain: Women's standing in the animal protection movement', *Society and Animals: Journal of Human-Animal Studies*, 9/1: 43–61.

Murray, G. and Waddington, J. (2005) 'Innovations for union renewal', *Transfer*, 4: 489–95.

National Education Association (NEA) (2006) 'Teachers unions merge in NY: NEA grows to largest union in U.S. history' 6 May 2006 (www.nea.org/newsreleases/2006).

National Mediation Board (2001, 2006) *Annual Performance Report*, Washington, DC.

Nelson, B. (2001) *Divided We Stand: American workers and the struggle for black equality*, Princeton, NJ: Princeton University Press.

NESDO (2006) *Migration Policy*, National Economic and Social Development Office, Dublin.

Ness, I. (2005) *Immigration, Unions, and the New US Labor Market*, Philadelphia, PA: Temple University Press.

Nissen, B. (2004) 'The effectiveness and limits of labor-community coalitions: Evidence from south Florida', *Labor Studies Journal*, 29/1: 67–89.

NLRB (1998–2006) *Annual Report of the NLRB*, Washington, DC.

NLRB (2000) *Dana/Metaldyne, Decisions of the National Labor Relations Board*, 351 NLRB No. 28, Washington, DC.

NMB (2001, 2006) *Annual Performance Report*, National Mediation Board, Washington.

Northrup, H. and Foster, H. (1975) *Open Shop Construction*, Philadelphia, PA: University of Pennsylvania Press.

O'Connell, P. J. and McGinnity, F. (2008) *Immigrants at Work: ethnicity and nationality in Irish labour market*, Equality Authority/Economic and Social Research Institute, Dublin.

Orozco, M. (2002) 'Globalization and migration: The impact of family remittances in Latin America', *Latin American Politics and Society*, 44/2: 41–66.

Ost, D. (2005) *The Defeat of Solidarity: anger and politics in postcommunist Europe*, Ithaca, NY: Cornell University Press.

Ost, D. (2006) 'After post-communism: Legacies and the future of unions in eastern Europe', in Phelan, C. (ed.) *The Future of Organised Labour*, London: Peter Lang, pp. 305–33.

Panitch, L. (1981) 'Trade unions and the state', *New Left Review*, 125: 21–43.

Pascual, A. and Waddington, J. (2000) *Young People: the labour market and trade unions*, Research Paper for the Youth Committee, ETUC, Brussels.

Payne, J. (1989) 'Trade union membership and activism among young people in Great Britain', *British Journal of Industrial Relations*, 27/1: 111–32.

PCS (2008) *National Organising Strategy*, PCS, London.

Penninx, R. and Roosbald, J. (2000) *Trade Unions, Immigration, and Immigrants in Europe: 1960–1993*, Oxford: Berghahn Books.

Pensions Board (2005) *National Pensions Review*, Pensions Board, Dublin.

Perkins, R. and Lovejoy, F. (2007) *Call Girls – Private Sex Workers in Australia*, University of Western Australia Press, Crawley, WA.

Perlman, S. (1928) *A Theory of the Labor Movement*, New York: Macmillan.

Peter D. Hart Research Associates (2005) *Labor Day 2005: the state of working America*, August, Washington DC.

Phelan, C. (2006) 'Worldwide trends and prospects for trade union revitalisation', in Phelan, C. (ed.) *Trade Union Revitalisation: trends and prospects in 34 countries*, London: Peter Lang, pp. 11–38.

Phelps-Brown, H. (1990) 'The counter revolution of our time', *Industrial Relations*, 29/1: 1–14.

Piore, M. (1994) 'Unions: A reorientation to survive', in Kerr, C. and Staudohar, P. (eds) *Labour Economic and Industrial Relations: markets and institutions*, Cambridge: Harvard University Press, pp. 514–29.

Pollert, A. (1999) *Transformation at Work in the New Market Economies of Central Eastern Europe*, London: Sage.

Pollert, A. (2003) 'Women, work and equal opportunities in post-communist transition', *Work Employment and Society*, 17/2: 331–57.

Portes, A. and Rumbaut, R. (1996) *Immigrant America: a portrait*, Berkeley, CA: University of California Press.

Portes, A. and Sensenbrenner, J. (1993) 'Embeddedness and immigration: Notes on the social determinants of economic action', *American Journal of Sociology*, 98/6: 1320–50.

Redman, T. and Snape, E. (2006) 'Industrial Relations climate and staff attitudes in the fire service: a case of union renewal?' *Employee Relations*, 28/1: 26–45.

Roberts, K. (1997) 'China's 'tidal wave' of migrant labor: What can we learn from Mexican undocumented migration to the United States?', *International Migration Review*, 31/2: 249–93.

Robinson, I. (2008) 'What explains unorganized workers' growing demand for unions?' *Labor Studies Journal*, 33/3: 235–42.

Roche, W. (2008) 'The trend of unionisation in Ireland since the mid-1990s', in Hastings, T. (ed.), *The State of the Unions*, Dublin: Liffey Press, pp. 17–45.

Roche, W. and Ashmore, J. (2001) 'Irish unions in the 1990s: Testing the limits of social partnership', in Griffin, G. (ed.) *Changing Patterns of Trade Unionism*, Sydney: Mansell, pp. 137–76.

Rodrik, D., Bradford, S. and Lawrence, R. (1997) *Has Globalization Gone Too Far?* Institute for International Economics, Washington.

Room, G. (2005) 'Policy benchmarking in the European Union: Indicators and ambiguities', *Policy Studies*, 26/2: 117–32.

Rosenstein, H. (2008) 'A new contract and a new kind of steward', *Labor Notes*, 347: 12.

Ross, S. (2007) 'Varieties of social unionism: Toward a framework for comparison', *Just Labour: A Canadian Journal of Work and Society*, 11: 16–34.

Ruhs, M. (2005) 'Managing the immigration and employment of non-nationals in Ireland', *Studies in Public Policy*, No. 19, Policy Institute, Trinity College Dublin, Dublin.

Ryan, S. (2001) 'Taken to the cleaners? The peculiarities of employment relations in the NSW contract cleaning industry', AIRAANZ conference, Wollongong.

Salazar Parreñas, R. (2001) *Servants of Globalization, Women, Migration and Domestic Work*, Stanford, CA: Stanford University Press.

Schenk, C. (2003) 'Social movement unionism: Beyond the organizing model', in Fairbrother, P. and Yates, C. (eds) *Trade Unions in Renewal: a comparative study*, London: Routledge, pp. 244–62.

Schütze, F. (1983) 'Biographieforschung und narratives interview' [Biographical research and narrative interview], *Neue Praxis*, 3: 283–93.

SEIU (2005) 'Nearly 5,000 janitors form union with SEIU', SEIU, 30 November (www.seiu.org/media).

SEIU (2006a) 'Janitors victory in Houston sparks hope for new era of economic gains for families in America', SEIU, 20 November (www.seiu.org/media).

SEIU (2006b) 'Janitors file more than a dozen new charges against cleaning contractors for illegal firings, threats, and harassment', SEIU, 6 November (www.seiu.org/media).

Simms, M. (2007) 'Interest formation in greenfield union organising campaigns', *Industrial Relations Journal*, 38/5: 439–54.

SIPTU (2006) 'SIPTU targets mushroom industry for massive clean up', press release, SIPTU, Dublin.

SIPTU (2007a) 'SIPTU to campaign for move from ERO to Registered Employment Agreement for mushroom industry to curb continued exploitation', press release, SIPTU, Dublin.

SIPTU (2007b) 'Milestone for the Mushroom Industry', press release, SIPTU, Dublin.

Sola-Corbacho, J. (2002) 'Family, paisanaje, and migration among Madrid's merchants (1750–1800)', *Journal of Family History*, 27/1: 3–24.

Sprenger, W. and Van Klaveren, M. (2004) 'Employability and career services', in Huzzard, T., Gregory, D. and Scott, R. (eds) *Strategic Unionism and Partnership: boxing and dancing?* Basingstoke: Palgrave Macmillan, pp. 343–50.

Sroka, J. (2007) 'Poland – industrial relations developments, 2006', EIROnline, Dublin.

Stalker, P. (2000) *Workers without Frontiers: the impact of globalization on international migration*, Boulder, CO: Lynne Rienner Publishers.

Stark, D. (1997) 'Recombinant property in east European capitalism', in Grabher, G. and Stark, D. (eds) *Restructuring Networks in Post-socialism: legacies, linkages, and localities*, Oxford: Oxford University Press, pp. 35–69.

Stenning, A. (2003) 'Shaping the economic landscapes of postsocialism? Labour, workplace and community in Nowa Huta, Poland', *Antipode*, 35/4: 761–80.

Stephenson, C. and Stewart, P. (2001) 'The whispering shadow: Collectivism and individualism at Ikeda-Hoover and Nissan UK', *Sociological Research Online*, 6/3: 1–15.

Stop Live Export (2008) *About Stop Live Export* (www.pacat.org/pacat_about.html).

Streeck, W. (1982) 'Organisational consequences of neo-corporatism in West German labour unions', in Lehmbruch, G. and Schmitter, P. (eds) *Patterns of Corporatist Policy Making*, London: Sage, pp. 29–82.

Stroud, D. and Fairbrother, P. (2006) 'Workplace learning: Dilemmas for the European steel industry', *Journal of Education and Work*, 19/5: 455–80.

Stroud, D. and Fairbrother, P. (2008a) 'Workplace learning: A trade union failure to service needs', *Journal of Workplace Learning*, 20/1: 6–20.

Stroud, D. and Fairbrother, P. (2008b) 'Training and workforce transformation in the European steel industry: Questions for public policy', *Policy Studies*, 29/2: 145–61.

Stuart, M. and Martinez Lucio, M. (2005) 'Partnership and modernisation in employment relations: An introduction', in Stuart, M. and Martinez Lucio, M. (eds) *Partnership and the Modernisation of Employment Relations*, London: Routledge, pp. 1–22.

Sullivan, M. (2007) *Making Sex Work: a failed experiment with legalised prostitution*, Sydney: Spinifex.

Sweeney, P. (2008) *Ireland's Economic Success: reasons and lessons*, Dublin: New Island.

Tansey, P. (1998) *Ireland at Work: economic growth and the labour market, 1987–1997*, Dublin: Oak Tree Press.

Taran, P. and Geronimi, E. (2002) 'Globalization, labor and migration: Protection is paramount', Conferencia Hemisférica sobre Migración Internacional, Derechos Humanos y Trata de Personas en las Américas, Santiago de Chile.

Tattersall, A. (2007a) 'Coalitions and community unionism: Using the term community to explore effective union-community collaboration', *Journal of Organizational Change Management*, 21/4: 415–32.

Tattersall, A. (2007b) 'Labor-community coalitions, global union alliances, and the potential of SEIU's global partnerships', in Bronfenbrenner, K. (ed.) *Global Unions: challenging transnational capital through cross-border campaigns*, Ithaca, NY: ILR Press, pp. 155–73.

Tattersall, A. (2009) 'A little help from our friends: Exploring and understanding when labor-community coalitions are likely to form', *Labor Studies Journal*, 34/4 (page numbers forthcoming).

Taylor, P. and Ramsay, H. (1998) 'Unions, partnership and HRM: Sleeping with the enemy?', *International Journal of Employment Studies*, 6/2: 115–43.

Tijdens, K. (1998) *Zeggenschap over arbeidstijden* [Participation in Working Hours], The Hague: Welboom.

Tijdens, K., Van Klaveren, M. and Van den Brekel, C. (1999) *The Absence of Women in the ICT Sector*, FNV Bondgenoten/University of Amsterdam, Amsterdam.

Tørres, L. and Gunnes, S. (2003) *Global Framework Agreements: a new tool for international labour*, Oslo: FAFO.

Touraine, A., Dubet, F., Wiewiorka, M. and Strzelecki, J. (1983) *Solidarity: the analysis of a social movement, Poland 1980–1981*, Cambridge: Cambridge University Press.

Towards 2016 (2006) Stationery Office, Dublin.

Trade Union Congress (1989) *Organising for the 1990s*, Special Review Body, Report No 2, Trades Union Congress, London.

Trade Union Congress (2001) *Partners for Progress: winning at work*, Partnership Institute, Trades Union Congress, London.

Traxler, F., Brandl, B., Glassner, V. and Ludvig, A. (2008) 'Can cross-border coordination work? Analytical reflections and evidence from the metal industry in Germany and Austria', *European Journal of Industrial Relations*, 14/2: 217–37.

Troy, L. (1986) 'The rise and fall of American trade unions: The labor movement from FDR to RR', in Lipset, S. (ed.) *Unions in Transition: entering the second century*, San Francisco, CA: ICS Press, pp. 75–109.

TUC (2003) *A Perfect Union? What Workers Want from Unions*, Trades Union Congress, London.

TUC (2004) *Young at Heart? Government, Unions and Young People – a Manifesto*, Trades Union Congress, London.

Turner, L. (2006) 'Globalization and the logic of participation: Unions and the politics of coalition building', *Journal of Industrial Relations*, 48/1: 83–97.

Turner, T., D'Art, D. and O'Sullivan, M. (2008) 'Union availability, union membership and immigrant workers: An empirical investigation of the Irish case', *Employee Relations*, 30/5: 479–93.

UAW (2006) *Department Reports: Submitted to the 34th UAW Constitutional Convention*, National Organizing Department, Detroit MI.

Undy, R. (1999) 'New Labour's Industrial Relations Settlement: the third way?' *British Journal of Industrial Relations*, 37/2: 315–36.

Upchurch, M. and Donnelly, E. (1992) 'Membership patterns in USDAW from 1980 to 1990: survival as success?' *Industrial Relations Journal*, 23/1: 60–8.

Upchurch, M., Taylor, G. and Mathers, A. (2009) 'The crisis of "social" democratic unionism: the "opening up" of civil society and the prospects for union renewal in the UK, France and Germany', *Labor Studies Journal*, 34/4 (page numbers forthcoming).

US BLS (2000, 2002, 2004, 2006) 'News: union members', Bureau of Labor Statistics, Washington DC.

US BLS (2008a) *Establishment Data: employment*, Table B-12, Bureau of Labor Statistics (bls.gov/pub/sppl/empsit.ceseeb12.txt).

US BLS (2008b) *News* 'Union Members', Bureau of Labor Statistics, Washington DC.

US Department of Commerce (USDOC) (1972, 1991, 1993, 2001, 2004–5, 2008) *Statistical Abstract of the United States*, US Government Printing Office, Washington DC.

USDAW (2006) *Young Workers' Report* (www.usdaw.org.uk).

USDOL (2000, 2007) LM-2 Reports, Department of Labor (www.del.gov).

Van Cruchten, J. and Kuijpers, R. (2007) 'Vakbeweging en organisatiegraad van werknemers' ['Trade union movement and employees' density rate'], *Sociaaleconomische Trends*, 1: 7–17.

Van Halem, A. and Wetzel, E. (2001) *Samen werken. Over arbeidsverhoudingen in de groothandel* [Working Together. On labour relations in wholesale], FNV Bondgenoten, Utrecht.

Van Klaveren, M. (2001) *De FNV en de regionale overlegeconomie: rapport voor de FNV* [The FNV and the Regional Consultation Economy: report for the FNV], STZ advies & onderzoek, Eindhoven.

Van Klaveren, M. (2002) 'The FNV "Industribution" project: Trade union learning in the Netherlands', *Concepts and Transformation*, 7/2: 203–24.

Van Klaveren, M. (2008) 'The retail industry: The contrast of supermarkets and consumer electronics', in Salverda, W., van Klaveren, M. and Van der Meer, M. (eds) *Low-Wage Work in the Netherlands*, New York: Russell Sage Foundation, pp. 148–76.

Van Klaveren, M. and Van de Camp, A. (1994) *Arbeidsorganisatie, kwalificatie en belangenbehartiging in het bankwezen. Rapport van een onderzoek voor de FNV Dienstenbond.* [Work Organisation, Qualification and Interest Representation in Banking. Report of research for FNV Services union], STZ advies & onderzoek, Amsterdam.

Van Klaveren, M. and Sprenger, W. (2004) 'Tiptoe through the tulips: The uneasy development of strategic unionism in Polder Country', in Huzzard, T., Gregory, D. and Scott, R. (eds) *Strategic Unionism and Partnership: boxing and dancing?* Basingstoke: Palgrave Macmillan, pp. 107–24.

Van Klaveren, M. and Sprenger, W. (2008) 'Call center employment: Diverging jobs and wages', in Salverda, W., Van Klaveren, M. and Van der Meer, M. (eds) *Low-Wage Work in the Netherlands*, New York: Russell Sage Foundation, pp. 237–66.

Van Klaveren, M., Posthuma, J. and Binkhorst, E. (1992) *'Voor jou tien anderen?' Verslag van een onderzoek naar arbeidsverhoudingen en werknemersbelangen in de media- en AV-sector* ['Ten Others for You?' Report of Research on

Labour Relations and Workers' Interests in Media and Audiovisuals], FNV Dienstenbond/Kunstenbond FNV, Woerden/Amsterdam.

Van Klaveren, M., Sprenger, W. and Van de Westelaken, A. (2002) *De praktijk van telewerken* [Teleworking in Practice], STZ advies & onderzoek, Eindhoven.

Verma, A., Kochan, T. and Wood, S. (2002) 'Union decline and prospects for revival: Editors' introduction', *British Journal of Industrial Relations*, 40/3: 373–84.

Visser, J. (1990a) *European Trade Unions in Figures: 1913–1985*, Boston, MA: Kluwer.

Visser, J. (1990b) 'De tropenjaren van de Nederlandse vakbeweging zijn nog niet voorbij' ['The heavy years of the Dutch union movement are not yet over'], *Zeggenschap*, 1/1: 30–42.

Visser, J. (2002) 'Why fewer workers join unions in Europe: A social custom explanation of membership trends', *British Journal of Industrial Relations*, 40/3: 403–30.

Visser, J. (2006) 'Union member statistics in 24 countries', *Monthly Labor Review*, 129/1: 38–49.

Vos, M. L. (2006) *Het arbeidersparadijs* [The Workers' Paradise], Amsterdam: Prometheus.

Voss, K. and Sherman, R. (2003) 'You just can't do it automatically: The transition to social movement unionism in the Unites States', in Fairbrother, P. and Yates, C. (eds) *Trade Unions in Renewal: a comparative study*, London: Routledge, pp. 51–77.

Waddington, J. (2006) 'Why do members leave? The importance of retention to trade union growth', *Labor Studies Journal*, 31/1: 14–38.

Waddington, J. and Whitson, C. (1997) 'Why do people join unions in a period of membership decline?', *British Journal of Industrial Relations*, 35/4: 515–46.

Waldinger, R. and Der-Martirosian, C. (2000) 'Immigrant workers and American labor: Challenge ... or disaster', in R. Milkman (ed.) *Organizing Immigrants: the challenge for unions in contemporary California*, Ithaca, NY: ILR Press, pp. 49–80.

Waldinger, R. and Lichter, M. (2003) *How the Other Half Works: immigration and the social organization of labor*, Los Angeles, CA: University of California Press.

Weeks, J. (1981) *Capital and Exploitation*, London: Edward Arnold.

Weil, D. (2005a) 'Individual rights and collective agents: The role of old and new workplace institutions in the regulation of labour markets', in Freeman, R., Hersch, J. and Mishel, L. (eds) *Emerging Labor Market Institutions for the Twenty-First Century*, Chicago, IL: University of Chicago Press, pp. 13–44.

Weil, D. (2005b) 'The contemporary industrial relations system in construction: Analysis, observations, speculation', *Labor History*, 46/4: 447–71.

Weir, S. (2004) 'USA – the labor revolt', in Lipsitz, G. (ed.) *Single Jack Solidarity*, Minneapolis, MN: University of Minnesota Press, pp. 294–309.

Wenzel, M. (2007) *Zwiazki zawodowe: Przynależność i ocena działalności* [Trade Unions: membership and the evaluation of their practices] (Report No. 3844), CBOS – Public Opinion Research Centre, Warszawa.

Wijmans, L. (1993) 'Werken aan een bindende bond' ['Working on a union bonding members'], in Warning, J. (ed.) *Voorbode van de toekomst: onderzoek naar werk in de dienstensector* [Herald of the Future: research on work in the service sector], Woerden: FNV Dienstenbond, pp. 119–29.

Willemsen, M. and Gründemann, R. (1999) *Rapport werkdruk in de contract-catering* [Report Work-Related Stress in Contract Catering], Hoofddorp: TNO Arbeid.

Willman, P. (2004) 'Structuring unions: The administrative rationality of collective action', in Kelly, J. and Willman, P. (eds) *Union Organization and Activity*, Routledge, London, pp. 73–88.

Wills, J. (2002a) *Union Futures: building networked trade unionism in the UK*, Fabian Ideas, No. 602, London: Fabian Society.

Wills, J. (2002b) 'Bargaining for the space to organize in the global economy: A review of the Accor-IUF trade union rights agreement', *Review of International Political Economy*, 9/4: 675–700.

Wills, J. (2005) 'The geography of union organising in low-paid service industries in the UK: Lessons from the T&G's campaign to unionise the Dorchester Hotel, London', *Antipode*, 37/1: 139–60.

Wills, J. and Simms, M. (2004) 'Building reciprocal community unionism in the UK', *Capital & Class*, 82: 59–82.

Wishart, J. (1992) *The Challenge for Unions: workers versus the new right*, Sydney: Left Book Club Co-operative.

Woodruff, T. (2007) 'Union organizing in difficult times', in *Never Work Alone, Organizing – ein Zuftkunftsmodell fur Gewerkschaften*, VSA (chapter available from SEIU in translation).

Woodruff, T. (2008) *Union Organizing in Difficult Times: how SEIU became the fastest-growing union in the United States*, SEIU, Washington DC.

Yates, C. (2002) 'Expanding labour's horizons: Union organising and strategic change in Canada', *Just Labour: a Canadian Journal of Work and Society*, 1: 31–40.

Index